With or Without

With or Without

Reading Postwar German Women Poets

✦

Charlotte Ann Melin

NORTHWESTERN UNIVERSITY PRESS

EVANSTON, ILLINOIS

Northwestern University Press
www.nupress.northwestern.edu

Permission to reprint material in this volume is gratefully acknowledged for the
following works:

Hilde Domin, "Drei Arten Gedichte aufzuschreiben," *Gesammelte Gedichte.*
Copyright © 1987 S. Fischer Verlag GmbH, Frankfurt am Main.

Ulla Hahn, "Gedicht," *Galileo und zwei Frauen.* Copyright © 1997 Deutsche
Verlags-Anstalt, München, in der Verlagsgruppe Random House GmbH.

Printed in the United States of America

10   9   8   7   6   5   4   3   2   1

Library of Congress Cataloging-in-Publication Data

Melin, Charlotte.
    With or without : reading postwar German women poets / Charlotte Ann
Melin.
        pages cm
    Includes bibliographical references.
    ISBN 978-0-8101-2966-5 (cloth : alk. paper) — ISBN 978-0-8101-2935-1
(pbk. : alk. paper)
    1. German poetry—Women authors—History and criticism. 2. German
poetry—20th century—History and criticism. 3. German poetry—21st
century—History and criticism. 4. Domin, Hilde—Criticism and interpretation.
5. Hahn, Ulla, 1946– —Criticism and interpretation. 6. Krechel, Ursula, 1947–
—Criticism and interpretation. I. Title.
PT167.M36 2013
831'.914099287—dc23
                                                                    2013018879

♾ The paper used in this publication meets the minimum requirements of the
American National Standard for Information Sciences—Permanence of Paper for
Printed Library Materials, ANSI Z39.48-1992.

CONTENTS

ACKNOWLEDGMENTS

Like many books, this project developed over time and benefited in numerous ways from the support of family, friends, and colleagues. With gratitude I acknowledge the library access extended to me on repeated visits by the Deutsches Literaturarchiv in Marbach am Neckar, particularly in summer 2000 when a critical portion of the research was conducted with support from the University of Minnesota through awards under the McKnight Summer Research Fellowship and Faculty Summer Research Fellowship programs. For her enduring friendship, keen scholarly insights, and willingness to look at whatever I was working on, I am deeply indebted to Cecile Zorach. My thanks extend as well to R. Blythe Inners for her editorial suggestions at the initial point when pieces of writing were merging into a common project, and to Marie-Luise Conen for her generous encouragement. For their comments on a very preliminary version of chapter 3, I thank Patricia Herminghouse and remember here the late Susanne Zantop. Support and advice of many kinds from colleagues at the University of Minnesota has been important for this project, especially from Arlene Teraoka, Ray Wakefield, and Jack Zipes. In addition, I want to express my appreciation for the attention given to the manuscript by the readers and all individuals involved with it at Northwestern University Press, especially Henry L. Carrigan Jr., whose faith in the project was critical to its realization at this point when scholarly publishing faces so many challenges. Finally, I dedicate this book to my husband, Matthew Rohn, whose companionship has carried me through all things, to our children (Eric and Anne) who have grown up while I worked on, and to my mother, Virginia Melin, who nurtured my earliest interests in poetry.

With or Without

"Just a few steps more . . . ," Ulla Hahn writes in the opening line of "Improved Version" ("Verbesserte Auflage"), from *Herz über Kopf* (*Heart over Head,* 1981).[1] The poem conjures up an ecstatic Orpheus poised to return Eurydice to life. Suddenly his muse startles him with a song of her own. He drops the lyre, and Eurydice boldly takes up the instrument herself. Hahn quips, "As to whether Orpheus followed her / the sources / are vague." Read as an allegory about the situation of poetry that pertains in many respects even today, these lines reflect perplexity about whether Eurydice can now lead Orpheus, and what that reversal might mean.

But that lack of clarity arises not simply because it is impossible to say with certainty whether the poetic genre—or the writings of women poets, or even more specifically, the work of German women poets—operates under new dynamics. The heady optimism and piquant satire of Hahn's lines drive us to fundamental questions not only about women poets but also more broadly about issues regarding the character of modernism and postmodernism that are central to understanding the ways in which poetry became construed as exemplary artifact in the twentieth century. Its unique construction as a genre depends on a similar curious relationship between individual experience and communal ideals that has shaped the condition of modernity itself, for modernism has been among other things intensely preoccupied with interpersonal expression. "Expressiveness" depends on viewer/reader/audience response, and that response, which is again determined by context, is highly prized. As Virginia Jackson proposes in summarizing the argument advanced by T. J. Clark in *Farewell to an Idea,* "one of the distinctive features of both modernism and criticism is the nostalgia for the expressiveness they retroactively produce as what they cannot themselves be" (Jackson 2005, 236).

New lyric studies ask us to be skeptical about claims that the lyric is a transhistorical and transnational form of expression, arguing instead for a deeper and more specific historical understanding of poetic activity (Culler 2008, 202–5). Hence, in reflecting on the special situation of postwar German poetry and women poets, I have found it useful to examine the various stipulative functions that theory and criticism exercise in defining aesthetic significance and the terms under which that literature operates in a particular literary environment. This analysis provides the basis for the case studies of three German women poets presented here, which focus attention on transformations in the social function of literature, practices of reading, and writerly attitudes that have broad significance at the end of the twentieth century. Many of my arguments are framed in part through reference to Anglo-American scholarship; this approach is not meant to imply that the problems identified can simply be removed from context. Rather, it acknowledges the fluidity of literary relations between Germany and its international counterparts after 1945. By reading poetry as a medium that on many levels operates in a transnational context yet still exhibits culturally specific manifestations, insight is obtained into how international forces such as feminism evolved, allowing the resulting interpretations to gain explanatory force.

While I am interested in recuperating the history of German women's poetry after 1945 and shedding light on the thinking of underappreciated theorists and feminists whose work contributed to this body of poetry, the larger agenda of this book has to do with the lyric genre itself—the way poems inhabit language, engage readers, and affiliate with aesthetic debates. Methodologically, that agenda requires the kind of double-reading strategy advocated by Rachel Blau DuPlessis in her essay "'Corpses of Poesy': Some Modern Poets and Some Gender Ideologies of Lyric" (DuPlessis 1994). For the lyric genre, this dual interpretive focus also points to the significance for poetological operations of textual rewriting, notional clusters, and performativity—a set of practices whose assumptions we need to explore before proceeding further.

Silvia Bovenschen's important essay "Über die Frage: Gibt es eine 'weibliche' Aesthetik?" ("About the Question: Is There a Feminine Aesthetic?") historically marked a watershed in German feminist thought that positioned scholars and poets to evaluate the complexity of revisionist practices at play in women's art. Here Bovenschen asserted: "Feminine art production represents itself, I believe, in a complicated process of new conquest or reconquest, appropriation and working over, as well as forgetting and subversion. In the works of women artists who have a connection to the women's movement, the traditions of art can be demonstrated as well as the break with them" (1976, 73). From this appreciation of the multiple ways in which creativity manifests itself, we learn how poiesis (the poetics of rewriting) participates in textual evolution by forcing discourse change that eventually leads to a paradigm shift, according to the argument Terry Threadgold cogently advances in *Feminist Poetics: Poiesis, Performance, Histories* (1997, 33). Moreover, we begin to see that in poetry, as Susan Stewart shows, this particular mode of creation renders the poem uniquely dialogic and fuels the sensual manifestation of its language, since "*poiēsis* as figuration relies on the senses of touching, seeing, and hearing that are central to the encounter with the presence of others, the encounter of recognition between persons" (2002, 3).

The indicators of rewriting/poiesis in poetry are, however, somewhat different from what surfaces in other genres, due to the way in which poems and poetics operate. In sorting out these dynamics in postwar German poetry, two concepts prove particularly useful—notional clusters and performativity. DuPlessis convincingly argues that among the most important materials available to women's poetry are tropes (that is, words marked as highly significant through chains of associations), for "the history of poetry shows that these—the foundational cluster, the tropes that Homans describes, the general gender narrative or pattern book of moves—are materials . . . in which a large cultural investment has been made" (1994, 71–72). Accordingly, I intend to explore key notional clusters that emerge from the materials under consideration, including the term "voice," which in the present discussion will illustrate the dynamics at play. Each word (including, I contend, categories of abstractions like gender, subjectivity, and authenticity, depending on how poets use these terms) represents a loaded choice that is incrementally connected by the poet to other meaningful discourse strands. Stewart is particularly adroit in describing how such associations gather larger significance. Taking one instance as an example, we recognize the value of realizing that when she points to "voice" as constituting much more than a poets' workshop cliché, Stewart interprets it broadly as "a reifying and mystifying version of subjectivity for what is in fact most profound and engaging about poetic voice—that is, the plays of transformation it evokes beyond the irreducibility of its own grain, its own potential for silence" (2002, 110). Voice, as will be seen, has a similar resonance in contemporary German poetry that goes beyond what occurs when a word functions as symbol.

Because notional clusters ontologically depend on the ways in which poetry constructs a sustained dialogue with readers to instantiate this larger meaning, performativity is a concept essential to understanding how these tropes work. As Judith Butler trenchantly explains, through performativity "acts, gestures, and desire produce the effect of an internal core or substance, but produce this *on the surface* of the body. . . . Such acts, gestures, enactments, generally constructed, are *performative* in the sense that the essence or identity that they otherwise purport to express are fabrications manufactured and sustained through corporeal signs and other discursive means" (1990, 136). Linking the construct of notional clusters with performativity through interpretive practice, I believe, allows us to comprehend the larger reach of discourse motifs (the figures we first see emerge within the work of single authors) and helps illuminate their significance in a wide range of poetological materials. In postwar German poetry, it is through such manifestations that we are prompted to attend to the ways in which poems variously engage us—as well as to the status of the lyric genre itself—and these dynamics raise questions about the nature of poetry that I will return to at the conclusion of this study.

In "Who Reads Poetry?" Jackson observes that "the history of the idealization of poetry has included many fascinating chapters, but we may be in the middle of one of the strangest so far" (Jackson 2008, 182). She proposes that the notion of what constitutes poetry has narrowed to only the lyric, while at the same time a curious idealization has generated "our current, spectral ideal of a genre powerful enough to overcome our habits of not reading it" (2008, 183). Indeed, Jackson regards Theodor W. Adorno as the salient example of how poetry's idealization served to elevate the lyric genre by assigning it special status for being able to transcend the social sphere.[2] She explains that Adorno in the influential essay "On Lyric Poetry and Society" constructs this detachment to make his discussion palatable to 1957 radio listeners (Jackson 2008, 182). While Jackson is correct that Adorno makes a special appeal, her reading of Adorno glosses over a number of specific concepts that are relevant to the current study and the position of German women authors. First, Adorno, like German postwar writers generally, reaches back to romantic conceptions of the artist as outsider. Secondly, the essay speaks after an era of fascism and during the Cold War, in other words in an intellectual context deeply marked by historical and geopolitical forces. Adorno's concern thus lies with advancing a paradigm for autonomous expression that paradoxically suppresses mere subjectivity while at the same time inviting poetry—a genre intimately linked to expressions of subjectivity—to become an agent for change. "The lyric work hopes to attain universality through unrestrained individuation," Adorno writes (1991, 38). The following chapters will explore the hypothesis that this synergistic paradox (constituted by the necessary coexistence of individual "subjectivity" and "universality") both creates expressive possibilities and constrains the lyric genre in ways that are especially significant for German women writers.

The particular circumstances that bind gender considerations to German poetry in the latter half of the twentieth century arise out of the aesthetic, historical, and social transitions that destabilized and altered mid-century European literary culture. Symptomatic of postwar flux are the proliferation of ephemeral publications, intense literary affiliations, contentious debuts, and verbose intellectual positioning. On the one hand, the war's end produce a heady, open literary environment where critical values, institutional structures, and literary canons are fluid—a climate in which at least in theory women authors could well establish themselves. Indeed, among the first poetry collections to appear after 1945 were in fact books by Marie-Luise Kaschnitz, Elisabeth Langgässer, Dagmar Nick, and Oda Schäfer. Ilse Schneider-Lengyal, whose house provided the site for the first meeting of Gruppe 47 (Lettau 1967, 21–23), wrote surrealist poetry and collaborated in the publication of the journal *Neues Europa* (Cofalla 1999, 83). The acclaim Ingeborg Bachmann received in Gruppe 47 as a lyric poet and for her poetry in the 1950s with *Die gestundete Zeit* (*Time Measured in Hours*, 1953) and *Anrufung des Großen Bären* (*Invocation of the Great Bear*, 1956) was followed by the honor to her of becoming the first lecturer in the prestigious Frankfurt Poetry Lecture series (1959–60). Living in Sweden, where she remained after the war, Nelly Sachs began publishing in Germany with the collection *In den Wohnungen des Todes* (*In the Houses of Death*, 1947) and was eventually awarded the Nobel Prize in Literature in 1966. These achievements, however, did little to alter the marginal status of German women poets.

The generation of authors that emerged a decade or so after the war was over (which included Elisabeth Borchers, Elke Erb, Sarah Kirsch, Friederike Mayröcker, Helga M. Novak, and Friederike Roth), however, benefited from revisionist tendencies that began to take hold more than a decade after 1945. Arguably they became the first cohort of women poets to gain acceptance from the literary mainstream. Their successes, identities as authors, and individual accomplishments owe much to shifts in literary tastes and the emergence of feminist scholarship and criticism in Germany.

For much of the immediate postwar era, women's experience—and with it their poetic voice and capacity for expression—was overshadowed on the German literary scene by the charged rhetoric of the *Stunde Null* (also known as *Nullpunkt*) or "zero hour" that, as Karen Leeder convincingly concludes, cast 1945 as a symbolic break with the past (2000, 200). This notion that German culture was starting anew was thoroughly entangled with the bold claims of modernism. Yet this abstract ideology of "newness" left unexamined many biases of the past and prevented scrutiny of old assumptions. Discomfort with the "zero hour" paradigm intensified in the 1960s and subsequently grew even more under pressure from postmodernism and globalization.

Recent appraisals of these German literary developments after 1945 have already productively contextualized the brash rhetorical claims of

cultural ideologies surrounding the *Stunde Null* (Brockmann 2004; Trommler 1977; Korte 1989; Schnell 1993), exposed ways in which aesthetic
paradigms actually contributed to the marginalization of women writers
(Leeder 2000), and remapped literary history to account more effectively
for the treatment of individual authors (Weedon 1997).[3] In concert with
these revisionist approaches, I propose that we need strategic readings of
the salient discourses about poetic theory, poetry, and literary institutions
(specifically anthologies) to elucidate more fully the complex status of
women writers. My effort here is directed toward describing an evolution
in perceptions about the lyric's capacity to project subjectivity, voice, and
authenticity. I argue that German women poets have a central role in this
evolution as they negotiate relationships to the literary mainstream (be
it modernism or the avant-garde), construct alternate literary traditions,
and propose new roles for both readers and writers.

With or Without: Reading Postwar German Women Poets looks at
the lyric genre as a dynamic medium that interacts with aesthetic, social,
and theoretical forces. To be sure, the relationship between gender and
poetry is never separate from other intellectual debates in Germany. The
Holocaust, Cold War tensions, regional conflicts, and many other issues
inspired reactions from German writers, who generally play a markedly greater role as public intellectuals than do their counterparts in the
United States. The tendency of these public intellectuals to equate political affinities with aesthetic programs, however, posed special difficulty for
women poets to the extent that their work was and still is frequently read
as involving private feelings rather than public concerns. Consequently, in
examining how postwar women poets individually seek to link feminist
and poetic discourses, I am interested in moving away from that ideological binary and toward interpretive perspectives that suggest where new
programmatic trajectories have developed for the lyric genre. This line of
inquiry yields a more differentiated, longitudinal measure of the literary
impact of feminism by pointing us toward areas in which women authors
have focused on similar problems across several decades.

It is common to find in German poetry anthologies, artistic manifestoes,
and critical or journalistic writing statements to the effect that poetry by
women suffers from unfortunate marginalization. Women poets are seen
as outsiders, their poetry viewed as subjective (often a blanket categorization), and the history of their work described as broken. From this
perspective (which is, of course, not novel to the postwar German literary
scene), women writers figure as isolated individuals, with the result that
the subtle role constructivist and relational thinking plays in their literary
self-construction tends to be eclipsed.[4] Feminist scholarship itself runs the

risk of inadvertently contributing to this constellation through intense focus on singular, exceptional writers, like the poet Ingeborg Bachmann.[5] However, the access we have to late-twentieth-century materials from the literary environment invites a critical rethinking of categories like marginalization and obscurity in the context of a larger, more disparate body of work by women authors. These materials are less fragmented by sheer historical neglect than the work of authors from previous centuries. Yet, as is well known, the lyric genre poses other, singular, interpretive difficulties.

Poetry has long been considered a dauntingly complicated and possibly unrewarding subject for feminist readings. Indeed, Renate Möhrmann in a seminal overview of contemporary writing by German women authors conceded her willingness to exclude the lyric genre from consideration on the grounds that it seems to have limited emancipatory force. She reasons that this exclusion is justified since although poems may have feminist traits to be analyzed, the lyric genre by nature makes these elements less clear to the observer (1981, 355). In *With or Without: Reading Postwar German Women Poets,* I argue for a more nuanced appreciation of the situation of lyric genre during the transformative period of the 1960s to 1980s. By analyzing representative poetic discourses, I want to address some of the problematical aspects of our current methodologies.

For German poetry after 1945, public poetic expressions of a sense of marginalization were deeply important for asserting the autonomy of the lyric genre. In that respect, at least, women's poetry was surprisingly comfortably situated within that literary mainstream. Objections, even today, to the absence of a history of German women's writing thus participate in a broader critique of various epistemological dichotomies (such as scholarship versus criticism, high versus low culture, and canon versus individual talent). Taking as my focus work by three West German poets who in crucial respects share a common literary environment—Hilde Domin, Ulla Hahn, and Ursula Krechel—I use close readings of poetological texts and poems to explore the evolution of attitudes about literature and subjectivity that test these dichotomies. As will be seen, feminine poetic writing is articulated in complex and sometimes contradictory ways by these authors through the manipulation of deictics, tropes, and traditional poetic forms.

For Domin, Hahn, and Krechel, gender dynamics are foundational to their understanding of literature, though the significance of gender in their works has been largely overlooked in scholarship to date. The reasons for this neglect have to do with both cultural and social dynamics. Writing about a woman author whose career began in an earlier historical period, Irmgard Keun (1905–1982), Krechel notes the underlying premise that "where masculine culture makes the claim of androgynous character, feminine cultural achievements that do not (even) approach the heights of those created by men remain dead [and] must be forgotten if the myth of the androgynous character of art is not to be endangered" (1979a, 122). The cultural formation observed by Krechel is reinforced by postwar social patterns analyzed by historian Dagmar Herzog in *Sex After Fascism*. Herzog persuasively documents how sexual politics, which had become an instrument for national and cultural identity during the Nazi period, continued to control postwar attitudes (2005). These gender politics exercised a decisive impact on the lyric genre as well, even before second wave feminism took hold.[6]

That impact sharpened in the 1960s, when German poetry underwent substantial transformation through the reception of international literature by German authors. By the late 1960s and early 1970s, interest in Anglo-American feminism and such writers as Virginia Woolf, Sylvia Plath, Adrienne Rich, and Susan Sontag stimulated discussions of women's writing. Meanwhile, the shallowness of the rhetoric of tolerance espoused by politically active intellectuals became increasingly transparent to feminists who encountered formidable institutional and social obstacles (as recently documented by Kersting 2003, 64–69; Lämmert 2003, 24–25; Schabert 2004). In the 1970s–1980s, groundbreaking scholarly essays (by Bovenschen [1976], Ursula Heukenkamp [1985], Barbara Lersch [1988], and others) and ambitious projects like Gisela Brinker-Gabler's anthology *Deutsche Dichterinnen vom 16. Jahrhundert bis zur Gegenwart* (*German Poetesses from the 16th Century to the Present*, 1978) marked theoretical and historical areas of engagement for feminist scholars and further legitimized women's writing.[7] These academic projects were well known to West German women poets, who frequently embarked on writing careers after extensive university study.

Yet the gains were not permanent.[8] When intellectuals began to speak about the "death of literature" in 1968, the phrase signaled less the demise of literary production than growing skepticism that literature could exercise a transformative influence on society.[9] While interest in more "objective" documentary forms of literature grew, these doubts combined with the turn to what Stuart Parkes terms "the apolitical German tradition of inwardness" (2000, 757) to yield a proliferation of personal writing. New Subjectivity in the 1970s created a climate in which more women writers entered the literary scene. Autobiographical works, prose fiction and drama that centered on protagonists who felt estranged from society, filmic writings, and small press publications helped define the trend's intimate qualities. However, its amateurish aspects irritated many critics, scholars, and established writers, generating complex hostility toward self-indulgent explorations of subjectivity and the seeming decline in artistic standards that came with the abandonment of modernist models. Women writers were particularly vulnerable to the critiques that inevitably followed this phase. Thus Krechel laments the backlash against them, observing, "The roll-back of the eighties caught the women's movement completely unprepared. It had slept through the overture" (1983b, 144). Poetry, in particular, became an imperiled genre, for reasons that I will discuss in subsequent chapters.

A dramatic shift then occurs in the 1990s with the startling resurgence of the lyric genre—a multifaceted renaissance that unfolds in journalistic media, anthologies, and performative venues (author readings, poetry slams, literary events, films, and literary marketing). Poetry experiments with the interface of high and low cultural modalities, with public and private dialogues, formal conventions and random montage. It becomes a lush proliferation of voices (see Rolleston 1997; Taberner 2005; Ryan 1997). Nontraditional publishing venues, unruly forms, and bold liberties with discourse are now rediscovered in women's poetry of the previous two decades.[10]

Against this background, it is striking to read a statement by author Gerhard Falkner that appears in his reflections on poetry, *Über den Unwert des Gedichts* (*On the Worthlessness of the Poem*, 1993). Falkner's volume argues fervently for an appreciation of poems in terms of what he sees as the lyric genre's fundamental qualities.[11] Here he defines poetry as an inherently gendered genre, but a masculine one, writing that "the poem is called forth by the idea of the passionate, one of the mainstays of [the] patriarchy. It is, contrary to popular opinion, something deeply unwomanly" (1993, 58).[12]

This comment, which claims the lyric genre as masculine and rhetorically effaces "feminine" writing, appears at a point when feminism was already well established, and precisely at the moment when the recent reunification of Germany was bringing identity politics to the fore in many domains. Surprisingly, it seems to realize a return to the hegemonic "androgynous character of art" that Krechel feared (1979a, 122). While it is beyond the scope of the present study to pursue the ramifications of this particular statement in greater depth, I am convinced that Falkner's remark signals a dramatic reformulation of canon, reader practices, and connoisseurship preferences at the twentieth century's end that we should notice. These reformulations cannot be appreciated without an awareness of the strategies of resistance, accommodation, marginalization, and self-assertion that emerged in German poetry in the 1970s and 1980s, particularly in the writing of women authors.

Critical orientation for my project came from approaches to poetry that integrate theory and close reading, particularly *Feminist Measures* (edited by Lynn Keller and Cristanne Miller, 1994). Terry Threadgold's discussion of poiesis is instrumental to the case I make for reading Hahn's poetics out of her poetry and essays (*Feminist Poetics*, 1997). The seminal work of Judith Butler (*Gender Trouble: Feminism and the Subversion of Identity*, 1990), as well as the research of Julia Kristeva (*Revolution in Poetic Language*, 1984), Gisela Ecker (editor, *Feminist Aesthetics*, 1985), Naomi Schor (*Reading in Detail: Aesthetics and the Feminine*, 1987), and Molly McQuade (editor, *By Herself: Women Reclaim Poetry*, 2000) have also helped me refine my understanding of how poets formulate their poetics.[13]

With or Without: Reading Postwar German Women Poets begins by considering the position of postwar German women writers as defined through problems of representational subjectivity. The first chapter maps this issue by charting the context chronologically marked off by Käte Hamburger's *Die Logik der Dichtung* (1957; *The Logic of Literature*, 1973) and the so-called *Fräuleinwunder* of the 1990s (Graves 2002).[14] Hamburger's concern with the underlying logic of the lyric genre reaffirms and deepens Adorno's definition of poetry as a form of verbal art that paradoxically links the impersonal distance of poems with their inherent subjectivity. I propose that the more specific association of subjectivity with women's writing made by Hamburger foregrounds one of the central representational problems for German poetry after 1945. At issue is the separation of the poet from the lyrical *I*, for that essential distinction acknowledges that poetry is constructed rather than unmediated, personal expression. Hamburger's treatment of lyrical subjectivity provides a theoretical antecedent to subsequent considerations of feminine writing because she insists that autonomous poetic expression depends not on a literal correspondence to reality, but rather on the capacity of texts to create their own world. Her analysis expresses important reservations about the competing interpretive frameworks represented by German academic scholarship and American New Criticism, the latter of which had been introduced in Europe through postwar cultural reeducation efforts. The chapter concludes with a discussion of how the aspirations of German intellectuals and writers after 1945 generated a dense aesthetic discourse about national, artistic, and private identity that posed ambiguous possibilities for women poets.

Turning to individual poets, I focus in the second chapter on the work of Hilde Domin, particularly her efforts in *Doppelinterpretationen* (*Double Interpretations*, 1966) to advance new principles for reading poetry.

My reading of Domin's project in relation to emerging feminist attitudes is consonant with Kathryn Thoms Flannery's analysis in *Feminist Literacies, 1968–75* (2005) of "reciprocating literacies describing the dialogic interaction between poet and reader" (2005, 143). Flannery determines that American feminist publications strategically promoted "unauthorized" reading based on the assumption "that readers would become writers and, at least on one level, that to show how poems could be put to use served the pedagogical function of demonstrating what work poetry could do, and what work new poems needed to do, to fuel cultural and political change" (2005, 129). I argue that for similar reasons Domin likewise invests poetry with transformative social value in advocating a poetry for readers.[15] Domin's intervention, however, stems from German efforts to reconnect with international modernism. In demanding an interface between poetic creation and active reading she promotes an intellectual autonomy and individualistic thinking that align well with democratic values. Close reading of her poem "Drei Arten Gedichte aufzuschreiben" ("Three Ways of Writing Poems") adumbrates a further development in Domin's conception of poetry, in part inspired by Virginia Woolf and Christa Wolf (Domin 1987b, 333–36). Through this interpretation I propose that Domin's interest in two notional clusters—poetic breath and civil courage (the latter concept traced by Domin to American poetry and the writings of Herbert Marcuse)—discursively connect her writings from the 1960s with later works that take up questions of feminism more explicitly.

The performative aspects of Domin's poetics, as well as personal connections, link her with Ulla Hahn, whose work is treated in my third chapter. Reading the feminized aesthetics developed by Hahn as a response to political and social tensions analyzed by Dagmar Herzog in *Sex After Fascism* (2005), I argue for interpretation of her work as a bold, often misunderstood effort to develop a feminine poetics. While Herbert Marcuse and Susan Sontag provide guidance for Hahn's projects, Adrienne Rich offers Hahn leverage in articulating power dynamics in the context of Hahn's ambitious anthology of women's poetry, *Stechäpfel* (*Thorn Apples*, 1992b). Exploring the emphasis Hahn gives to feminine poetics in the 1990s, this third chapter analyzes the poet's lecture series "Poesie und Vergnügen—Poesie und Verantwortung" ("Poetry and Pleasure—Poetry and Responsibility," 1994) and also engages in a close reading of the meta-poem "Gedicht" from the collection *Galileo und zwei Frauen* (*Galileo and Two Women*, 1997a). Concluding remarks on the new formalism represented by Hahn foreground her efforts as an anthologist to change fundamentally readership habits related to poetry.

The fourth chapter focuses on the poetry and essays of Ursula Krechel. Krechel, unlike Domin and Hahn, makes an early, explicit commitment to feminism through journalistic writing with *Selbsterfahrung und Fremdbestimmung: Bericht aus der Neuen Frauenbewegung* (*Self-Experience and Outsider Designation*, 1975), and this allegiance is sustained in subsequent essay collections (1975/1983). My analysis explores the concept of authenticity articulated in Krechel's "Leben in Anführungszeichen: Das Authentische in der gegenwärtigen Literatur" ("Life in Quotation Marks: The Authentic in Contemporary Literature," 1979b), relating it to crucial postwar discussions of literary representation. Discussion continues with an examination of *Lesarten* (*Ways of Reading*, 1982) and *Mit dem Körper des Vaters spielen* (*Playing with the Body of the Father*, 1992), where Krechel returns explicitly to the topic of feminine writing. Close readings of poems from Krechel's poetry collection *Verbeugungen vor der Luft* (*Air Bows*, 1999) explicate techniques of linguistic experimentation deployed to challenge the expectations of readers. The chapter concludes with a discussion of *In Zukunft schreiben* (*Writing into the Future*, 2003) that confirms Krechel's commitment to individual expression.[16]

With the fifth chapter, I move from individual poets to an examination of representative anthologies from the postwar period. Poetry was highly prized during the war period, and the cultural utility of poetry anthologies gave them strategic significance after 1945.[17] In the postwar era, anthologies became influential tools for conveying aesthetic and political values (Melin 2003, 38–55). Although publication records document numerous poetry anthologies between 1945 and 2000 (approximately one hundred), only about a dozen take German women authors of the postwar period as their subject.[18] From this group, I examine the poetic agendas defined in the six collections that are most representative and explicit about their canon-defining aims—*Gezeiten: Neue Frauenlyrik aus der BRD* (*Tides: New Poetry by Women from the FRG*, 1981), *Mörikes Lüfte sind vergiftet* (*Mörike's Skies Are Poisoned*, 1982, ed. Göbelsmann), *Wenn wir den Königen schreiben* (*When We Write to the Kings*, 1988, ed. Rosenkranz), *Stechäpfel: Gedichte von Frauen aus drei Jahrtausenden* (*Thorn Apples: Poems by Women from Three Millennia*, 1992b, ed. Hahn), *Gedichte berühmter Frauen* (*Poems of Famous Women*, 1996, ed. Borchers), and *Frauen dichten anders* (*Women Write Differently*, 1998, ed. Reich-Ranicki). This comparison shows that the canon and programmatic agendas defined by the collections are strikingly consistent and argues that they thus serve an important consolidating function. Given the crucial role postwar anthologies played (in establishing literary tastes, describing social roles for poets, and introducing new poetic styles), my analysis finds that in emphasizing a renewed appreciation of texts, rather than developing a coherent poetic ideology, these anthologies make their most important contribution by attempting to redefine readerships and habits of reading.[19]

With or Without: Reading Postwar German Women Poets concludes with a consideration of the trope of belatedness in mid-century German poetry by women in relation to Butler's notion of performativity. This troping, I propose, frees gender from becoming a restrictive, identitarian category and opens space for discussion of attitudes about language, voice, influence, and the possibility of expression that are foundational to the lyric genre. As such it confirms the observation by American poet Alice Notley that "there are no forms of poetry that are entirely 'owned' by women: what studies of women's poetry seem to show are predilections for shapes and subjects, what our poetry tends to be like" (Notley 2005, 167). The trope of belatedness constitutes such a predilection—a mask that allows the poet to speak with both emotion and a sense of intellectual distance. It is a mode of displacement that has been familiar in German poetry since romanticism, which makes its salience for women poets in the 1970s and 1980s all the more striking.

The individual case studies that comprise this book attempt a strategic foray into postwar poetry, rather than marking a comprehensive historical study. I have restricted the focus to West German writing in the interest of situating the analysis in a more or less unified literary environment. Key poems are interpreted as examples that indicate areas of flux in the lyric genre, rather than dramatic turning points. Indeed, the situation of German women poets is full of paradoxes. Caught between the desire to construct a continuous tradition that embraces women's writing and an agenda of rejecting the status quo in the name of feminism, women poets find no easy answers. Encouragement for their projects comes from Anglo-American feminism and writers like Virginia Woolf and Adrienne Rich, with this reception mixed freely with German creative sources that range from hymnals to Else Lasker-Schüler and Ingeborg Bachmann. The transformation of the literature industry in the second half of the twentieth century has had both positive and negative impact on the status of German women writers. Without an appreciation of how the volatile interplay between collective aesthetic values and creative individualism after 1945 productively shapes women's poetry—and with it New Subjectivity—it would be difficult to explain the "sheer diversity" of the contemporary German literary scene (compare Taberner 2005, 1), and to account for the striking renaissance of poetry since the 1990s.

Chapter One

✦

Poetic Sense, Feminine Sensibility

In *Die Logik der Dichtung* (1957), revised and translated as *The Logic of Literature* (1973), Käte Hamburger paradoxically defines the lyric genre as a mode of expression rooted in subjective experience, while simultaneously insisting that readers distinguish between the empirical *I* of the poet and the constructed lyrical *I* (1973, 286).[1] Further complicating this twist of logic, Hamburger acknowledges that we find ourselves unable to conceive of these two identities as unrelated because the lyrical *I* is inherently constructed as the expression of the poet (1973, 272). Hamburger's theoretical conundrum points to what I see as one of the most important unresolved problems for postwar German poetry, especially with respect to women's writing, namely conflicting attitudes about the nature of subjectivity.

If we were to define subjectivity following the reasoning presented in Hamburger's theoretical discussion of the lyrical *I,* we would arrive at a narrow definition of it as linguistic expression that constructs feeling or reflects the mind's shaping perspective (Preminger and Brogan 1993, 1229), or perhaps, in a more generous interpretation, determine that it is a quality that "depends on the expression of personality or individuality of the artist" as constructed in a literary work of art (Robbins 2005, 7). The apparent neutrality of these explanations, nonetheless, does not adequately fit the German cultural context, for reasons that will become clear. These limited definitions do not take into account dimensions of meaning at play in expressions of subjectivity, including the instability of identity and the affective response of readers, and, more crucially for the present discussion, they do not address the ways in which social and cultural institutions either value subjectivity or find it suspect.[2]

To a greater degree than its American counterpart (particularly in comparison with the emotional verve and personal discourse explored by beat and confessional poets), German poetry and the discourse that surrounds it after 1945 postpones engagement with questions about the significance of individual voice that are intimately connected to the ways in which subjectivity becomes manifested.[3] In the years immediately after the Second World War, discussions by writers and intellectuals focused with a surprising degree of depersonalization on a posited *Vergangenheitsbewältigung* (coming to terms with the past), stylistic reintegration with international modernism, and questions of artistic legitimacy.[4] At the same time, abstractly defined concerns with originality and translation, voice and artifice, proximity and distance, home and exile mirrored a worrisome instability in collective experience.[5] The instability that was masked by tendencies toward impersonal abstraction makes the tentativeness of the subjective very apparent, even within the lyric genre.

Conventional wisdom holds that subjectivity became the centerpiece for German literature after the "death of literature" was declared in 1968 by New Left authors eager to transform society through revolutionary measures.[6] In this context of social upheaval, subjectivity was equated with narcissistic and often trivial preoccupations attributed to writers. Taking stock of German poetry during the period 1965–1985, Harald Hartung in *Deutsche Lyrik seit 1965* (*German Poetry Since 1965*) dates the subsequent reemergence of an openness to subjectivity around 1975, placing it against the background of "disorientation and depression" that followed the collapse of the student protest movement (1985a, 12). The modernist aesthetic paradigms that had defined German poetry since 1945, according to this account, were perceived as exhausted (1985a, 8–9).[7] As Hartung explains:

> After the "progressive," collective *We* had run aground, the possibilities of the *I* were considered. But what kind of an *I* was that after all? Was it the old bourgeois, individualistic *I* that everyone thought had been conquered—or could something like a new *I* exist that had passed through the experience of revolt and collectivity? That was what the discussion about the New Subjectivity in poetry was about. (1985a, 11)

A trenchant reader of contemporary German verse who astutely diagnosed the proliferation of poetic voices that occurred in the 1980s, Hartung found symptoms of this change in the turn of poetry away from theory and toward a strangely empty, egotistical preoccupation with the feelings of an "ichloses Ich," a selfless *I* (1985a, 48–65).

While I agree with much of Hartung's explanation, which is supported in general by other appraisals of New Subjectivity (Ryan 1982; Korte 1989, 157–66; Parkes 2000),[8] we need a wider view of postwar German literature to come to terms with the complex reasons why subjectivity keeps resurfacing as a problem for the contemporary lyric genre. Long before this psychologically motivated subjectivity turned into a flash point for debates in the 1970s–1980s and became recognized as one of the most distinctive features associated with women's writing, the attention that the lyrical *I* receives in Hamburger's study indicates that it represented an underlying problematical concept that was of central importance to German poetry. My concern in this chapter lies in examining the qualities of subjectivity advanced by Hamburger in her discussion of poetry in *The Logic of Literature,* which I see as one of the pivotal documents in this theoretical debate.[9] In connection with this analysis, I also want to explore the implications Hamburger's shifting theoretical perspectives have for the literary context in which her work appeared, following the interpretive model developed by Terry Threadgold in *Feminist Poetics: Poiesis, Performance, Histories.*[10]

Threadgold suggests that rewriting is a defining practice of feminist poetics that should be discerned through the careful reading of texts and discourses that "may vacillate between citation, reproduction, system-integrated innovation . . . and the production of something now entirely new, but 'undisciplined' " (Threadgold 1997, 33). Turning to *Die Logik der Dichtung,* we find, in fact, that Hamburger takes issue with the philologically based poetics that preceded her project and that she systematically questions the assumptions of other contemporary scholars, meticulously rewriting their interpretive paradigms in very distinctive ways. In Hamburger's critical practice, such rewriting constructs a protracted dialogue with earlier theorists. Threadgold regards such exchanges as especially indicative of significant philosophical rifts and argues that in the twentieth century they not only reveal the constraints of distinct theoretical systems but also enable fundamental conceptual shifts. For Threadgold, the very shift "from a focus on the *poetics* to the *poiesis* of textuality, a move from the analysis of the verbal text as autonomous artifact to much more complex understandings of the embodied and processual making of meanings in complex social and cultural contexts" signals a paradigmatic change in response to the influence of feminism and post-structuralism (Threadgold 1997, 85).[11] The purpose in recognizing the emergence of this new paradigm is not to claim that one paradigm simply supplants another. Rather, Threadgold contends, that change is characterized by a dynamic relationship between old and new paradigms, as is clearly the case with respect to Hamburger's project and the evolving status of postwar German women's poetry.

Termed a "Pionierarbeit" (pioneering work) when it appeared in 1957 (Hahn 2003, 130), Hamburger's *Die Logik der Dichtung* resonates with later discussions of poetic craft and feminine writing, so it provides a useful point of departure for interpreting debates about subjectivity in the 1970s–1980s.[12] The peculiar ontological status that Hamburger attributes to poems amplifies the difficulty of developing any poetic theory, let alone one that addresses a category of non-mainstream work, such as women's poetry. Hamburger acknowledges indeterminacy as a fundamental characteristic of the lyric genre, asserting that the poem as a structure is paradigmatically open to reality, experience, and meaning. She sees "the poem" as an entity constituting a statement of reality (*Wirklichkeitsaussage*) because she regards the lyrical *I* as a genuine subject of expression within the experiential field of its own statement (1957, 190). As an experiential phenomenon, the poem thus exists in concrete specificity, not theoretical abstractness. To understand poems, then, we are required to negotiate a balance between tangible perception of the text itself and theoretical framework.

Difficult to achieve, such balanced reading rarely surfaces in German literary debates over connoisseurship values.[13] Hamburger's theory displays admirable idealism when compared with journalistic discussions of German poetry in the first decades after World War II, where only limited self-reflection informs consideration of questions about whether evaluative standards represented as universal are invested with ideological bias.[14] Hamburger appears to struggle in this study with the clash between a quest for enduring aesthetic values and a fascination with what would prove to be ephemeral qualities in emerging contemporary literature. We see evidence of this contest through comparison of the 1957 *Die Logik der Dichtung* with the revised English-language edition, *The Logic of Literature*, which exhibits significant differences in Hamburger's choice of exemplary texts. In particular, Hamburger expands her discussion of contemporary German literature, especially experimental poetry, and affirms the transformative conception of poetry articulated by Hilde Domin in the 1960s.

To consider the implications of that expansion, this chapter accordingly concludes with a schematic consideration of the position of women poets in German cultural life after 1945 that connects the positions articulated in *Die Logik der Dichtung* with questions about poetry's functions, contents, and readerships that will be pursued in subsequent chapters. The postwar West German literary climate was characterized by contradictory demands from literary tradition, academic scholarship, and journalistic criticism. Far from being a protected enterprise, poetry unfolds in this context as a politicized project that responds dramatically to an overdetermined, yet richly international, aesthetic environment. While the rhetoric of a fresh start and break with the past captures much literary attention well into the 1960s, the writings of Hilde Domin, Ulla Hahn, and Ursula Krechel express important reservations on the part of women writers about this type of oppositional avant-gardism, which Peter Bürger placed at the center of twentieth-century artistic innovation.[15] Absent this antagonistic hubris, women's poetry is better aligned with the model Rainer Rumold proposes for the German avant-garde, which he concludes was "considerably less given to programmatic break with the institution of art than to a mediation of modernity and tradition" (2002, xix). What I want to propose, then, is that women writers powerfully expand the lyric genre's possibilities by struggling against that postwar literary context in a way that incrementally redefines notions of subjectivity, representation, and canon.

Theory Moves and Genre Troubles

Die Logik der Dichtung (1957) proceeds out of dissatisfaction with theory. As Hamburger observes in explaining her commitment to meta-criticism in the second, revised edition in English translation, *The Logic of Literature* (1973):

> Hitherto neither genre analysis of poetics nor the interpretation of individual literary works has taken into account the fact that narrative and dramatic literature afford us the experience of fiction or of nonreality, whereas this is not the case with lyric poetry. However, that which is mediated as experience has its cause in the mediating phenomenon itself. The phenomena are lyric, epic, and drama, and also every single representative of each of these types. That epic and drama impart the experience of nonreality, while the lyric imparts that of reality, is alone due to the logical and hence the linguistic structure which underlies them. For this reason the logic of literature is also the phenomenology of literature. (1973, 5)[16]

From this perspective, the lyric genre aims to create a heightened reality of constitutive elements (the kind of opaque representations that for Johann Wolfgang von Goethe are both phenomena and theory), an effect that is intensely experienced on its own terms by the recipient of the text. The epic and drama, on the other hand, lavishly use deictics,[17] past form narration that simulates present actions, speech representations, and simulations of time and space that display the artifice of their construction, according to Hamburger's analysis.

What is at stake for Hamburger is clearly something larger than the philological study of the rules and history of a particular genre. Her project is not about the formal literary properties that Wolfgang Kayser described in *Kleine deutsche Versschule* (*Little German Verse School*, 1946), nor the preservation of the genre boundaries of lyric, epic, and drama mapped by Emil Staiger in *Grundbegriffe der Poetik* (*Basic Concepts of Poetry*, 1946), nor even the oppositional qualities of modern style that Hugo Friedrich defined in *Die Struktur der modernen Lyrik* (*The Structure of Modern Poetry*, 1956).[18] Hamburger instead steps outside this body of literary scholarship and into phenomenology as a presumptively neutral sphere of intellectual exchange. All the same, she is at the outset particularly interested in distinguishing her project from that of Staiger, who is described by Hamburger as arriving at new ways of interpreting literature "by distilling from the traditional formal concepts of lyric, epic, and drama the lyrical, the epic, and the dramatic, understood as consolidations of existential attitudes: as recollection, representation and tension" (Hamburger 1973, 4). Departing radically from the conventional division of literature into three genres, Hamburger proposes instead two fundamental categories of literature—the fictional or mimetic genre (encompassing epic, drama, and film) and the lyrical genre.[19] In poetry, Hamburger emphatically asserts, "What we expect to experience and empathize with is experience itself, not merely something factual, but something palpable" (Hamburger 1957, 180).

My aim in examining Hamburger's project as a prelude to later discussion of German women's writing is in part to bring into focus a gendered asymmetry that inhabits postwar aesthetic debates pertaining to interpretive authority, even when that factor remains unstated in the assertions made about poetics and poetry.[20] By virtue of its publication date (1957), *Die Logik der Dichtung* offers a salient test case for studying the latent biases of aesthetic claims of its era because it appears at a historical moment when pretensions to critical neutrality are at an apogee (see Zimmermann 1988, 393). Revisionist appraisals of the work of postwar German literary scholars, as well as feminist analyses of modernism, have progressively elucidated how exclusionary ideological assumptions become embedded and naturalized in discourses about aesthetics, abstraction, and universality.[21] Indeed, Rita Felski observes that "saturation of cultural texts with metaphors of masculinity and femininity is nowhere more obvious than in the case of the modern" (1995, 1). The particular strain of modernism that takes hold in postwar Germany is advanced as both a neutral, aesthetic universalism and as a progressive political attitude. However, that apparent universalism masks underlying power dynamics that have a constraining impact on women writers and other marginal groups.

Committed to creating an unassailable intellectual framework, Hamburger's project runs the risk of taking the objective neutrality promised by traditional scholarship for granted. Even fresh impulses from American New Criticism, which had been imported into Germany as part of initial postwar cultural reeducation initiatives with the intent of promoting democratic values, offered little challenge to these tendencies.[22] Along with international modernist poetry, New Criticism possessed the cachet of political correctness. Its seductive illusion of unprejudiced readers opening themselves to texts—a comfortable premise for Hamburger's work—is, of course, not really possible.[23] Publication of *Die Logik der Dichtung* predates the formulation of hermeneutics in Hans Georg Gadamer's *Wahrheit und Methode* (*Truth and Method,* 1960), which ultimately did recognize that close reading is always framed by the nonobjective interpretive horizon of the reader (Gadamer 1965). Coming before this more circumspect iteration of hermeneutic interpretation theory, Hamburger admirably tackles instead the question of how literary language itself represents reality by focusing on the construction of the lyrical *I*. This analysis of subjectivity in many respects anticipates the later emphasis on expressiveness that comes to define women's writing. Moreover, though her examples draw primarily on the established literary tradition (notably Goethe, Friedrich Schiller, Georg Trakl, and Rainer Maria Rilke), and despite the fact that Hamburger displays no special interest in promoting women writers, she indirectly establishes an important precedent. *Die Logik der Dichtung* contributes to a reformulation of canon through its abundant references to Virginia Woolf, Annette von Droste-Hülshoff, Nelly Sachs, Ricarda Huch, Else Lasker-Schüler, Marie Luise Kaschnitz, and other women authors, validating a framework for future discussions of women's writing.

Divided into five parts, *The Logic of Literature* begins with the premise that literature has an underlying gestalt. Hamburger's insistence on only two genres, which are defined by distinctive modes of representation, signals a radical intention to rethink literature in fundamental terms. She relaxes the apparent strictness of these categories by including anomalous forms (ballad and first-person narrative) and film as objects of analysis. Characterizing the study as "an attempt to extrapolate from the realm of general literary aesthetics a more specific logic of literature" (1973, 1), Hamburger anchors her arguments in the work of philosophers and linguists, taking G. W. F. Hegel's insights into the complex nature of aesthetic representation as a productive starting point, though finding in the Hegelian dichotomy that Benedetto Croce subsequently delineates between intuitive and theoretical knowledge an inadequate foundation for a theory of literary language (1973, 14–17). While she concludes that Croce's conceptual rubrics are too broad, Hamburger also critiques as too narrow Roman Ingarden's organization of the mimetic work of literature into strata of statement types (a schema that draws on Husserl's theory of judgment), because in her view it simply labels properties of literature without resolving the problematical relationship between literature and reality (1973, 18–23). She is more receptive to efforts by Susanne Langer to describe in holistic terms how art creates meaning, yet still objects to Langer's proposal that art constitutes an articulation of abstracted memory (1973, 86–89). These critical gestures firmly detach Hamburger's approach from the interpretations of literary scholars (like Staiger) and journalistic criticism. Yet although this strong theoretical orientation grounds Hamburger's definition of her project as systematic phenomenology, it also represents a particular constellation of intellectual commitments and dispositions that favors rational philosophical thinking as a basis for critical aesthetic authority.

Whereas the elite authority of the literary scholar continued to be asserted by Staiger and other literary scholars debated in *Die Logik der Dichtung*, Hamburger herself actually begins to envision literature as accessible to anyone who understands its underlying principles, even though her dense argumentation and complex explanation of representational dynamics make substantial demands on readers that prohibit the general adoption of her theory that she imagines.[24] Hamburger shrewdly makes plain that Staiger had aligned genre with existential attitudes—a position clearly suited to the immediate postwar ethos. When all of its conflicting assumptions are weighed, however, her theory likewise reveals itself patently as a product of its time. Like New Criticism, it reflects only tangentially on problems of literary valuation. It does not dare to ask whether literature should properly be involved in social critique, yet offers a dedication to Thomas Mann, for whom political engagement was an enduring dilemma.[25] With prescience, too, *The Logic of Literature* argues rigorously for the transparency of literature to readers—a non-elite understanding of texts, and poetry in particular, something that really only achieved broad currency for German writers in the mid-1960s.

Emphasizing the aesthetic properties of literature, Hamburger elevates the act of reading itself to central importance, speculating that unmediated access to text can occur even if the work's creator is unable to explain its underlying structures. "Creative artists themselves are not conscious of this logical structure or inherent order," Hamburger observes, "just as we, when we are thinking and speaking, are little aware of those laws of logic which we must follow if we are to make ourselves understood. However, these laws, once disclosed, provide the literary interpreter with a key to many hidden doors, doors behind which the secrets of the creative process and therewith the forms of literature themselves lie concealed" (1973, 7).

At the same time Hamburger, who confidently occupies the role of the cogent interpreter (very much in the spirit of American New Criticism), states that it is completely acceptable for the artist to be a naive talent who simply revels in the medium. That concession presents certain difficulties. The sovereign free play of the imagination as an activity essential to the creative mind was for good reason a potentially suspect value in postwar literary discourse. Spontaneous creativity, after all, can allow the medium to drive the work, absent accountability. It may radically free the artist from intellectual constraints, and potentially turn art into a subversive project.[26] After 1945, experimentalism's heady potential attracted the creativity of many younger poets writing in German, including concrete poets (such as Eugen Gomringer and Helmut Heissenbüttel), the Vienna group (including H. C. Artmann, Ernst Jandl, and Friederike Mayröcker), and satirists (like Peter Rühmkorf and Günter Grass). At the same time, radical artistic autonomy to the point of nihilistic experimentation remained suspect with poets who remembered the example of Gottfried Benn, whose brief association with fascism served as a reminder that his greatly admired calls for aesthetic sovereignty had a darker side. Nonetheless, by the 1960s, the liberating aspects of play would hold increasing appeal that indelibly marked the writings of Hilde Domin, Hans Georg Gadamer, Herbert Marcuse, and others.

For Hamburger, notions of play and creativity are inseparable from questions of linguistic verisimilitude. Hamburger argues that poetry in its generative playfulness uniquely gains the capacity to create its own reality. This assertion rests on a critique of merely representational language. Her objection to the constructed fiction of mimetic genres implicitly calls into question the validity of the literary realism that had dominated the immediate postwar scene. Common to discussions of literature in Germany between 1945 and 1960 were calls for writing that expressed the shock of the war's aftermath (*Trümmerliteratur*, "literature of the rubble") and showed an attempt to deal with the recent past (*Vergangenheitsbewältigung*).[27] Citing Susanne Langer's *Feeling and Form* (1953), Hamburger instead draws attention to the fact that literature has the capacity only to give the *illusion* of real events in creative ways—that literature is never reality (see Langer 1953).

With regard to this problem of literature's incapacity to represent reality, Hamburger expresses particular skepticism about collective memory. Hamburger comments, "Memory is primarily linked to what we have experienced ourselves. What I can remember is only my own individual past" (1957, 42). So, to speak of memory as a sense of history, Hamburger concludes in agreement with Langer, actually means to engage in metaphorical extrapolation (1957, 43). Hamburger's subsequent discussion of poetry widens the gulf between acts of memory and simplistic realism by sharply distinguishing the use of language as a tool for communication (*Mitteilungsinstrument*) from the poetic use of language as expression (*Ausdrucksinstrument*).[28] "Between the lyrical *I* and the historical, that is to say theoretical or pragmatic *I*, runs a divide that is only recognizable from the perspective of logic, a border that we can characterize as context, a context that announces the will of the expressive subject to be a lyrical *I*" (1957).[29] Thus for Hamburger, poetry matters as experience, but it needs to be freed from ideological and aesthetic constraints of the kind that had been imposed on it in the postwar German context.

Poetry as Documentary or Transformation

While on the surface this debate about the instrumental capacities of language seems tangential to the situation of women's poetry, in the postwar years representation is powerfully bound to gender, for what is valued as worthy of representation is, as it turns out, a quite narrow set of experiences. The position occupied by *Trümmerliteratur* (as well as the cultivated ethos of democratic liberalism that was associated with starting German literature over from the clean slate, from the *Nullpunkt* or zero hour, of 1945) privileged certain types of writing in postwar Germany. As Leeder puts it:

> The premium placed upon the bald documentation of war and its aftermath, the naked saying of the essentials in a language cleansed and simplified, meant that the experience of men—at the front, returning from the trenches—became the dominant poetic paradigm. However, whereas this poetry served to support the myth of a fundamental postwar caesura, much German poetry (perhaps more than other genres) is striking for the continuities which established themselves across the years of the Third Reich. The 1940s and early 1950s also saw a great deal of very different poetry: much of it written by women. (Leeder 2000, 200)

It was not just that ethos or existential positions determined preferred content, but that a perceived and very urgent sense of cultural (and often financial) scarcity drove the literary scene toward self-preserving mainstream trends. Writing a philosophical account of literature in 1957, Hamburger is not positioned to deliver a sweeping correction to the presumptive *Nullpunkt* orientation of postwar German literature, yet to her credit her uncompromising analysis refuses to accept its vaunted realism uncritically. Hamburger thus forcefully opens an important new creative and interpretive space for the lyric genre by shifting attention to larger questions of how representation relates to subjectivity.[30]

Into that space, Hamburger inserts a discussion of poiesis that evolves out of her notion of "die Beschaffenheit des lyrischen Ich" (translated as "the constitution of the lyrical *I*"). Arguing that literature "as the art of language" must not be understood as simply a "verbal art work," Hamburger argues that texts qualify "quite literally as *creative* language [*dichtende Sprache,* in other words creating language or language in the act of creation]" with logico-linguistic functions that "govern it [language] as it produces forms of imaginative literature" (1957, 7). Acknowledging that the difficulty of defining the lyric genre is due to the tautology that the genre is itself defined by the lyric poem (1957, 162), Hamburger explicitly separates poetic expression from mere statement. She further emphasizes, "The lyrical form is the expression of the will of the declarative subject not to have its expression understood as being directed toward a connection with reality, be it a historical, theoretical, or pragmatic connection" (1957, 164).[31]

In attempting to define more explicitly the lyrical *I*, especially through her treatment of the problem of objective interpretation and the ontological status of the lyrical *I* in love poetry (1957, 182–84), Hamburger embarks on a series of qualifying clarifications that seek to avoid the critical pitfalls that arise if one assumes that poetic texts should be read as strictly biographical. Most conspicuously, she takes pains not to banish biographical-historical information artificially from close readings of texts, as could hypothetically occur with New Criticism.[32] To this end, she defines a variable spectrum for the appreciation of qualities of objectivity and subjectivity in works of poetry. Rejecting the notion that it would be possible to disassociate iconic writers like Goethe, Immanuel Kant, and Martin Heidegger from their prose works, Hamburger concludes that the same standards of interpretation should be applied to poetry:

> Therefore the lyrical statement-subject is identical with the poet, just as well as the statement-subject of a work in history, philosophy,

or the natural sciences is identical with the author of the respective work. That is, identical in the logical sense. But, whereas in the case of such reality-documents this identity-factor presents no problems, because the statement-subject plays no role in their content—their being completely object-oriented—in the case of the lyric I it must be modified to a certain degree. Logical identity does not imply that every statement in a poem, or even the entire poem, has to correspond to real experience of the creating subject. (1973, 276)

Hamburger's assertion that the boundary between author and text is fluid in poetry ingeniously dispenses with simplistic biographical readings. By hypothesizing a harmonic consonance between experience and subjectivity—rather than an exact correspondence—she locates securely within the metalanguage of the poem. Hamburger insists on a rigorous "logic" in analyzing all types of discourse and yet she simultaneously works toward a radical notion of the specialness of poetic language.

Long after Hamburger, this tenet that lyric poetry is not simply the unmediated expression of an author's feelings resurfaces as an issue in late-twentieth-century German poetry. It is taken up with greater vigor two decades later when feminism challenges gender roles forged in the Cold War era and, in fact, becomes one of the central flash points in the discussion of women's writing, as the critical controversy surrounding Ulla Hahn attests. Circling in on this fundamental problem of poetic representation, Hamburger exercises prescient insight in 1957 into a literary problem that will continue to fester by reminding us that it is impossible to read subjective discourses with detached objectivity. Her discussion of subjectivity, which foregrounds the theoretical issues that underlie postwar debates about representation, also allows us to track how these tensions were realized as part of an evolving literary history, if we consider the choices Hamburger makes as she cites exemplary texts.

If, as Hamburger argues, poetic language has a special relationship to reality, then it would follow that the discovery of this principle ultimately demands practices of reading more adequately attuned to the dynamic social function of literature. Hamburger herself pushes forward in this direction. In the heavily revised English edition of *The Logic of Literature,* Hamburger makes noteworthy refinements. Her choice of examples changes to address the situation of contemporary poetry with its emphasis, according to Hamburger, on "the purely linguistic artistic phenomenon" (1973, 232). Gone are many exemplary texts from the traditional German canon—poetry by Joseph von Eichendorff, Hans Carossa, and Theodor

Storm. Quotations are abridged as well, although Goethe, Rilke, Trakl, and Eduard Mörike continue to illustrate Hamburger's arguments. Gottfried Benn's "Was schlimm ist" ("What's Terrible"), quoted in *Die Logik der Dichtung* (1957, 174–75), disappears. By contrast, one of Bertolt Brecht's poems about Hitler ("Wenn der Anstreicher durch die Lautsprecher über den Frieden redet . . ." "When the house painter talks about peace through the loud speaker . . .") is now cited in *The Logic of Literature* (1973, 264–65).

These editorial changes tacitly reflect the cultural ascendancy of Brecht over Benn in the 1960s and simultaneously register shifting notions of readership. As an advocate of esoteric, monologic poetry, Benn inspired German poets with his lecture series "Probleme der Lyrik" ("Problems of Poetry," 1951), especially writers who chose to pursue hermeneutic poetry with its perceived detachment from politics. Brecht, who returned to East Germany from U.S. exile in the late 1940s, experienced a more delayed reception, but the accessibility of his language and his sharp political critique made his work a model for socially engaged younger poets in the subsequent decades.[33] Turning to Brecht, then, Hamburger displays an inclination to accept a rhetoric of engagement not used in the 1957 German edition, thus embracing a notion of political poetry, which she construes in broader terms to encompass poetry of the Holocaust by Nelly Sachs and Paul Celan (1973, 263).

Hamburger remarks on the vitality of experimental literature as well, a change that represents more than a simple updating of the project. Citing Max Bense's conviction that words respond to objects (Bense, a contemporary literary theorist, was keenly interested in questions raised by automatic writing) and commenting that this semiotic relationship is the basis for twentieth-century innovation in poetic language by such authors as Stéphane Mallarmé, Arno Holz, and Gertrude Stein, Hamburger also inserts a poem by Holz (a naturalist author who had dedicated himself to advancing a radical transformation of writing through pioneering literary writing and theoretical work). She deems Holz the epitome of "another expression for the lyric statement process in general," albeit an extreme development (1973, 257). Nonetheless, Hamburger generously finds that Holz's work produces a "verbalization of the thing meant" (1973, 259) that now conforms to both her own and Bense's definition of poetry. Considering the more recent development of concrete poetry, however, she argues against its inclusion in the lyric genre:

> The predominance of language, its being made absolute or "concrete" seems to be the reason for the abolishment of the lyric form

qua form—a process extending into the most recent developments
in "concrete poetry," which works on the graphic plane with words,
syllables and letters, and produces "visual texts." With such manipulation of linguistic elements as graphic material, the frontier is
reached where lyric subject-object correlation is no longer valid
or applicable, and precisely for this reason, it appears to us, this
concrete-visual form of poetry no longer falls within the category
of the lyric. (1973, 262)

Lyric poetry, Hamburger emphasizes, "transforms reality into a reality
of subjective experience" (1973, 286). Made of language, poetry is not
simply words.

This insistence on an even more robust subjectivity to support adequate literary representation motivates the conclusions Hamburger then
draws in her chapter about the lyrical genre for the English edition.
Although the final pages of this section again overlap with the contents of
the German edition, Hamburger first inserts an important new reference
to Hilde Domin.[34] These remarks connect Hamburger's scholarly theory
with ongoing developments in German contemporary poetry criticism.
Referring to Domin's anthology *Doppelinterpretationen* (*Double Interpretations,* 1966), which juxtaposed poems with commentary by poets
and critics, Hamburger deliberates about Domin's invitation to make
poetry a vehicle for interpretation:

> The lyric poem is an open logical structure because it is constituted
> by a statement-subject, and this is as such the reason "for the ulti-
> mate inexplicability from which and in which (the poem) lives," as
> one modern poetess, Hilde Domin, formulates it, tracing the inter-
> pretive variability of the poem back to just that. A poem is open as
> to interpretation and this is true in principle even for the simplest,
> most directly approachable poem. (1973, 286–87)

This firm assertion frames Hamburger's meta-interpretative project as
compatible with the distinctly populist approach advocated by Domin,
which will categorically authorize anyone to interpret poetry. In the context of the other affinities Hamburger displays toward accessible poetry
(reflected, for example, in the substitution of Brecht for Benn), this
remark carries an implicit critique of artificial divisions between "high"
and "low" culture. Hamburger brooks no recourse to mere connoisseurship in matters of poetry. Instead, *The Logic of Literature* promises, along
with a rigorous gestalt-oriented methodology, an appreciation of texts on

their own terms—an interpretive stance that potentially aspires to open the literary field to writers outside the mainstream.

Subjectivity and Postwar Poetry

Hamburger's obvious appreciation for the material of poetry—words, linguistic overtones, experimental creativity—commits her project firmly to a deeper appreciation of the lyric genre. Pursuing the underlying gestalt of literature, Hamburger seeks to overcome the limitations of historical scholarship, tendentious existential attitudes, and normative genre studies, and aspires instead to a transcendent form of interpretation that will account for subjectivity. Because Hamburger asserts that the lyric genre uniquely depends on the cerebral construction of its meaning by an active reader, she is not prepared to accept as inevitable a radical disjuncture of signifier and signified. However, she also does not seek to make poetry merely an abstract object of study. Rather, Hamburger ultimately claims that the understanding of literature depends on collective experience that must develop through the participation of a wide audience of individual readers, a principle that we will find elaborated by Hilde Domin in *Doppelinterpretationen*. Hamburger's *Die Logik der Dichtung* is thus, in many respects, finally an aspirational project that arises out of the hope of creating community through reading.

Returning now to the problem of how to reconcile the lyrical *I* with the empirical *I* of the poet, which is in essence a matter of how individual readers respond to texts, we can better appreciate the reasons why in the German context the question of autobiographical fallacy is not simple, even for sophisticated critics and interpreters.[35] Viewed as a question about how the institution of literature is shaped by history and theory, the recurrent tendency toward the conflation of persona with work can be seen to pose a problem not just for individuals, but also for women writers in general, who as a group remain perennially vulnerable to this particular form of misprision.[36] In fact, it is more than a hypothetical issue. Analyzing the recent case of the so-called *Fräuleinwunder* in the late 1990s, Peter J. Graves rightly objects that the label gives more weight to the physical attributes of the woman author than to her books (2002, 206).[37] This journalistic label, he ventures, was in essence shrewd marketing—a slogan coined to play up the charismatic, physical attractions of young German women writers. In drawing this conclusion, Graves invokes Virginia Woolf's lament about the constraints faced by women writers and regrets that at a time when postures of feminine reticence and male extroversion seem outdated—indeed, in an arguably post-feminist era—such categorical labels inevitably overstate affinities while muffling the voices of individual authors (2002, 196–97, 207).

The nervousness that both Hamburger and Graves display about biographical cul-de-sacs points to an intractable dilemma, namely the recurrent claim made to justify literature is that its purpose lies in transforming reality. That claim is taken to transcend national, historical, and cultural context. Though we need not enter into an analysis of such justifications here, we should acknowledge the repeated invocation of this rationale by German literature after 1945, where commitment to social transformation became one of the hallmarks for defining aesthetic success.[38] Confidence in the ability of art to effect that transformation is, however, inflected quite differently in the paradigms of 1950s modernism and of postmodernism on the leading edge of the twenty-first century. The overarching assertion that art transforms makes the value of subjectivity one of the most contentious issues for German poetry throughout the long postwar period, even when it is seemingly overshadowed by other discourses. On the one hand, pure inwardness (an extreme form of subjectivity that sporadically resurfaces throughout this period) is repeatedly seen as an abandonment of the notion that artistic expression transcends the individual and can effect transformation in broader society. On the other hand, "genuine" self-expression (a more general type of subjectivity) acquires positive worth due to its perceived uniqueness and transformational impetus. This second type of subjectivity, so it is assumed, has the capacity to build pressures for change, even though it may originate from marginal sources that at first glance appear to have little effect.

After Hamburger, the poets Domin, Ulla Hahn, and Ursula Krechel, whose work will be the focus in subsequent chapters, explore further how individual expression intersects with collective practices of reading to become transformative. In many respects the success of these women in advancing this agenda is surprising, considering the cultural history of the postwar period. Given the rampant proliferation of poetry immediately after the war (Schnell 1993, 90), the marginal situation of women working in the lyric genre starkly mirrors the era's awkward divisions. Marianne Vogel concludes that during the postwar years women participated only on a limited basis in literary debates and were rarely the subject of these discussions (2002, 227). Still, Günter Häntzschel offers the more positive finding that women were surprisingly well represented in literary publishing venues at the start of the 1950s, even though they were overlooked in standard literary histories.[39] While such circumstances did not necessarily limit private writing, they certainly affected public reception.[40]

In this environment, Käte Hamburger's pioneering effort to engender a broad theory about what constitutes the lyric genre reminds us that writing is not simply about self-expression and autonomy, but rather always involves larger cultural forces. Her striking emphasis on subjectivity as the source of poetic creativity and a trait fundamental to literary expression animates a discourse strand in poetics that anticipates cultural debates of sustained significance for German women writers. Though in many respects a marginalized scholar, Hamburger herself remains unconcerned about the marginalization of poetry. Instead, she envisions a transformation of the ways in which the lyric genre is seen to operate that in principle renders it more accessible. Throughout her discussion about the dynamic subjectivity of the lyrical *I*, she insists on the unresolved openness of poetic language. Finally, Hamburger recognizes the paradoxical possibility of the coexistence of the "objective" aesthetic theory and the "subjective" experience of poems. Thus in her effort to bridge that interpretive divide, Hamburger invites a deeper response to the pleasure and complexity of poetry by embracing its ineffable creativity.

Chapter Two

◆

Sighs and a Longing for Solidarity:
Hilde Domin and Feminism's Volatility

"That women write in a fundamentally different way, that I don't see," Hilde Domin emphatically declares in her second poetry lecture at the University of Frankfurt (1987–88). Even so she quickly adds, "And yet: what woman would not at times have issued the exasperated sigh of the Droste, 'If only I were a man then at least / the heavens would counsel me'" (1988a, 48).[1] Not only do these statements clash, Domin's subsequent rejection of *Frauenlyrik* (women's poetry) as a category, and her insistence that an approach of *Sachlichkeit* (realism or objectivity) alone can break down intellectual ghettos (1988a, 52), would also have been unpopular in feminist circles, so Harald Hartung observes (1994, 189).[2] It is a curious position, considering that in the decade preceding these lectures feminist scholarship had renewed interest in Domin's work (Lermen and Braun 1997, 7). Domin's contradictory stance, however, is intrinsic to the German literary scene in the late 1980s.

Although the disjuncture stems at least in part from the loosely associative, autobiographical quality of Domin's lectures, that element of contradiction is a good measure of the volatile relationship between postwar German poetry and feminism. Of course, the problem is not simply a German one. As Denise Riley puts it in writing about feminism and the field of history, "The apparent continuity of the subject of 'women' isn't to be relied on; 'women' is both synchronically and diachronically erratic as a collectivity, while for the individual, 'being a woman' is also inconstant, and can't provide an ontological foundation. Yet it must be emphasized that these instabilities of the category are the *sine qua non* of feminism" (1988, 2). If we accept Riley's premise, however, we still need to come to grips with the meaning this variability has for the work of individual artists. What interests me about Domin is precisely the fact that she begins to write in what is arguably a pre-feminist context and that her career subsequently unfolds at a point when feminism is beset by such instabilities.[3] Her writings thus reflect a high uncertainty about gender politics, but they also draw strength by foregrounding the subjective perspective of the "woman."

The exercise of reading Domin's work with attention to gendered aspects leads directly into the shifting currents of German postwar culture, where the contradictory attitudes presented by mid-century modernism encountered new pressures for aesthetic change in the 1960s. In her theoretical writings, Domin responds to these tensions by engaging in the "poiesis of rewriting" supplied in Terry Threadgold's account of the complex patterns of reaction, appropriation, and invention that can be observed in women's writing (1997, 1). Apart from the kind of dialogic theoretical reflection that Threadgold's critical model explains, Domin also engages in an even more fundamental praxis of poiesis to the extent that she uses poetry itself to bind various discourse tropes to gender. Such latent work, Threadgold argues, constitutes some of the most powerful theory-making because it is performed not through explicit statements, but rather through literary gestures that implicitly model new conceptual paradigms (1997, 28). This writerly approach to theoretical aesthetic problems allows Domin to keep her distance from preliminary and essentialist conceptions of feminism while positioning her to articulate a new poetics based on her convictions about the link between gender and creativity in general.

Before turning to these issues, my analysis begins with Domin's poetry/criticism anthology *Doppelinterpretationen* (*Double Interpretations*, 1966) and the programmatic essay collection *Wozu Lyrik heute* (*Why Poetry Today?* 1968) to get at the terms of political engagement, modernist aesthetics, and poetic identity that shaped the German literary scene surrounding her. While these publications connect with the dominant postwar conceptions of the lyric genre, Domin's projects, I argue, diverge from the views of her contemporaries and seek to change the aesthetic climate in fundamental ways. The distinct position she occupies with her notion of intellectual engagement becomes obvious when her views are compared with those articulated by Hans Magnus Enzensberger and Herbert Marcuse. Following this discussion, a close reading of Domin's "Drei Arten Gedichte aufzuschreiben" ("Three Ways of Writing Poems," dating from 1967–68) determines that this key poem sequence for Domin invokes a discourse of gender that has explanatory power in defining women's writing. The chapter concludes with an analysis of Domin's Frankfurt poetry lectures, "Das Gedicht als Augenblick von Freiheit" ("The Poem as an Instant of Freedom"), which explores Domin's belated support for feminism and finds in her work evidence of discursive patterns and representational practices characteristic of women's writing in the late twentieth century.[4]

Double Interpretations

German intellectual discourse after 1945 valorizes expressions of political engagement as the hallmark of a progressive society. Yet for many reasons, feminine voices articulating women's concerns were often perceived as a weak partner in this public debate. So, despite the certitude with which scholars and critics have interpreted Domin as a writer whose oeuvre seems to participate predictably in the postwar ethos, something remains ineffably puzzling about her work. While her reputation today benefits from the alignment of her biography with conventional postwar narratives about how marginalization motivated corrective ethical engagement, and her poems appear straightforward and accessible in that context, "perfection in simplicity" according to Walter Jens (1998, 53), their impact nonetheless remains hypothetical. And Domin herself seems to downplay the force of her own words.[5] Writing in "Geburtstage" ("Birthdays"), a poem that begins somberly on the occasion of her deceased mother's birthday, the poet notes that poems are like the newborn fawn (*Reh*) that stands on its own immediately after birth:

> Ich habe niemand ins Licht gezwängt
> nur Worte
> Worte drehen nicht den Kopf
> sie stehen auf
> sofort
> und gehn (1987c, 312)

> I have not forced anyone into the light
> only words
> words don't turn their head[6]
> they stand up
> right away
> and go

Taking the corporeal act of birthing as a starting point, Domin distances the lyrical *I* in this poem from female physicality by replacing the reflex of human maternal attachment with a gender-neutral creation of words. The

power of words to influence is rhetorically predicated on a renunciation
of biological feminine identity, for the poet, we read, is not a human birth
mother. Given her spare use of imagery in poems, it seems particularly
significant that Domin uses the strangeness of this animal birth to access a
more abstract notion of creativity that renders creation itself autonomous
from the artist. Domin's care in avoiding a direct depiction of the poet as
the pregnant doe mirrors an ambivalence about gender that surfaces as
well in her remarks about women writers. Released into the real world,
words' freedom in the abstract gives them unlimited potential in collective life, but also an uncertain fate. Domin's text provides no comfortable
resolution to these problems.

Born in 1909, Hilde Domin lived into the twenty-first century, through
and beyond the upheaval that two world wars brought to Europe.[7] Her
studies (of such subjects as law, economic theory, sociology and philosophy), marriage to and collaboration with the classical archaeologist Erwin
Walter Palm (to whom many poems are dedicated), years as a language
teacher, and even work as a translator seem strangely detached from her
public identity as a highly respected writer. Indeed, these accomplishments scarcely figure in most discussions of her work. Instead, her exile
after 1935 (in Italy, England, and Santo Domingo), return to Germany in
1954, and connections to other Jewish writers like Nelly Sachs and Paul
Celan opened her work to readings that focus on biographically framed
questions of exile, *Heimat* (home), identity, language, and memory (Lehr-
Rosenberg 2003; Wangenheim and Metz 1998; Lermen and Braun 1997;
Bühler-Dietrich 2002; Wangenheim 1982).[8] A latecomer to poetry whose
first attempts at verse date from the early 1950s, Domin seems to applaud
this reading by telling readers, "Ich befreite mich durch Sprache," she
"freed herself through language" or speech (1988b, 14). It is a position
that readily found space in the postwar German cultural landscape under
the category of engaged literature, but political engagement was not her
only concern.

In 1966 Domin published a remarkable collection, *Doppelinterpretationen*. The title explains the book's design: for each poem in the
anthology, the poet provides self-commentary that is paired with the
independent reaction of a critic. The appearance of *Doppelinterpretationen* coincides with a precarious time for German poetry. The scholar
Walter Höllerer and poet Karl Krolow are engaged in heated debate
about the future of the lyric genre. They argue over the merits of long
poems, which Höllerer promoted out of enthusiasm for American models
like Williams Carlos Williams's *Paterson* and Krolow decried as an ero-
sion of poetic craft.[9] The "Goll controversy" was simmering, provoked

by later-dismissed charges of plagiarism that were leveled by Claire Goll (widow of modernist writer Yvan Goll) against the acclaimed younger poet Paul Celan.[10] Meanwhile, the much-vaunted Gruppe 47 had become a fragile coalition by the late 1950s, due to combative critiques, literary marketing, and political disagreements. Though showing temporary signs of fresh vigor in the early 1960s, the group's last regular meeting was to occur in 1967. Domin was not a part of Gruppe 47, but many of the authors in *Doppelinterpretationen* were (see Arnold 2004, 103).[11]

Somehow in the midst of this turmoil, Hilde Domin managed to bring sixty collaborators together (1966, 340) for a collection that she envisioned as a conciliatory *Treffpunkt* (meeting point) for poets and readers (1966, 11).[12] Furthermore, Domin insisted on rules that place critics and poets on equal footing, setting terms of reciprocity that produce startling results. To everyone's surprise, even the most secure respondents found these arrangements unsettling (1988a, 87–88).

Domin's non-elitist, theoretically inclusive conception of poetry cum interpretation reconnects with the intense sensory experience sought by romantic and symbolist poets.[13] Moreover, she boldly promotes poetry as a performative art—an experience realized through reading out loud—a practice she herself had honed in exile (1988a, 37). Above all, Domin rejects dogma and the pose of the ivory tower poet, announcing that for writers encounters with reality are more complex than ever (1966, 16). These terms echo the appraisal of the lyric genre articulated in Hans Magnus Enzensberger's 1960 anthology *Museum der modernen Poesie* (*Museum of Modern Poetry*), yet also signal a crucial departure from the status quo of postwar aesthetics.

Doppelinterpretationen opens with a dense introductory essay, "Über das Interpretieren von Gedichten" ("On the Interpretation of Poems"), that takes stock of postwar German poetry, then systematically advances aesthetic values that had begun to blossom in the mid-1960s. Asserting that poems appeal to both eye and ear, Domin embraces the principles of reader-response theory elaborated by Hans Georg Gadamer in his discussion of hermeneutic interpretation in *Wahrheit und Methode* (*Truth and Method*, 1965). This model for unmediated interaction between reader and text emboldens her confidence in poetry's capacity to work transformatively on its audiences. Steadily, she builds to a crescendo of optimism about the future of poetry that presumes its continuity and transcendent value. "There is no 'zero hour,' nor can one exist: it is nothing more than a mirage. . . . The Eternal, Always-the-Same, Never-the-Same, becomes newly made each moment. Readers do this as fully as those who are writing. This is why art exists; this is why poems exist," Domin asserts (1966,

48). The procedure she applies to reach this lofty conclusion bears careful examination because here Domin dismantles some of the most fundamental, but until then largely unquestioned, assumptions upon which postwar German poetry had been founded, namely the tenet that it broke with the past and cleansed itself by embracing international modernism. Domin's distinct goal is to assert the value of individual experience over abstract modernist rhetoric. The argumentative tactics she adopts include shorthand citation of postwar poetological discourses, movement away from ethically detached positions, and assertion of a more inclusive poetic canon.

Her overview of German postwar poetry first presses the question of how poetry is received by limiting the selection of texts to contemporary works and then by inviting new forms of readership with Domin's declaration that the book is "no anthology in the usual sense of the word" ("keine Anthologie im üblichen Sinne") (1966, 11). From the first pages, Domin makes clear that what interests her about encounters with poets is the powerful synergy poetry produces between the free play of the imagination and rational thought (1966, 12). Her model for the resulting clarity (*Nüchternheit*) is first and foremost Bertolt Brecht, although her position is amply supported by references to Friedrich Hölderlin's Orphic poetry and Theodor W. Adorno's trenchant theoretical insights into the significance of poetry for society (1966, 11–12).

This focus allows Domin to introduce the contrast of Brecht with Gottfried Benn; thus it invokes the preeminent dichotomy that had shaped German verse since the early 1950s. Explaining her examples, Domin expresses skepticism about the coldly rational working procedures espoused by Benn, particularly in his influential *Probleme der Lyrik* (*Problems of Poetry,* 1951), and observes that they can only be understood within the esoteric confines of artistic work (1966, 12). She then challenges the prevailing categories of contemporary German verse, declaring that it is in fact neither merely cerebral like Benn's work, nor politically engaged, á la Brecht (1966, 13–15). Mainstream German poetry, as Domin sees it, is "pure" (*rein*); it depends on the creativity of individual poets rather than rigid aesthetic programs (1966, 15–16).

The thrust of this argument is Domin's dramatic assertion that German poetry has moved beyond the notion of *Kahlschlag* (the "clear cut" that signified a total break with the past, represented by 1945). In fact, she goes so far as to declare that "German poetry, more than the politicians, is 'finished' with the 'past'" (1966, 15), a statement of strategic significance for Domin's project. Despite Domin's claim, rejection of the notion of *Kahlschlag,* a term synonymous with the concept of a *Stunde Null* or "zero hour," was in fact still as yet only faint in mainstream literary discourse.[14] This act of publicly rewriting the conceptual framework for the lyric genre by pronouncing an end to this rhetoric of postwar aesthetics is a bold maneuver on Domin's part. When she asserts that the continuity of German literature is more significant for the writers themselves than is any rupture signified by some "zero hour," Domin emphatically challenges one of the most basic assumptions of the postwar literary scene. It is a break with the dominant view that poets should in a sense be the moral watchdogs of society, a move that liberates poetry from a particular set of stylistic and content burdens.

As Stephen Brockmann observes in his detailed study of the period, *German Literary Culture at the Zero Hour,* "In the literary history of postwar Germany, Weyrauch's primarily literary *Kahlschlag* came to be inextricably associated with Richter's and Andersch's insistence on cultural-political and generational *tabula rasa,* conflating the primary areas of German culture, from politics to literature to morality, in an attempted—but failed—radical new beginning" (2004, 196). Brockmann, of course, is concerned with the major contours of this period, rather than the growing significance of peripheral trends that occupy us here. The concept of the "zero hour" that Domin evokes refers to features of this dominant social dynamics, not the least of which is a generation gap that is often expressed as a rebellion of the "youth," a term that barely disguises the extent to which this tension was figured as gendered, a masculine father-son conflict (compare Brockmann 2004, 170–207). Thus while *Doppelinterpretationen* pays tribute to the best aspirations of modernism, its reservations about postwar rhetoric point to ways in which these modernist discourses had with time become the newly entrenched establishment. The ideological attraction of the *Stunde Null* concept depended on the linkage between a favored democratic ethos and ostensibly universal aesthetic values. To correct the impasse inadvertently created by this conflation of ideas, Domin argues that poetry must tolerate ideological as well as formal diversity, and she therefore promotes a conception of the lyric genre grounded in the authority of individual experience.

In my view, Domin's *Doppelinterpretationen* accomplishes this task convincingly by spelling out that vision for poetry as an autonomous ethical act. She conceives of the anthology as a collective project freed from any single ideology, including the notion of the "zero hour." The texts she chooses, as she explains in a concluding essay about the selection process ("Rechenschaftsbericht," an accounting), have been written in the past fifteen years. In other words, they represent German lyric poetry *after* both Benn and Brecht through works published between 1950 and 1965 (1966, 338). "This book is intended to serve understanding of the contemporary German poem, concretely and through individual examples," Domin writes, defining her goals (1966, 16). These remarks politely, though firmly, put space between Domin's project and theoretical writings that defined German literary culture in the 1950s, notably Hugo Friedrich's *Die Struktur der modernen Lyrik* (*The Structure of Modern Poetry*, 1956), with its reading of modern poetry as inherently dissonant and resistant to interpretation, and Adorno's *Prismen* (*Prisms*), which contained his famous pronouncement that to write poetry after Auschwitz would be barbaric (1955a, 31).[15]

Domin sustains her effort to lay the past to rest by countering contemporary poetological discourses that in her view had reached the limits of their usefulness for contemporary writers. Whereas Paul Celan spoke of the poem as being "ever mindful of its dates" (1986, 34), Domin applauds an ongoing process of constructing meaning that keeps a text fresh rather than consigning it to archive the past (1966, 47). In doing so, she rhetorically aligns her project with Hans Magnus Enzensberger's conviction that poetry is an atelier for working poets (1960b, 766–67). Unlike Enzensberger, however, Domin voices confidence that German poetry is not provincial and has achieved international stature (1966, 15). Through this assertion, Domin reframes the purpose of anthologies as programmatic documents, making it clear that her project no longer needs to be part of an intellectual catch-up program to reposition German poetry in an international context—a program saliently articulated in *Museum der modernen Poesie* by Enzensberger, one of the contributors to *Doppelinterpretationen*.[16]

Rewriting these discourses, Domin frees the lyric genre from a one-dimensional construction of poetry as the agonizing response to horrific events. In the process, she also relaxes the hold of academic authority over it. Through a lengthy exposition on how to read and interpret poems, Domin gradually strips the participants in *Doppelinterpretationen* of special authority based on academic standing. Domin first pronounces contemporary poets no more qualified as intellectuals than writers of the past, commenting, "The modern poet is not a more trained mind, no more a *poeta doctus* [erudite poet], than were, for example the romantics or the poets of the renaissance, although the common prejudice, whether voiced in praise or rebuke, labels us 'more reflective'" (1966, 16). The remark sets aside the credentials of the *poeta doctus,* a moniker often used to validate the significance of contemporary authors. By then pointing out that scholarly misinterpretations are relatively common, Domin further downplays the authority of critics and reviewers (1966, 34–35). Finally, she describes the interpreters who contributed to *Doppelinterpretationen* as being selected for their perceived interest in the authors and texts, rather than for any prestigious academic stature (1966, 339). These principles frame *Doppelinterpretationen* as a playing field that offers remarkably level terrain for poets and critics/scholars.

However, its construction was openly provocative in the way it crossed matchmaking with blind submissions. Of the thirty-one poets chosen to represent the contemporary scene, eight are women, a generous proportion for anthologies of the era. Interestingly, all of the interpreters/readers are men, many leading scholars of the time (including Clemens Heselhaus, Hans Georg Gadamer, Hans Mayer, and Benno von Wiese). According to Domin, one *Spielregel* (rule of the game) for participants was inviolable: the poet must not be informed about the identity of the critical respondent until after his reaction was submitted (1966, 338). Interpreters, on the other hand, were asked to choose an author of interest from a list of names and, according to Domin, were matched with texts for which they would be sympathetic readers (1966, 339). This recipe could easily make poets feel vulnerable, if their authority to speak about their work was not given equal standing with the contributions of interpreters. But Domin strives to create a balance of powers by defining interpretation as co-construction of text by author and reader.[17] Making clear that she sees *Doppelinterpretationen* as an innovative, collective project, Domin questions the very authority by which postwar poetry speaks. Theory and praxis in *Doppelinterpretationen* upend the conventional balance of powers among poem, poet, and reader. This intervention shakes up public/private sphere distinctions and thereby supports Domin's secondary aim of describing a poetics adequate to contemporary writing.

Here we must pause to reflect on the nature of Domin's arguments as well as the content of her statements. Since the points she makes result from processual rewriting, a tone of negotiation rather than confrontation characterizes her positions. From the vantage point of 1966, this logical structure clashes with the dialectical argumentation style preferred by many fellow writers, notably Enzensberger. Instead Domin exercises a capacity for integrative thought and high awareness of context that is congruent with the explanation of the feminine constructivist thought process described in *Women's Ways of Knowing*, which builds on the research of Carol Gilligan (Belenky et al. 1986). For such constructivists, the authors assert, "it is in the process of sorting out pieces of the self and of searching for a unique and authentic voice that women come to the basic insights of constructivist thought: *All knowledge is constructed,* and *the knower is an intimate part of the known*" (1986, 137). Integration, rather than antagonism, shapes the interpretive negotiations of poet and reader that Domin sanctions in *Doppelinterpretationen*. Synthesis becomes the precondition for establishing the relationship necessary for the experience of poetry according to the terms of poetic experience that Domin promotes. That drive toward that synthesis and eventual reconciliation, rather than antagonism, emboldens her to move beyond the constrained aesthetics of *Kahlschlag* and take the potential of experimental forms of poetry seriously. Accordingly, many of the conceptual moves Domin makes in *Doppelinterpretationen* occur through poetological tropes rather than direct critique, emerging as latent arguments and discourse strands that resonate across her work.

The latter half of the introductory essay, where we see this form of argumentation at work in particular, focuses on the ways in which poems must be understood to come into being in and exist as a dynamic medium. Domin rejects the notion that poetry is static by describing how poems manipulate the dynamic fluidity and coexistence of contradictions (word/image, meaning/form, mind/body, objective rationalism/subjectivity) (1966, 22–23). Invoking concepts of sight, breath, and handicraft (*handwerkliches Vorgehen*) as poetically central (1966, 41),[18] Domin emphasizes unequivocally that we possess a capacity for *perceptual* thinking. For Domin, "sehen lernen, hören lernen, lesen lernen" (1966, 19), literally "learning to see, to hear, to read," is fundamentally linked to learning by seeing, hearing, and reading. And such sensuous learning is required to really experience art, an experience that is, in turn, according to Domin, a precondition for its interpretation. Accordingly, Domin explains, authors who qualify as "Sprachingenieure" ("language engineers"), like concrete poet Helmut Heißenbüttel, are perhaps overrepresented in the collection (1966, 14) because they push the boundaries of the lyric genre and, hence, their work poses special challenges for interpretation. "It is certain," Domin writes, "that the modern poem in its duality, more than earlier poetry, must be heard as well as read. Eye and ear complement each other, they cannot replace each other" (1966, 27).[19]

For Domin, poetry's dynamic, kinesthetic energy, which she also equates with the power of breath, defines the lyric genre. "The modern poem," Domin writes, "is something fundamentally optical, that is probably the prevailing opinion (Benn et al.). It must be experienced with the eyes. That is certainly correct. But it is only a part of the truth. It must be breathed in" (1966, 21). In making this claim about the physiological experience of the text, Domin prepares for a discussion of poetic breath (one of her key tropes for representing the power of poetry) that aligns contemporary German work with that of the Americans Charles Olson[20] and Robert Frost.[21] However, the significance Domin attaches to breath is less a formal matter of emphasizing line or syntax than of marking an absolutely crucial ontological direction: the turn of breath (*Atemwende*) that Paul Celan claimed for poetry and inscribed as the title of his 1967 poetry collection by that name (1972, 141).[22]

Domin's appeal to this aesthetic discourse emphasizes that for the lyric genre as a whole artistic expression depends on physical performance and collective interaction.[23] Breath, for Domin, is not simply a convenient metaphor signifying some abstract relief. Like the physical gestures captured in Jackson Pollock's action painting, it is the intense embodiment of subjective expression in the process of being produced—a manifestation of the forceful creative act of the poet that anticipates the kind of expression that "New Subjectivity" will try to develop.[24]

Acknowledging that poems seem to have the status of a *Denkmal* (monument) fixed in memory, Domin nonetheless asserts their capacity to stimulate the reader with very sensual, even sexual, living effects (1966, 24–25). Domin, here reviving symbolist aesthetic principles, argues that the *Erregung* (stimulation) that the poet feels when writing a poem is directly experienced by the reader through breath. Frozen (*eingefroren*) in the poem, according to Domin, "the breath of the reader, led by the breath of the poet, is thawed out, and, in its own, original manner, brought to flow again" (1966, 25). Through its sensuous iteration, the poem becomes a seemingly contradictory fluid monument, a "lingering fleeting, [an] object of observation—capable of being experienced, always new, as identification" (1966, 25). Domin thus invests poetic breath with primal significance. Breathing, as Luce Irigaray observes, is a reflex of both profound autonomy and interdependence, since "breath exists before and beyond all representations, words, forms, all kinds of specific figurations or even idols, all sorts of rituals or dogmas, and thus allows a communication between cultures, sexes and generations" (2004, 146). For Domin, both reader and poet are in a sense only made alive through the poem's generative breath. Indeed, breathing becomes tantamount to an ethos of collectivity. Separately explaining poetic language in "*Salva nos*" ("Save Us"), she boldly claims:

> Diese ist unsere Freiheit
> die richtigen Namen nennend
> furchtlos
> mit der kleinen Stimme

einander rufend
mit der kleinen Stimme
die Verschlingenden beim Namen nennen
mit nichts als unserm Atem (1987c, 240)

This is our freedom
naming the correct names
without fear
with the small voice

calling each other
with the small voice
the ones who devour calling by name
with nothing but our breath

"*Salva nos,*" like *Doppelinterpretationen,* argues for the possibility of synthesis, dialogue, and the free play of the imagination outside the restrictions of society. Its ethical space becomes available through the "Aneignung, Einswerden" (appropriation, becoming one) that is mediated by the breathing together of poet and reader (1966, 25). The fundamental tension of the modern poem, Domin emphasizes, is dynamic connection, rather than rupture. She sums up: "The newly won concept, which I am provisionally calling the 'concept of simultaneity,' would not consist of thesis, antithesis, synthesis, but rather it would remain a sort of quivering force field" (1966, 23–24).[25] In "*Salva nos,*" breath creates freedom through language, thus binding the poet's subjectivity to the sheer feel of poetic language.

Latent in the notion of breath explored in *Doppelinterpretationen,* as we have seen, is a fundamental conviction that the experience of art mediates profound human relations. Domin's concern with how poetry in this way can ultimately contribute to social discourse is subsequently brought into sharper focus by *Wozu Lyrik heute* (1968). This ambitious essay collection takes as its point of departure the question of whether poetry plays a meaningful role in the contemporary world. Domin is clearly not interested in vague commitments to political action. Instead, her arguments in favor of dismantling traditional social structures specifically predicts their replacement by postmodern conditions, conditions that, Domin asserts, will produce new forms of poetry (1968, 20–21). Two leitmotifs in *Wozu Lyrik heute*—the value of poetry grounded in a conceptual framework supplied in part by Marcuse and the critique of the literature as an industry or institution (*Literaturbetrieb*)—are especially important for discerning Domin's response to feminism.

Substantial portions of the collection predate *Doppelinterpreta-tionen,*[26] although one chapter on interpretation is transferred in from that anthology. *Wozu Lyrik heute* nonetheless reflects more the specific historical context of 1968 than the earlier postwar attitudes previously described.[27] Domin's diagnosis of a shift from diachronic to synchronic society (1968, 20) echoes the analysis of Jürgen Habermas in *Technik und Wissenschaft als "Ideologie"* (*Technology and Science as "Ideology,"* 1968).[28] Likewise, her thinking resonates with Enzensberger's "Commonplaces on the Newest Literature," which seemed to some readers to pronounce an end to literature as an aesthetic project (1968a).[29] Unlike *Doppelinterpretationen,* which gave poets the upper hand in mediating aesthetic debates, *Wozu Lyrik heute* cites a considerable secondary literature (including social and literary theorists Adorno, Walter Benjamin, Hans-Georg Gadamer, Georg Lukács, anthropologist Arnold Gehlen, American social journalist Vance Packard, and others). Domin's references to Herbert Marcuse, however, are the clearest indication of the changed ethos of the 1960s, for in Marcuse Domin finds more robust validation for her belief in the transformative power of art.[30]

Rejecting a conception of the lyric genre as either a flight from reality or a conservative utopia, Domin asserts that poetry belongs

> to the basic requirement for the active shaping of human interaction. And that is completely independent from the content of the poem, it is politically engaged in the narrow sense or simply a seismograph of the time, that is upsetting and at the same time consciousness-raising, heightening the impulse for life. It is directly a guarantor of freedom in this sense. Diametrically opposed to the *one dimensionality* (Herbert Marcuse) of functioning to fit in without contradiction. (1968, 23)[31]

This Herder-inspired argument that poetry is essential to collective life mirrors Marcuse's analysis of "the denial of idealistic culture" (1964, 234). Moreover, despite reservations about what she terms the "parole of the *hippies* or even of the messianic Marxist Herbert Marcuse" (1968, 23), it is clear that Domin shares his concern that "Imagination has not remained immune to the process of reification" (Marcuse 1964, 250). For Domin, poetry is also more than a solipsistic recourse to writing as psychological therapy (1968, 14). Instead, she recognizes the harm caused by the historical separation of sensuousness and rational philosophy, very much as did Marcuse in his discussion of aesthetics in 1955 (Marcuse 1966, 172–96), and breaks these artificial divisions to advocate

imaginative freedom that derives from sensuousness.[32] Thus reaffirm-
ing after *Doppelinterpretationen* the capacity of art to covey meaning
through sensuous form with an immediacy unconstrained by culture,
Domin stresses, "Lyric poetry gives only the essence of that which befalls
the human being. It connects us again with the part of our being that is
untouched by compromises, with our childhood and the freshness of our
reactions" (1968, 14). Poems above all, she concludes, allow their creators
"in einem Augenblick des 'Innehaltens' " (in a moment for pause) space
for true expression, an instant of highest identity and freedom (1968, 32).
This freedom, or "Atemraum für etwas wie Entscheidung" is quite literally "breathing space for making decisions" (1968, 32).

Appearing in 1968, Domin's aesthetic project in *Wozu Lyrik heute*
unfolds against a complex backdrop of social turmoil in which passions
for political causes and women's liberation have not yet diverged as
much as they would later. In a trenchant analysis of postwar discourses
related to gender, *Sex After Fascism,* Dagmar Herzog observes, "Just as
the sexual conservatism of the 1950s was not only about sex but also
served as well as a strategy for mastering the Nazi past, so too, albeit
again in contradictory ways, the sexual revolution of the 1960s and
1970s became a major locus at which intergenerational conflicts over
the events of the 1930s and 1940s were at once engaged and evaded"
(2005, 181–82). Herzog's reading of how sexual and political tensions
become entangled offers a way, I believe, to expose the underlying direction of Domin's reasoning. As Domin experiments with the lens of gender,
tropes of sensuousness become tantamount to the association of sexual
dynamics with creativity. In analyzing Marcuse's contribution to intellectual debates of this era, Herzog observes that although his studies of
sex and power are currently overlooked, as the present analysis of poetological discourses confirms, Marcuse was, according to Herzog, "one
of the first to specify how Nazism's hubristic racism was inseparable
from its attempts to reorganize sexual life, how central the politicization of the previously more private realm of sexuality was to the Nazis'
political agenda, and how it was that sexual excitation could become a
mechanism for social manipulation" (2005, 18).[33] This powerful combination of gender and politics unquestionably makes Domin more
attuned to feminism, as the subsequent close reading of the poem "Drei
Arten Gedichte aufzuschreiben" ("Three Ways of Writing Poems") will
argue.[34]

While tropes (that is, notional clusters), such as the one of breath,
facilitate Domin's individualistic expression of a subjective feminine
perspective, Domin's personal attitudes about women's liberation also

emerge in *Wozu Lyrik heute* through her discussion of how the German *Literaturbetrieb,* or literature industry, sets standards of taste, arbitrates value, and exercises institutional force to promote or suppress writers. Domin treats these subjects in a three-part series of essays grouped under the weighty academic title "The Construction of Literary Opinion: The Dialectic of Judgment, Prejudice, and the Creative Process in the Controlled Society."[35] More detailed than the opening piece "Wozu Lyrik heute" ("Why Poetry Today"), these essays synthesize and extend discussions of literature as an institution by Frankfurt school theorists Adorno and Benjamin, as well as Enzensberger (1964a), and Gadamer (1965).

The first essay in this series, "Urteil als Risiko" ("Judgment as Risk"), which was originally given as a university lecture in Munich in 1967, protests against the commodification of art.[36] Domin objects to the impact of mass production on German literary culture, a postwar phenomenon exemplified through the short shelf life of books (1968, 34). The machinery of literary production demands rapid style change, increasing relativism in aesthetic judgment, and ultimately degradation of the climate for literature. This "crisis of good taste" equates for her with the reduction of art to crass standards (1968, 36), although Domin refrains from critiquing high/low cultural divides. Focusing instead on the setting of taste within literary circles, Domin's analysis repeatedly takes note of the status of women writers and their vulnerability within the cultural system. As part of this analysis "Urteil als Risiko" also discusses how the reputation of an author can be unjustly savaged by critics through a reference to Virginia Woolf's essay "How It Strikes a Contemporary" (1968, 36).

Evoking Kant's disdain for taste as a subjective category and Hans-Georg Gadamer's rejection of external critical standards in favor of the genuine encounter with art (1968, 37), Domin examines a broad spectrum of problems related to the institutional aspects of art—artistic ideologies, writers' groups (from the George circle to Gruppe 47), and de facto self-censorship. Domin cites, for example, Ingeborg Bachmann's reflections in her Frankfurt lectures on the "unofficial terror" used by artistic groups to police taste and Nathalie Sarraute's critique of literary taste in the novel *Les fruits d'or* (*The Golden Fruits*) (1968, 44–47), but does not explicitly relate these issues to gender dynamics.[37]

She minces no words in deploring the marginalization in critical discussions of poets who write with emotional pathos, notably Nelly Sachs, Paul Celan, and Ingeborg Bachmann (1968, 49). On this point Domin concludes with an impassioned affirmation that authenticity, nonconformity, and even failure have aesthetic value. Culture, she wants her audience to understand, must not be legislated by arbiters of taste (1968, 54). We will return to questions of the marginalization raised by Domin's treatment of literature as an institution in the concluding section of this chapter.

After this analysis of art cliques, Domin turns to a discussion of art's objective value under the title "Werten und 'Gebrauchen' von Kunst" ("Valuing and 'Using' Art"). Proceeding from a rejection of the notion that art can be produced by rigid criteria, Domin embarks on a discussion of *Automatik* (automaticity) that revolves around the question of whether training (rational, muscular, or aesthetic) yields artistic achievement (1968, 56–58). From a twenty-first-century perspective, her preoccupation in this section with computers and their programmability to generate art output may seem quaint, despite salient references to Walter Benjamin's treatment of this problem in "Art in the Age of Mechanical Reproduction" (1968, 56).[38] However, considering the era, Domin grapples boldly with the implications of information technology. The conclusions she draws become the basis for her subsequent rejection of controls that suppress subjectivity. Many aesthetic judgments, in her view, constitute an undesirable *Grenzkontrolle* (border control) for art (1968, 59). Much as in *Doppelinterpretationen,* where she introduces the trope of breath to promote the sensuous value of art, Domin analyzes the example of automaticity to consider more broadly desirable qualities of authenticity and originality that she sees as intrinsically tied to art's special function in society as "Partner, Treffpunkt Freiheit" (partner, meeting point freedom) (1968, 62–64). In both cases, examples serve to confirm her point that for art to thrive it needs to exist independent of the controls of the culture industry (1968, 56–58).

The third essay in *Wozu Lyrik heute,* "Die Institutionalisierung der Literatur und der Aufbau der Meinungsmaschine" ("The Institutionalization of Literature and the Construction of the Opinion Machine"), takes on these issues directly, reprising Domin's discussion of the ideological character of artistic standards (*Maßstäbe*) and the literature industry (*Literaturbetrieb*) from *Doppelinterpretationen* before embarking on a detailed examination of literary marketing. Domin hopes to counter a reduction of art to "culinary matters, decoration, ware, object rather than subject of an encounter" (1968, 74), in other words to resist its trivialization as artifact.[39] Sharing the skepticism of Enzensberger about avant-garde movements (1976), Domin's particular interest lies in reasserting the autonomy, spontaneity, and complexity of art. With insider knowledge as a well-connected writer, she expresses grave concern about the emergence of managed opinion steered by literary cliques as a form of control that reduces artistic individualism and results in false displays of political solidarity (1968, 83–86). The essay that follows, "Lyriktheorie, Interpretation, Wertung" (which originally appeared in 1967 in the literary journal *Neue Deutsche Hefte*), reinforces this discussion by again asserting a privileged, autonomous position of poets with regard to the creation, theorization, and appreciation of poetry.

Though women writers are not their main focus, *Doppelinterpretationen* and *Wozu Lyrik heute* register many gendered tensions in the literary sphere. Domin's rejection of the predominantly masculine *Kahlschlag* aesthetics—with its past histories, rigid dichotomies, critical hierarchies, and ideological constraint—leads her to propose instead dialogic interactions, sensuous artistic media, and an ethos of collective solidarity. In *Wozu Lyrik heute,* the rejection of automaticity and commodification supports an appeal for artistic autonomy and authenticity that would afford marginalized writers, like herself and other women, a greater public space. Both works follow a pattern of adumbrating important aesthetic issues indirectly through tropes and examples; thus it is hardly surprising that Domin's poetry extends this use of tropes to articulate gender dynamics with similar indirectness. Indeed, closer analysis of the poem "Drei Arten Gedichte aufzuschreiben" ("Three Ways of Writing Poems"), written near the time of these two publications, reveals that Domin's apparently minimalistic poetic texts are in fact multilayered constructions that strategically examine forms of agency, subjectivity, and symbolic practice available to postwar women poets through symbolic invocation.

Other Ways of Writing Poems

On July 1, 1968, the first two sections of "Drei Arten Gedichte aufzuschreiben" (dated April 1967) appeared in the newspaper *Süddeutsche Zeitung* under the title "Postulat" or "Postulate" (Lermen and Braun 1997, 115). It was a year after the death of the student activist Benno Ohnesorg on June 2, 1967, an event that drove the Red Army Faction to acts of terrorism in West Germany that were felt deeply in intellectual circles. But these poems seem to avoid this political context and speak of nature as one of the most fundamental sources of poetry. The third section of this poem, which appeared separately in the *Frankfurter Allgemeine Zeitung* in June 1968, then moves the reader unexpectedly into the public sphere. Here Domin calls for a poem the size of the poet, thereby pointing to the original occasion for this poem: the Literaturforum in

Frankfurt arranged by Horst Bingel, where poems were displayed in large poster format.[40] The intimate spaces of lyrical verse are now replaced by the political space for poetry that Domin advocated in *Wozu Lyrik heute*. Let us further explore these seeming contradictions in this cycle, which Domin chose to read publicly in 1988 at the conclusion of her penultimate talk for the Frankfurt Poetry Lectures (1988a, 102–4):

"Drei Arten Gedichte aufzuschreiben"

1.
Ein trockenes Flußbett
ein weißes Band von Kieselsteinen
von weitem gesehen
hierauf wünsche ich zu schreiben
in klaren Lettern
oder eine Schutthalde
Geröll
gleitend unter meinen Zeilen
wegrutschend
damit das heikle Leben meiner Worte
ihr Dennoch
ein Dennoch jedes Buchstabens sei

2.
Kleine Buchstaben
genaue
damit die Worte leise kommen
damit die Worte sich einschleichen
damit man hingehen muß
zu den Worten
sie suchen in dem weißen
Papier
leise
man merkt nicht wie sie eintreten
durch die Poren
Schweiß der nach innen rinnt

Angst
meine
unsere
und das Dennoch jedes Buchstabens

3.
Ich will einen Streifen Paper
so groß wie ich
ein Meter sechzig
darauf ein Gedicht
das schreit
sowie einer vorübergeht
schreit in schwarzen Buchstaben
das etwas Unmögliches verlangt
Zivilcourage zum Beispiel
diesen Mut den kein Tier hat
Mit-Schmerz zum Beispiel
Solidarität statt Herde
Fremd-Worte
heimisch zu machen im Tun

Mensch
Tier das Zivilcourage hat
Mensch
Tier das den Mit-Schmerz kennt
Mensch Fremdwort-Tier Wort-Tier
Tier
das Gedicht schreibt
Gedicht
das Unmögliches verlangt
von jedem der vorbeigeht
dringend
unabweisbar
als rufe es
»Trink Coca-Cola« (1987b, 333–36)

"Three Ways of Writing Poems"

1.
A dry riverbed
a white band of pebbles
seen from a distance
here I wish to write
in clear letters
or a rocky pile
scree

slipping under my lines
landsliding
so that the tricky life of my words
their "and yet"
may be an "and yet" with every letter

2.
Small letters
precise
so that the words come quietly
so that the words creep in
so that one must go there
to the words
seek them in the white
paper
quietly
one does not notice how they enter
through the pores
sweat that runs toward the inside

fear
mine
ours
and the "and yet" of every letter

3.
I want a strip of paper
as tall as I am
a meter sixty
on which a poem
that cries out
as soon as someone passes by
cries out in black letters
that demands something impossible
civil courage for example
this spirit that no animal has
em-pathy for example
solidarity instead of herd instinct
foreign-words
made familiar in deed

human
animal that has civil courage
human
animal that knows em-pathy
human foreign word-animal word-animal
animal
that writes poem
poem
that demands the impossible
from everyone who goes past
urgently
not to be refused
as if calling
"Drink Coca-Cola"[41]

In a close reading that richly elucidates many details about the context in which "Drei Arten Gedichte aufzuschreiben" appeared, Michael Braun interprets this text as a triptych that mediates on questions fundamental to poems: which surface to inscribe, how to write, and what purpose writing serves (Lermen and Braun 1997, 115–20). Braun develops an existential analysis that casts the poet as engaged in a struggle to find language to assert individual identity, even in the face of potential nuclear annihilation. He persuasively connects Domin's text to the work of Paul Celan, especially the long poem "Engführung" (or "Stretto"), and with justification emphasizes that the struggle against silence that preoccupies German poets after 1945 must inevitably be linked to Adorno's admonishment that to write poetry after Auschwitz would be barbaric (1955a, 31). This line of reasoning supports his interpretation of the noun *Zivilcourage* (civil courage) and the categories of *Mensch/Tier* (man/animal) in the third section as an expression "eine Poetik des Dennoch" (a poetics of "and yet")—*dennoch* (either capitalized as a noun or appearing in lower case as an adverb) being a word that Domin repeatedly foregrounds in prose statements about poetry as well—a poetics that voices faith in humanity and optimism that transcends even the horrors of the twentieth century (Lermen and Braun 1997, 120).

While I find the interpretation advanced by Braun convincing in many respects, his reading does not attend to Domin's cultivation of feminine modes of expression. Moreover, Braun's characterization of the first section as "the shortest of the poem and the only one with masculine cadence" is an awkward patronization of women's writing of a kind Domin herself acknowledges in her essay "Über die Schwierigkeiten, eine berufstätige Frau zu sein" ("On the Difficulties of Being a Working Woman" from 1974) (see Lermen and Braun 1997, 116). Here she remembers with some irritation having been called "unter Poeten ein Mann" ("among poets a man") by a colleague who intended the remark as a compliment, one which Domin does accept finally, after reasoning through the other's perspective (1992h, 75). More significantly, however, Braun by tracing the notion of *Zivilcourage* back to Bismarck and viewing the poem in terms of Gottfried Benn's writings and *Kahlschlag* aesthetics (alluded to by the reference to Adorno) deflects attention away from how "Drei Arten Gedichte aufzuschreiben" expresses a different, post-"*Nullpunkt*" construction of poetics and social engagement, for the key to this construction lies in the feminine discourse of the poem (compare Lermen and Braun 1997, 118–20).

Domin's discursive treatment of poetics and engagement is particularly concentrated around the terms *dennoch* and *Zivilcourage,* which, as we will see shortly, cannot be read in their full complexity without recourse to the dimension of gender. With "Drei Arten Gedichte aufzuschreiben," Domin creates language that has crucial performative functions. Using words, line, and the economy of poetic thought, she explores the autonomy of art in feminine terms. This coded language foregrounds sensuous experience, equates poetic creation with the labor of breath, and finally makes the abstract rhetoric of aesthetic discourse an iteration of the body.

"Drei Arten Gedichte aufzuschreiben" opens with two contrasting surfaces divided by the coordinating conjunction *oder.* The first is a dry riverbed on which the poet would like to write in clear letters. The second is a loose deposit of stones and boulders (*Schutthalde, Geröll*) that seems to crumble away beneath the lines the poet is writing. The poet finally chooses the latter medium, for in that avalanche, the *heikle Leben* (the tricky life or existence) of the poet's words becomes truly possible. The term *Dennoch* ("and yet") is repeated multiple times, as we will see, with increasing significance.

The desolation of the scene serves a function similar to the seemingly dead landscape encountered famously in Stefan George's poetry.[42] Along with the poet, the reader is wholly immersed in the physical texture of two rocky landscapes, each of which is doubly named as *Flußbett/Band von Kieselsteinen* and *Schutthalde/Geröll.* Exploration of that terrain mirrors the act of inscription through writing. The poet's and reader's mental exercise is articulated in the poem as physical movement, with repetitive elements used to orchestrate pauses for thought. For example, when the letters that the poet wishes to write on the white stones (*Lettern*) are echoed in the last line of the poem through the term *Buchstaben,* the reader stops to consider what distinctions might exist between those otherwise synonymous terms. But what does this connection of stones, letters, and poem imply?

After speculatively relating the imagery of stones by general association to Christian symbolism, nuclear wastelands, and the surface of Mars, Braun more plausibly suggests a connection between this landscape and Paul Celan's poem "Engführung," from *Sprachgitter* (*Speech-Grille,* 1959).[43] White stones appear, for example, in the first section of "Engführung" (1975, 197). I contend that even more proximate to the publication of "Drei Arten Gedichte aufzuschreiben," however, are poems from Celan's *Die Niemandsrose* (*The No-Man's Rose,* 1963) that return to this stone imagery, such as "Radix, Matrix" (Celan 1975, 239).[44] In *Die Niemandsrose,* these stones evoke the traditional Jewish act of placing a stone in a loved one's memory, particularly at memorials to the victims of the Holocaust. These stones also express a sense of ponderous weight because they are immutable objects that represent memory and grief.

But the sliding rubble requires a different explanation. Depicted as in motion, its instability contrasts with the static positioning of the white stones, reminding the reader of how difficult it is to capture the messy stuff of reality in words, a point that the term *Dennoch* will reinforce. Accordingly, the tension between stones and rubble is one between representations that freeze the moment and those that are, in the language of Domin's prose, dynamic and thus explicitly constructed in relation to an empathetic viewer/audience. In short, this section of the poem addresses a long-standing aesthetic debate about the nature of art, one to which Domin also alludes in her Frankfurt poetry lectures by linking Lessing and Christa Wolf (1988a, 53).[45] Interpreting this passage in the spirit of Goethe, who valued the paradoxical tension between permanence and change, Braun argues that the poem emphasizes how "writing itself is an eminent act of holding fast and at the same time of flowing (of words, reality)" (Lermen and Braun 1997, 116).[46] It is my contention, however, that Domin structures her conception of writing as a choice between lucid writing and the dynamic, if unstable, conditions represented at the conclusion of the stanza by the *Geröll* (scree, pebbles, or rubble). For her, this rock slide is clearly the more poetically generative and positive image; its qualities signal an interpretive path that leads toward Annette von Droste-Hülshoff and Virginia Woolf.

In Annette von Droste-Hülshoff's famous poem "Die Mergelgrube" ("The Marl-Pit"), the poet descends into the *Schutthalde* (rocky debris) to discover fossils, isolation, and ultimately poetry in the naive song of a shepherd (1973, 45–48).[47] Rich in minerals, marl is, in fact, used as a fertilizer. Domin connects with this imagery through the term *Geröll*, which echoes Droste-Hülshoff's description of how clumps of earth disintegrate in her hand and under her feet, revealing small gleaming stones.

The two poets react to these rolling stones quite differently. While in "Die Mergelgrube" the poet sinks herself into the experience of the rocky ravine so completely that she becomes transfixed by the idea that she is either the first or the last person on earth, Domin swiftly transports her reader from the loose stones to a transformed frame of mind signified by the word *Dennoch*. Used here as a noun rather than more conventionally as an adverb or conjunction, *Dennoch* interjects a reflective pause in the penultimate line of the first section, since the word contains a sharp division of syllables (*den/noch*) made more dramatic by the aspiration that occurs when *noch* is pronounced. Its repetition again in the final line signals a definitive change. Moreover, the verb *sei,* which Domin uses in the sense of a wishful imperative "let it be," optically mirrors the semantically very different subjective form *sei,* used to mark indirect speech in the concluding line of "Die Mergelgrube."

The linkage of Domin's stone imagery to Virginia Woolf is more oblique. In her essay "Über die Schwierigkeiten, eine berufstätige Frau zu sein" ("On the Difficulties of Being a Working Woman"), Domin names only four women authors specifically, and both Droste-Hülshoff and Virginia Woolf are the focal points (1992h, 75–76). Earlier, Domin had written about Woolf in a 1964 essay, where she noted, "They found her walking stick on the bank of the Ouse, just like the shoe that Empedocles left at the crater Aetna. She had written a lot about water: about being washed over, drowning, indifferent as to whether it was the sea or a pond or a river or even just water" (1992i, 97). Woolf's fateful walk into Ouse River with pockets full of stones is vivid for Domin, and Woolf was a writer whose imagery reached in the direction of figuring language as stones. Woolf in *The Waves* even made one character answer another's monologue on the organic unity of the English language by saying, "Those are white words . . . like stones one picks up by the seashore" (Woolf 1977, 14).

When Domin posits a choice between the more difficult terrain of the garbled scree and the pristine whiteness of the dry riverbed unrolling like a white stone scroll, she raises another issue: the marginalization of the "other." Domin observes in her Frankfurt lectures that "the persecuted and women [have been] so perceptible in the last 40 years" (1988a, 47). Discursively, the imagery of stones in "Drei Arten Gedichte aufzuschreiben" connects with Domin's reflections both on the nature of writing and on the difficulty of being a writer, for in her meditations on otherness of many kinds, the authors Woolf and Droste-Hülshoff represent two of the most prominent examples.

The bold linkage of persecuted individuals and women (*Verfolgte und Frauen*) has its roots in Domin's publications from the 1960s, where she considers the mental despair experienced by writers. "Virginia Woolf's books," Domin observes, "start with the lost paradise, with the notion that everything is broken, that the absolute is no longer possible: perfect love, complete devotion, absolute happiness" (1992i, 98). What fascinates Domin are the isolated moments in Woolf's work where time seems to stand still and happiness exists for just a moment, even though her life ended in suicide (1992i, 99). Throughout the 1960s, however, Domin regards such tragic despair as a matter of the human condition.

During this time, Domin turns repeatedly to the example of Woolf. Dedicated to Woolf, the poem "Tunnel" (published in *Was für ein Zeichen mache ich über die Tür,* a collection written in Heidelberg in 1962–64) seems to speak with sisterly reassurance to a companion traveler (1987d). Both "Tunnel" and Domin's essay on Woolf respond to Edward Albee's play *Who's Afraid of Virginia Woolf* (1962), which, Domin writes, startled her with its animosity toward the deceased writer (1992i, 94). Domin, in fact, challenges the title by commenting that to make the same kind of statement in Germany, one would have to ask, "Who's afraid of Enzensberger?" (1992i, 94). Subsequently in Domin's speech upon receiving the literary prize of the city of Bad Gandersheim (1974), Woolf is linked with the tenth-century poet Roswitha (for whom the award is named), Annette von Droste-Hülshoff, and Lady Murasaki (1992a, 70). She is furthermore fatefully placed beside Ingeborg Bachmann, whom Domin mourns at the conclusion of the speech, along with Paul Celan and others (1992a, 71). Finally, the poem "Ausbruch von hier" from the cycle *Die Haut des Planeten* (*The Skin of the Planet*) memorializes writers whose lives ended in suicide—Celan, Peter Szondi, and Jean Améry—by pronouncing them free now to find a truly viable language (1987a). Woolf never seems far from Domin's thoughts about poetry, certainly not in "Drei Arten Gedichte aufzuschreiben."

This chain of associations (stone/language/women writers) in "Drei Arten Gedichte aufzuschreiben" defines a trajectory of reflection that has epistemological significance, for it opens questions about who can legitimately write and how, and ultimately about whether the writer is capable of taking a moral stance. Moreover, the gravity of those questions is signaled by the pause and aspiration enacted through pronunciation of the word *Dennoch*. So definitive is this very real change in breath, it literally causes the reader to pause to think and reflect. The word, by its very performance in speech, makes us attentive, not just to the sequence of words, but to every individual letter.

This interpretation of the meaning of *Dennoch* for Domin is enhanced when we explore the aesthetic principles Domin elaborates in the fourth and fifth of her Frankfurt lectures, where she talks about that word. In the fourth lecture, Domin treats the topic of *Lesepraxis* (reading practices), emphasizing that reading is not intended to achieve a complete interpretation, but rather to open democratically, to any reader, the simple pleasure of the act. Reminiscent of the kind of reciprocal interpretation adumbrated in *Doppelinterpretationen,* this lecture stresses that the reader gains possession of the poem through reading and negotiated exchange with the author as the individual linguistic logic of a text is pursued. This lecture ends with her recitation of "Drei Arten Gedichte aufzuschreiben." The subsequent fifth lecture returns to the poem, adding Domin's further reflection on the notion of *Dennoch* as a "Metapher der Widerständigkeit" or "metaphor for the nature of resistance" (1988a, 106). Here Domin connects the word *dennoch* with a meditation on the myth of Sisyphus, the eternal stone mover, as a parable for the work of the writer in a century when writers in exile faced daily struggles to continue their work (1988a, 106). The disparate leitmotifs (*Dennoch,* stones, exiles, and marginalized writers) are thus rhetorically concentrated into a single meditation and thematic constellation.

In the second section of "Drei Arten Gedichte aufzuschreiben," the attention to precision signaled by *Dennoch* continues, underscored by the opening line "small letters." The vertical configuration of letters on the page (especially *K, l, B, h, t, b*) produced by these two words emphasizes the physical material of language, the production of text-forming words and the linear/sequential reading of words. This section is further marked by abrupt line breaks and one-word lines that similarly draw attention to the reading process.

Domin's choice here, and also in the first section, of the noun *Worte*—a plural for semantically connected words, rather than *Wörter,* used for the disconnected words of a dictionary—emphasizes meaning over decontextualized labeling. Words like *hingehen, suchen,* and *eintreten* (go there, seek, enter) spatially enact a drama in which poet and reader physically meet at the reader's instigation, as was the intention of the notion of *Treffpunkt* hypothesized in *Doppelinterpretationen.* The poem is thus not fragmented expression or an interior act of inscription, as posited by Braun (Lermen and Braun 1997, 117), but rather an outward gesture of venturing forth into coherence, the reader's move out of himself or herself and into the poem, met by the poem's own advance toward the reader.

The sense of stealth and subversion that enters the poem through the reflexive verb *sich einschleichen* (to steal/creep/sneak) makes the encounter more charged. Stealth intensifies the resistance signaled by *Dennoch,* and is reinforced when the reader is prompted to experience the eerie covert existence of words in the line *Man merkt nicht wie sie eintreten* (one does not notice how they enter). As the poet describes a cyclical process whereby words infiltrate the skin's membrane and flow inward with the intensity of sweat, tactile sensations envelop the reader.

The terms *klein* (small) and *leise* (quiet) emphasize the subtlety and subconscious power of poetry, but underscore self-awareness of feminine weakness and diminishment. This terminology of smallness echoes phrasing found in "Wie wenig nütze ich bin" ("What Little Use I Am"), from Domin's first collection of poetry, *Apfelbaum und Olive* (*Apple Tree and Olive,* written 1955–57), where the poet muses: "What little use I am, / I lift my finger and leave behind / not the smallest mark / in the air." Indeed, the poem continues, perhaps the poet leaves only "the small sound of my voice . . . on a scrap of paper" (1987c, 30–31). Smallness, however, should not be read as a negative quality in Domin's work, for diminutive writing figures quite positively as symbolic of a fresh beginning in a text from *Lieder zur Ermutigung* (1960). "Trust, this most difficult / A B C," the poet begins in describing the difficulty of finding language and a basic sense of security (1987c, 222). With these simple letters the sign she will make where a new haven, the city of Jerusalem, need only be discreet: "I make a small sign / in the air, / invisible" (1987c, 222). In "Drei Arten Gedichte aufzuschreiben," this reflex of contraction is reversed in the final section when the poem becomes the physical size of the poet.

As in the opening section of "Drei Arten Gedichte aufzuschreiben," the second breaks into two distinct parts, as the latter half making an unexpected turn with the word *Schweiß* (sweat) tilts bodily exertion over into fear. This angst is, however, not the worry of a single individual (*meine*). It is also collective fear (*unsere*). Domin resists the viscous cycle of intense anxiety that motivates Erich Fried's poem "Angst vor der Angst" ("Fear of Fear," 1964) (1982), where fear generates fear about thinking about fear.[48] At the same time, her final line refuses to dismiss fear; the crucial connective *und* does not subordinate it to other considerations. Fear exists, and "yet," that strategic connective creates the space for the poet to insert her utopian concept of the *Dennoch,* the inherent, heroic resistance to pessimism of every single letter and word she writes. Remembering that the title under which these two first sections originally were published was "Postulat," it appears that Domin's postulate emerges in the space opened up by *Dennoch.* The first section postulates writing not as concrete, but sliding; the second hypothesizes it as standing up to fear, despite all threats. The third section embarks in a new direction that finally takes us beyond the pause invoked by *Dennoch*.

Through exuberant unfurling as the act that dominates in section three, the longest of the poems contained in "Drei Arten Gedichte aufzuschreiben," Domin affirms the capacity of art to create true solidarity. The language chosen for this section foregrounds performative acts—the poster poem screams (*schreit*) and demands deeds (*verlangt Zivilcourage*). While *Zivilcourage* can be understood in terms that mesh with general postwar German discourse about the social engagement of intellectuals as "acting ethically," in fact, the word finds a more specific usage in Domin's work, as she elaborates her understanding of *Zivilcourage* in two essays. In "Über die Schwierigkeiten, eine berufstätige Frau zu sein" ("On the Difficulties of Being a Working Woman," 1974), Domin poses the question of whether women demonstrate civil courage and answers herself, "perhaps" (1992h, 78). Women may have a type of civil courage in some cases, "but when women are involved, they seldom have courage [when it comes to doing something for themselves]" (1992h, 78).[49] In other words, true bravery in the public sphere seems to fail them in matters pertaining to women. A second essay from 1983, "Zivilcourage: Ein Fremdwort" ("Civil Courage: A Foreign Word"), provides further clarification. Here, Domin links civil courage with demonstrable solidarity, particularly in times of totalitarianism. "Civil courage and solidarity, they belong together" (1992c, 236).

Thus Domin envisions "civil courage" not as extraordinary battlefield bravery, but as a daily exercise in ordinary life.[50] As Domin explains later, "Civil courage is something relative, to be measured against the shyness that one has, because a person is shy, or the shyness that one has because a person feels intimidated by others" (1992c, 237). The essay "Zivilcourage: Ein Fremdwort," in fact, ties courage to conditions in modern consumer society. Domin refers to a discussion with a school director about his reluctance to require students to pick up their Coca-Cola containers because he fears a conflict with them (1992c, 236–37). Both the adult and the students in this case, Domin observes, thereby fail to exercise *Zivilcourage,* a failure that points to the convergence of an abundance of consumer goods and a loss of ethical orientation.

That commodification is a matter of concern for poets may not be an obvious point, but it was much on the mind of postwar German writers. Ingeborg Bachmann's powerful poem "Reklame" ("Advertisement"), Hans Magnus Enzensberger's "Landessprache" ("Language of the Land"), and a host of other poems from the period of the *Wirtschaftswunder* (economic miracle) era are written with apprehension that the metaphoric power of language, so necessary for poetry, will be irrevocably diminished and finally subsumed in marketing slogans and advertising.[51] Recalling Domin's interest in Marcuse's social theory, we may well recognize the consonance of their thinking in this instance. "Art's separation from the process of material production," Marcuse observes in 1977 after this trend has advanced much farther, "has enabled it to demystify the reality reproduced in this process. Art challenges the monopoly of the established reality to determine what is 'real,' and it does so by creating a fictitious world which is nevertheless 'more real than reality itself' " (1978, 22). The subversive, stealthy qualities of poetry were seen as a corrective to the insidious effects of commodification.

Returning to the poem, we can now see that what Domin seeks in section three is a new exercise of *Zivilcourage*. This search, let us remember, takes place against the backdrop of political and social turmoil in 1968. The smallness of the writing and quietness of voice in the second section contrast hugely with the third section of the poem. That contrast amplifies the courageousness exhibited in the act of making the poem into a poster—a widely visible, public statement.

The poem's performative display of civil courage depends, I believe, on a gendered discourse of engagement. Clearly, *Zivilcourage* is meant to transcend the masculine shadings of political concerns, for the poem equates it with a display of emotional *Mit-Schmerz* (empathy). Though common empathy has stereotypically been associated with the temperament of women, Domin further elevates this *Mit-Schmerz* to a higher plain of human value beyond gender. Her skillful manipulation of line breaks in the second stanza articulates the ennobling poetic assertion that humankind is distinguished from animals through the conscious exercise of civil courage. But Domin couples this acknowledgment of our fundamental humanity with the realization that humans cannot escape the physical and instinctual any more than animals. Given that paradox, her recourse to the feminine subjective perspective serves the heuristic function of producing a new context in which ethical actions can occur.

Finally, the emboldened poet strives to create a poem whose words possess the full instrumental power of language—exemplified by Domin's startling quotation of an advertising slogan. Such a poem commands its recipient (the reader) to act, calling even upon the ubiquitous authority of the quotidian. The ad, which admonishes us to "Drink Coca-Cola," cloaks its commercial message in the guise of a seductive woman, not unlike sensuous poetry.[52] Thus we can interpret Domin's choice of this strange imperative as yet another invitation to exercise civil courage, one that reminds us that gritty reality affronts *Zivilcourage* every day.[53] For good reason, reality, authenticity, and truth are the bywords of post-1968 literary debates, given the increasing impingement of the public sphere on private space about which this slogan reminds us. Weaving elements into the poem that are coded as feminine, Domin discerns generative possibilities in this new proximity. In advertising she finds another model that elucidates the give-and-take between poem and reader, and, by extension, all human interactions. Invoking traditional "feminine" elements and confronting reality, "Drei Arten Gedichte aufzuschreiben" explores the multifaceted ways in which gender relates to creativity across the broadest possible spectrum, from sublime inspiration to commercial persuasion.

Writing Polemics or Poetry

"Drei Arten Gedichte aufzuschreiben," in many ways the centerpiece of Domin's Frankfurt poetry lectures, expresses her deep concern with the status of poetic texts not as sterile aesthetic artifacts, but rather as tools for reshaping a whole culture of reading and writing. As is evident from her essay collections *Doppelinterpretation* and *Wozu Lyrik heute,* Domin's larger artistic aim is to create in the public sphere a broad literary/intellectual collectivity based on constructive dialogue. Although this preoccupation grew out of literary discussions of the 1960s that were freighted with the intellectual burdens of the postwar ethos, her intricate critical counterpoint against the writings of Benn, Celan, Enzensberger, Gadamer, and Marcuse makes clear that these discussions were pivotal to her thinking. By contrast, Domin's poetry exhibits more autonomy, relying on resonant words and spare images meant to engage readers in dialogue with her art. Within this framework, poems are not conceived as representing an idealized sublime. Rather, they become experiential catalysts in which expression is intended to launch conceptual interactions that continue beyond the text itself.

With her Frankfurt lectures, Domin finds herself in an actual performative context that both foregrounds the centrality of poetry reading and authorizes her academically.[54] Here, in fact, she becomes overtly polemical about the ethical functions of literature and is emboldened to articulate opinions about feminism more directly. Though wary about feminist essentialism in other essays, Domin moves in this unique public venue to address questions of representation and the situation of women writers in terms that show their status as core aesthetic issues in her work.

The process by which this occurs directs our attention again to the history of the period.

By Domin's account in *Das Gedicht als Augenblick von Freiheit,* 1974 was a particularly significant year for poetry. Marcel Reich-Ranicki inaugurated the *Frankfurter Anthologie* (a project that published poetry in one of the leading German newspapers, the *Frankfurter Allgemeine Zeitung*), and *Kursbuch,* the leading German New Left journal, voiced disillusionment with political activism (see Domin 1988a, 20).[55] The two publications marked the beginning of a renewed interest in the lyric genre and signaled disenchantment with political activism, both issues of interest to Domin. That same year, "Über die Schwierigkeiten, eine berufstätige Frau zu sein" was published in Domin's collection of auto-biographical essays, *Von der Natur nicht vorgesehen* (*Not Anticipated by Nature,* 1974).[56] It is an uncharacteristically polemical piece—a blunt list of twenty observations peppered with anecdotal evidence testifying to the obstacles faced by women.[57]

Republished in Domin's *Gesammelte Essays,* the piece might arguably have found a home in the parallel volume of her collected autobiographical works, given the personal stories it relates (compare 1992c, 1992b). The text has a poetic feel since the opening and closing are bracketed with the gestural statement, "Wir sind alle Hermaphroditen" ("We are all hermaphrodites"). By this declaration Domin means that creative individuals embody both feminine and masculine qualities (1992c, 73, 78). In the essay Domin lists the difficulties of the working woman, including the division of work by sex (points 2–3), the affronts to female intelligence (4–6), the precarious status of women writers (7–12), and the gender tensions within contemporary society (13–19). She is sharply critical of blatant contradictions—"second shift" housework oppressing career women, Ibsenesque households headed by committed Marxists, and sexual liberation that devolves into meaningless sex (1992c, 76–77). "The woman," Domin summarizes, "is allowed to participate in almost anything today: provisionally" (1992c, 78).

On the specific topic of women authors themselves, Domin notes that women tend to find men to be spokesmen for their issues and worry about whether their writings will be altered by men who undertake their publication (1992c, 74–76). Her frank critique of the marginalization of women cites the words Virginia Woolf sent in 1942 to an American women's organization: "Die Frauen sind wie Juden unter Nazis" ("Women are like Jews under the Nazis") (1992c, 76). She furthermore attributes a similar statement from around 1968 to Sartre. Despite these harsh words, Domin concludes on a more conciliatory note, locating common human concerns beyond social constructions of gender, "All of us have fear of loneliness. . . . Our bones will become almost the same. Our dust will not be different in any way" (1992c, 78–79). In death, Domin muses, everyone becomes both hermaphrodites and ultimately ungendered, thus finding a solution to gender inequities by transcending mortal issues.

In the second of her Frankfurt lectures a decade later (1987–88), Domin returns to this formula to distance herself from a simplistic interpretation of gender, telling listeners that she believes that both sexes manifest dual gender traits (particularly in the case of creative individuals). Her earlier term for this situation, *Hermaphrodit* (hermaphrodite), is now equated with the term *androgyn* (androgynous), downplaying sexual identity even further. This discussion of whether one can distinguish female from male sensibility is connected to reflections about Christa Wolf. Wolf's own Frankfurt poetry lectures from 1982 powerfully asserted that women should have a voice in the public sphere.[58] Clearly inspired by her, Domin warns against the ghettoization of women writers that might be precipitated by feminism:[59]

> Women's poetry, recently it's been called "feminine poetry," is it a category in and of itself? I doubt it. I address myself to all listeners, men and women, especially to the critics among you. Intellectual ghettos need to be broken down. It's quite simple. One only needs objectivity. Objectivity is a word of freedom. (1988a, 52)

With this politically cautious declaration, Domin renews her efforts to reclaim a general notion of "authenticity," which she views as the principle by which writing achieves the truth.

By the late 1980s, when this lectures series occurred (some two decades after "Drei Arten Gedichte aufzuschreiben" voiced optimism about the vitality of poetry), "New Subjectivity" had resulted in such extreme artistic preoccupation with everyday material detail that the aesthetic verve of the quotidian was undermined. The casual style associated with the movement had degraded the worth of "frank" expression and trivialized notions of authentic voice. Between "Über die Schwierigkeiten, eine berufstätige Frau zu sein" and the Frankfurt lectures, Domin's abiding reservations about feminism resurface as well. Now Domin's reference to "weibliche Lyrik" (feminine poetry) becomes a performative overture that recalls for her audience the pragmatic efforts of the women's liberation movement, but she uses it to deflect attention to the intimate interdependence between author and audience that she sees as the fundamental aesthetic problem. The representational structure for this relationship is characteristically paradoxical. Domin names it using an oxymoron, "unspezifische Genauigkeit" (unspecific exactness), to explain poetic— yet not reductive—precision (1988a, 71).

Domin's lecture swiftly turns away from further political questions about feminism, launching into a disquisition in which Domin compares her own sense in 1932 that catastrophe was imminent to the mythic Cassandra's prophetic powers. Eventually, this musing leads, strangely enough, to the recitation of two love poems, one by Marie Luise Kaschnitz and the other by Eric Fried. Were it not for the fact that Domin opens her third lecture with a reading of the poem "Gleichgewicht" ("Balance"), which unifies these disparate themes, the talk would seem sheer rambling.

These digressions, however, have a purpose. Employing again a short-hand treatment of contemporary literary debates, Domin dramatically steers the focus in the third lecture to the abstract problem of truth and literature. "Writing—and therefore reading, too—is a training in truth-fulness," Domin declares. "That is one of the points where I agree with Enzensberger. 'Means of production for recognizing the truth,' Enzens-berger says, whereas I speak more cautiously about 'truthfulness'" (1988a, 62–63).[60]

Domin's transformation of Enzensberger's term *Wahrheit* (truth) into *Wahrhaftigkeit* (truthfulness) reflects a nuanced understanding of the representative capacities of writing and heightened appreciation of the distance separating subject, writer, and reader. Her "correction," however, should not be understood to constitute a substantial disagreement with Enzensberger (1988a, 62).[61] Rather, Domin uses her rhetorical qualifica-tion to negotiate very careful terms for the twin-like relationship between author and reader, a relationship that she has repeatedly adumbrated, as we have seen, in her writings since the 1960s. Both the autonomy of writerly practice voiced when Domin speaks about the poem as "der unverbrauchbare Gebrauchsgegenstand" ("the non-consumable com-modity") (1988a, 57), and the social context in which such poetry occurs, are important for authors in general. This latter investment is made clear by Domin's choice of terminology in the lectures, which references both Enzensberger's discussion of poetic practice in *Landessprache* and the poetics of Bertolt Brecht.

Neither Enzensberger nor Domin takes *Wahrheit* (truth) and *Wahr-haftigkeit* (truthfulness or authenticity) at face value. We can look at the term *Wahrhaftigkeit* as Domin uses it here in terms of both content and context. On the one hand, truthfulness expresses an attitude toward the contents of poetry. Domin displays an acute sense of how subjectivity operates—an awareness that poems are constructs rather than simple mimesis, with the results depending on where the poet chooses to situate herself. As much as the poet would like it to be otherwise, poems do not connect us with unvarnished truth, even when they aspire to that absolute. On the other hand, the poet who pursues *Wahrhaftigkeit* is already admitting that writing poetry is a shaky proposition, demanding three kinds of courage (*Mut*), according to Domin: courage to write, to speak, and also to assert one's own identity (1988a, 63). *Wahrhaftigkeit* thus implies distance and yet it conjures up closeness. Domin links this *Wahrhaftigkeit* to poetry as pure interpretation, describing how poems stay alive (*lebendig*) through the experience of readers (1988a, 65), and even citing an anecdote about how a young woman had used one of Domin's poems to achieve reconciliation with her mother (1988a, 66–67).

The overall effect of Domin's lectures is thus one of contradictory circularity. Domin categorically rejects "feminine poetry," but chooses to use again the very same terms that appear in her earlier writings on gender issues (*Zivilcourage, Mut, Dennoch*). Here we should pause to reflect on the strategies that Domin uses. Invested in the ideal that poetry reveals truthfulness, Domin invents her own Platonic vocabulary as a way of encapsulating her views and differentiating her values from others'. In this way the representational position of the lyrical *I* that we previously encountered in Hamburger's theory continues in Domin's work. Her poems are clearly not conceived as unmediated expression, for *Wahrhaftigkeit* (truthfulness) makes the expressive relationship between language and content more tenuous. Yet that representational distance opens up the possibility that expression may be an assumed mask, hence not genuine. This conceptual dilemma, as we will see, raises even more complex challenges in the poetics of Ulla Hahn. I therefore understand Domin's project in these lectures to be, in fact, the creation of a new social context for literature that resembles the reciprocal, dynamic literacies that Kathryn Thoms Flannery in *Feminist Literacies, 1968–75* finds realized through the mutually interconnected development of American feminist periodicals, polemic, poetry, performance, and pedagogy (2005). In terms of a larger conceptualization of women's writing, what we encounter with Domin is a situation in which feminine writing per se is less important for our understanding of her work as women's writing than an entire set of feminine aesthetic attitudes and practices centered around notions of performance and heightened sensitivity to performance contexts.

The difference between Flannery's examples and Domin, of course, is that Domin remains deeply reluctant to identify herself as a "woman writer." This particular reluctance also seems more pronounced in the German postwar literary context, where idealism exerted a powerful influence. Trusting individual self-assertion, Domin seeks to cultivate a sense of collective, ethical purpose that transcends gender by hypothesizing a dynamic community of readers. Domin's locus for exploring feminine agency becomes corporeal performance that is alive with breath, pause, courage, and intense reading, and explained by her use of related leitmotifs to illustrate these principles. "Performance," Peter Middleton observes, "is a moment when social interaction can study and celebrate itself, and the poet is given significant new materials with which to extend the signifying field of the poem. Authorship and intersubjectivity collaborate with the implicit allegorization of poetry's potential and actual place in everyday life" (2005, 103).

Performance as an act with universal civic value, rather than a singular testament to feminism, gives Domin the means to show that writers enjoy the freedom to define their own voices. "The longing / for justice / does not diminish / But the hope," Domin laments in the poem "Älter werden" ("Growing Old"), a text which is subtitled a response to Christa Wolf (1987c, 360). Even so, when she concludes with the lines "Hand in Hand mit der Sprache / bis zuletzt" ("Hand in hand with the language / to the end"), Domin reaffirms with the sensuous image of handholding not just the partnership of language and poet, but also ultimately of poet and reader, and of individual and community (1987c, 363).

Chapter Three

✦

"The Path Emerges as We Go": Ulla Hahn's Poetics and Politics

On a cool fall evening in 1982, an attentive audience packed the lecture hall at the Deutsches Literaturarchiv in Marbach am Neckar to listen to a poet who had recently debuted her first collection, *Herz über Kopf* (*Heart over Head,* 1981), published by the nearby Deutsche Verlags-Anstalt in Stuttgart. Outside dry leaves dappled the sidewalks leading past the statue of Schiller, a monument reminding visitors that tiny Marbach was in fact his birthplace. The Neckar River, poetically celebrated by Friedrich Hölderlin, snaked gracefully through the valley below. Following applause for the reading, the public was cordially invited to ask the poet questions. Several poetry lovers responded with the expected adulatory requests for insight into the creative inner life of writers. Then one audience member challenged the author head-on. Why, he reproved gruffly, would a poet today use insipid traditional forms, pen saccharine love poems, indeed, apparently promote neoconservative, apolitical values? The poet so addressed was Ulla Hahn.

My recollection of this incident, observed from the back of the hall, is that Hahn maintained her decorum through a brief answer. Certainly, Hahn was no stranger to the ritualized tensions of public literary debate. Poems about readings from throughout Hahn's career treat these situations ironically. "Meine Damen und Herren" ("Ladies and Gentlemen") from *Unerhörte Nähe* (*Unheard-of Proximity*) satirically represents the poet disabusing her audience of misconceptions about poetry (Hahn 1988a, 64), and "Dichterlesung" ("Poetry Reading") from *So offen die Welt* (*So Open the World*) evinces understanding for restless listeners, this time students, even going so far as to poke fun at the poet herself:

> Eine Schulklasse kichernd in den hinteren Reihen
> Lyrik Leistungsstufe eins: Bildlich gesprochen

Und nun suchen sie live zu erfragen:
Was will uns der Dichter damit sagen?

Da sitzt sie buchstäblich, ziemlich klein
und schon grau und die Schuhe! (2004, 41)

A school class giggling in the back rows
Poetry at the introductory level: figuratively speaking
And now they're trying to discover live:
What is the poet trying to say?

There she sits literally, rather small
and already gray and those shoes!

What interests me about this type of exchange is what such tense, staged, or playful negotiations explain about the situation of the lyric genre in the second half of the twentieth century. As we have seen in the case of Hilde Domin, interactions with readers play a crucial role in the life of poetry.[1] Yet readers, like that outspokenly dissatisfied audience member in Marbach, bring very specific preconceptions to lyrical texts, including views antithetical to the poet's. In Hahn's case, these interpretive negotiations play an important role in her poetics and are often staged within individual poems, in ways that are especially pronounced in areas involving the relationship of contemporary poetry to tradition, the perceived degree of political engagement, and the articulation of gender perspectives. For Domin, confidence in poetry's *Wahrhaftigkeit* (truthfulness) was sufficient to assert its value and provide confirmation of the authority of lyrical subjectivity. In considering Hahn's work, we become acutely aware that the poem is an artifact created by a poet who can assume many masks, thus the kind of representation it engages in ("truthful" or otherwise) cannot be taken for granted. For Hahn, the poem is very much an intimate work on a page, but it is also hypothetically a mass media item, social intervention, staged performance, or something else altogether.

The lyric genre in West Germany after 1968 faced many challenges—first the abandonment of poetry in favor of political activism, then the disillusionment with politics and decline into solipsistic "New Subjectivity" scribbling. Yet this short history does not explain its stubborn continuation very well. Why, under these conditions, has anyone continued to write or read poetry? For lost, according to this narrative, is the belief in poetry's force that Domin optimistically proclaimed in "Drei

Arten Gedichte aufzuschreiben" ("Three Ways of Writing Poems"). Such a summary of post-1968 trends does not go far in explaining an author like Ulla Hahn. By virtue of when her career starts, Hahn is immersed in the conflicting ideologies of this period and caught up in the shifting conditions for the production and consumption of poetry. Measured against conventional expectations about how German writers should respond under such conditions, she negotiates these divergent pulls quite idiosyncratically—appropriating and yet also radically rewriting literary tradition, rejecting demands for the politicization of art while applying activist techniques, and constructing a stylized feminine artistic persona while engaging with feminism. If we take Hahn's work seriously, as indicative of the evolving status of the lyric genre, then this post-1968 period is key to interpreting the renaissance of poetry in the 1990s and the ensuing proliferation of styles.

Although it is not possible to do entirely without the common explanations of how New Subjectivity arose after political activism collapsed, my goal in this chapter is to reexamine the details of literary history of the period with greater attention to important theoretical issues raised by the poetry and prose of Ulla Hahn. This analysis, which begins with a discussion of Hahn's *Literatur in der Aktion* (*Literature in Action,* or *Activist Literature,* 1978) and other literary essays, suggests that for Hahn and others, the 1960s and 1970s were a time of crucial incubation in the lyric genre that fed the progressive development of postmodernism. The polarized gender dynamic registered in Hahn's work gives evidence of growing pressures on the literary establishment for stylistic and conceptual expansion of the lyric genre, changes that were gradually realized. A close reading of the poem "Gedicht" ("Poem") from Hahn's *Galileo und zwei Frauen* (*Galileo and Two Women,* 1997) reveals how in retrospect these tensions become a productive source for Hahn's poetics. The chapter closes with a consideration of what is at stake in Hahn's wide-ranging literary projects, which in the last decade have expanded to include the promotion of poetry performance through the recitation, memorization, and delivery of works in audio format.

Poems as Seismographs

Contemporary German women's poetry, it could be argued, divides into poets whose forte is a mastery of traditional poetic craft (like Sarah Kirsch, Karin Kiwus, and Ursula Krechel, who pursue meticulous handling of line, metaphor, and content) and those adept at avant-garde, textually experimental forms (like Friedrike Mayröcker, Elke Erb, Brigitte Oleschinski, and Barbara Köhler, whose texts exhibit linguistic fragmentation, typography, and non-representational expression). Hahn straddles this division, for her use of traditional conventions of rhyme, form, and register masks her eclectic procedures for radical rewriting (Melin 1997). Examples of these qualities are replete in her work. For instance, Hahn muses ironically in a poem from *Epikurs Garten* that "progress" means that "Es ist / für Wort und Spiele keine Zeit" ("there is / for word and play no time") (1995, 83). Then she unabashedly rhymes *Zeit* with the neologism "*Sekundenseligkeit*" (which means something like "momentary bliss"), emulating the lyricization that Mörike and Mallarmé achieve, even while defiantly terming them passé.

Such subversion pervades Hahn's poetry. Although superficially her work focuses on initiating, sustaining, and terminating personal romantic liaisons, the confrontational posturings exhibited in many of the poems amplify political ideals elaborated in her early academic study *Literatur in der Aktion* (*Literature in Action,* 1978). Indeed, a bold playfulness, rather than an outright rejection of convention, asserts Hahn's feminist agenda in poetry. Similarly, her essays about women authors argue for their prestige within the framework of the existing cultural system, even while she applauds authors from the 1940s and 1950s in particular for covert acts of opposition.

"Poems are reputed to be aesthetic seismographs of emotional and social changes," Ulla Hahn commented in 1989, a year whose events ended the Cold War and ushered in the sweeping transformations that closed out the twentieth century (1989a, 41). Her choice of words echoes Hilde Domin's previously discussed observation in *Wozu Lyrik heute* (*Why Poetry Today*) that poetry, even when not blatantly political, is a "seismograph of the time, hence unsettling and at the same time consciousness-raising" (1968, 23). It is perhaps not surprising, then, that apart from a few isolated poems that could be categorized as clearly political—"Hildegard L. Kommandanturstabsmitglied der SS in Majdanek" ("Hildegard L. Command Staff Member of the SS in Majdanek") or "Fernsehbild vom Foto einer jüdischen Frau im KZ" ("Television Picture of a Photograph of a Jewish Woman in Concentration Camp") from *Herz über Kopf*—Hahn's work seems to appeal primarily to the emotions. Yet this apparently apolitical response consistently drives toward feminist issues (of identity, sexuality, and agency), and there is a steady stream of poetry collections, novels, anthology projects, and essayistic prose in which Hahn appeals for social change in unexpected ways.

Ulla Hahn's literary debut in the 1980s with popular love poems led to the problematic and persistent categorization of her work as "feminine" writing, a mode assumed by detractors to be detached from political commitment and theoretical acumen. This categorical dismissal has obscured the fact that Hahn, in experimenting ironically with the intimate, expressive capacities of the lyric genre, unorthodox forms, and unliterary elements that sometimes irritated readers, has worked from the beginning with a keen awareness of the factors hampering German women poets of her generation. Essayistic texts by Hahn dating from the 1970s make clear that her theory of composition, conception of canon, and understanding of power dynamics in fact contain much self-conscious reflection about the imbrication of social issues and aesthetic values. Apart from the light these essays shed on the partisan reception of Hahn, what intrigues me about them is the extent to which they critically reveal the unquestioned functioning of norms regarding politics, gender, and class, and how these norms have shaped the climate for German poetry.

In the 1990s, German poetry became a field in which oppositional voices (Ryan 1997), diversity and resistance (Rolleston 1997), and a combination of language experimentation with cool hermeticism (Elm 1999) were seen to mirror social-political shifts. Real-world transformations included the reunification of the two Germanys, the emergence of postmodernism, and the spread of new technologies. In this context, Hahn, by now an established author, writes to consolidate a strategy for revitalizing cultural life, fusing an arguably idiosyncratic commitment to feminism with an appreciation for traditionalism. Her 1992 international anthology *Stechäpfel: Gedichte von Frauen aus drei Jahrtausenden* (*Thorn Apples: Poems by Women from Three Centuries*), presents itself as an ambitious project to recover forgotten women writers. Indeed, the 1998 anthology *Frauen dichten anders* (*Women Write Differently*) (Reich-Ranicki 1998) positions Hahn herself as a major poet by including fourteen of her poems as well as an impressive number of her own commentaries on women authors.[2] At the decade's close, Hahn embarks on a general project to capture a new audience for poetry by issuing the 1999 collection *Gedichte fürs Gedächtnis* (*Poems for Memorizing*), which presents a traditional canon annotated with up-to-date Internet references.

Though Hahn became famous for explicitly "feminine" poetry (especially love poems), exploration of her prose, from her study of protest literature (1978) to commentaries on women's writing in the 1990s, makes evident the complex relationship between the lyric genre and gender embodied in her work from the start. Comprehensive appraisal of these texts leads me to conclude that her aesthetic project is, in fact, a type of activist art fashioned to challenge readers' assumptions by prob-lematizing the intimate, expressive capacities of the lyric genre. For Hahn, the complementary relation of poetic theory and praxis has a strongly heuristic character, a self-educating character that runs counter to critical expectations that writers should strive to produce works that only display theoretical consistency. "The path emerges as we go" (2003, 86–87), Hahn observes about poetry, an assumption about writing as a heuristic process of evolution that I argue also informs her ideological commitments.

Hahn, who was born in 1946 and grew up in the Rhineland in a working-class environment, studied literature, history, and sociology in Cologne and Hamburg. Her poem "Mein Vater" ("My Father"), written in 1974, portrays a young author on whose desk photographs of Salvador Allende and Angela Davis flank the unsmiling, but cherished, image of a man who was a "Bauernkind, eines von zwölf, / und mit elf von der Schule" ("Peasant child, one of twelve, / and at eleven out of school") (1993, 6). Hahn's initial publications comprised political verse and academic prose, including *Literatur in der Aktion: Zur Entwicklung operativer Literatur-formen in der Bundesrepublik* (*Literature in Action: On the Development of Operative Literary Forms in the Federal Republic*, 1978). After a brief career as a university lecturer in Hamburg, Bremen, and Oldenburg, she worked at Radio Bremen in 1979 and turned to poetry (Braun 1986b).

At a time when much loosely written free verse was being produced, it is notable that Hahn took up neglected poetic conventions: carefully crafted verse, love poems, and rhymed forms such as the sonnet. These modes dominated her numerous volumes of poetry *Herz über Kopf* (*Heart over Head*, 1981), *Spielende* (*Game End*, or *Players*, 1983), *Freudenfeuer* (*Bonfire*, 1985), *Unerhörte Nähe* (*Unheard-of Proximity*, 1988), and *Liebesgedichte* (*Love Poems*, 1993). Two subsequent collections, *Epi-kurs Garten* (*Epicure's Garden*, 1995) and *Galileo und die zwei Frauen* (*Galileo and the Two Women*, 1997), experimented with the languishing traditions of nature poetry and ballads. Her more recent collection of poetry, *So offen die Welt* (*So Open the World*, 2004), displays continuing formal experimentation with language, rhyme, and free verse forms. Pub-lication of her collected essays (*Dichter in der Welt*, 2006), fiction, and multiple anthology projects testify to Hahn's sustained and multifaceted productivity as a writer.[3]

Parallel to these writings, Hahn published both academic prose and commentaries on authors that appeared in venues outside the literary mainstream. The location of these texts, either in specialized scholarly journals or standard newspapers, left them apparently disconnected from her creative work. However, through these publications, too, rather than in her poetry alone, Hahn responds explicitly to the disaffection with political protest after 1968, the rise of feminism, and the onset of post-*Wende* tensions, the term *Wende* or "turn," meaning the end of the GDR. Thus, to read fully Hahn's poetic experiments with linguistic manipulation and postmodern handling of form—traits that left readers bewildered about whether she was pursuing a conservative or radical agenda—the prose cannot be ignored. Against that background, abrasive declarations like the lines in "Ihr Kampfgenossen all" ("All You Comrades in Battle") that "You can kiss my ass / my grin already is hanging out of my mouth I'd / rather go into the rushes" read as rhetorical provocation rather than declarative statement (1981a, 69).[4] Such literal decree that politics should be jettisoned is in fact a calculated act, not a naive remark through which Hahn accidentally leaves her views open to harsh ideological scrutiny. Instead of allowing interpretation to be blocked by an unquestioning appropriation of the critical values of the early postwar period, this more expansive reading of Hahn's oeuvre positions us to appreciate the power and vulnerability of the lyric genre after 1968.

Essays about women's poetry from the 1980s by Renate Möhrmann, Gisela Elsner, and others illustrate the unsettled conditions under which Hahn debuted, but offer only partial explanation of her contested status, for they exclude the lyric genre from considerations of feminist trends in literature. Möhrmann implies that the lyric genre had limited emancipatory force (1981, 355), a suspicion that seems confirmed by Theodor Tauchel's announcement that Hahn had won the Leonce-and-Lena Prize. In words that stress tradition and decorous femininity, Tauchel chastised Hahn's male competitors for "a depressing slide into the profane and apoetical" and applauded her use of "the taboo, antiquated, mocked rhyme" (1981, 125). The following year Elisabeth Alexander advocated a larger role for women authors, but in similarly latently conservative terms. Concerned about potential fractionalization, Alexander warned against an apparent antagonism to women's interests in their own poetry, which she attributed to a fundamental lack of unified vision among women (1982, 116). For her, reinvigorated tradition appeared preferable to the contemporary "fashionable intellectual language" (Alexander 1982, 115).

By contrast, Gisela Elsner cautioned in the leftist journal *Kürbiskern* that by posturing "as if they were persuaded that subjectivity, irrationality, inconsequentiality, human warmth, the capacity for suffering and the ability to display understanding for everyone were writerly qualities," women writers could potentially ghettoize themselves and feed the prejudices of male critics (1983, 143–44). Elsner's charge that emotional displays inadvertently pandered to the existing stereotypes describes in effect Hahn's reception. Hahn won the approval of the influential critic Marcel Reich-Ranicki, garnered literary prizes, and sold an astonishing 80,000 volumes of poetry (Hahn 1988b), yet many still dismissed her verse as sentimental and trivial—categories encoded as "feminine."

Such objections proved tenacious. Jörg Drews's selection criteria for the major 1995 anthology *Das bleibt: Deutsche Gedichte 1945–1995* (*That Remains: German Poems 1945–1995*) still excluded Hahn by rationalizing, "Besides it was clear that a more or less arbitrary general poetry market would endure on and on, unbothered by literary-theoretical problematizations of the poetic genre, and that Ulla Hahn e tutti quanti, i.e., quante would continue to find their numerous readers: naturally the operation would somehow roll on" (1995, 258). Literary scholar Michael Braun also repeatedly chastised Hahn for her popularity and ostensible naïveté. Reviewing *Epikurs Garten,* Braun begins with acid enthusiasm that in this volume Hahn has left "the beaten path of guaranteed success" and decided for once not to present herself as the model pupil of poetic canon with solid "riche rime" and "proper sonnets" ("als Musterschülerin des poetischen Kanons mit solidem Reimereich und 'anständigen Sonetten' präsentiert"), but rather attempts to find her own voice apart from folk song language and decorative fairy-tale tone ("dekorativem Märchenton") (1996, 149). Nonetheless he concludes that the collection falls into a banal "flânerie in the flower garden" that leaves it seriously flawed (Braun 1996, 149–50). Such wholesale dismissal hinges on the perplexing traditionalism of Hahn's verse, but underestimates the challenge she issues to contemporary poetics. As Hahn counters in her 1994 Heidelberg lectures, which are partly concerned with the antagonisms between writers and critics, her opponents have missed the point. Quoting her early poem "Ars poetica," which contains an allusion to the destructive singing of the Lorelei, Hahn remarks on her intended irony, and the fact that it can be observed in the radical line breaks, exaggerated rhyme, and carefully manipulated poetic clichés that the reader encounters (1994, 11–12).

Several scholars have refined the analysis of Hahn by considering her work in connection with the factors that shape literary culture: evaluative categories in criticism (Wittkowski 1988), intertextuality (Rohlfs 1993), belated German reception of postmodernism (Anz 1996), and clashes between marginalized (especially feminine) aesthetics and dominant tastes (Melin 1997). Persuasively arguing that, for Hahn, poetic quality is defined by the ability to express existential suffering in beautiful form, Wittkowski concludes that the emphasis she places on individual voice that presents itself as private or nostalgic expression inevitably exposes her poetry to the charge that it is more kitsch than art (1988, 63). Further,

Wittkowski has noted that the prepublication dissemination of Hahn's work in such prominent public venues as the *Frankfurter Allgemeine Zeitung* generated unique conditions for its evaluation because "unlike any other author in the literary history of the Federal Republic of Germany, she owes her prominence to the newspaper medium" (1991, 170). Recognizing that the matrix of German literary culture equates these qualities of decorative surface and the aura of popularization with low art, we can discern that Braun, Drews, and others frequently disparage Hahn's poetry from precisely this standpoint, using diminutives, effete terms, and feminized designators like *Musterschülerin,* i.e., "model schoolgirl" (Braun 1986a, 119) and *dekorative[r] Märchenton,* in other words, decorative fairy tale tone (Braun 1996, 149).

The representation of Hahn in the voices of critics and the news media (where status quo gender assumptions clearly persist), however, creates a ventriloquized version of her poetics. The author herself describes her project quite differently. The discourse in essays that predate Hahn's poetry publications indicates that the artistic program she pursues has roots in her political activism and scholarship as a trained Germanist. In particular, the very effacement of boundaries between high and low art, as well as public and private expression vaunted as the hallmark of "operative" (that is, activist) literature corresponds to the pressures in her poetry on the fixity of categories of private/public and female/male. Contrary to the prevailing assumption that Hahn abruptly broke with her earlier commitments, this evidence points to important continuities between *Literatur in der Aktion* and subsequent poetic projects (see also Hahn 1984, 93).

Literatur in der Aktion, originally a dissertation study of protest and agitprop (or propagandistic) texts, endorsed the view that literature has a political function by emphasizing the role of authorial intention. Advocating a dismantling of the culturally constructed (bourgeois) separations of the personal from the political (1978, 165), Hahn celebrates literature with broad appeal. Much a product of its times and written in dry, academic prose, *Literatur in der Aktion* discusses performance, linguistic manipulation, and accessible subject matter in ways that anticipate her later subversion of poetic conventions of the "beautiful." Commenting on workers' literature and Peter Schütt, Hahn goes so far as to equate aesthetic quality with instrumental value: "Critical for the efficiency of the texts is not only the more or less successful literary realization of their enlightenment intention. Every attempt to assess the effect of these texts must take into account the place, the point in time of the publication and the potential addressees" (1978, 165). Hahn argues that literary judgments must now register class distinctions, connoisseurship values, and audience response because literature articulates an exchange between dominant and marginalized forces. This exchange exposes productive tensions between private and political elements, high and low culture, and socially engaged and "purely aesthetic" artworks. Many of the pieces analyzed in *Literatur in der Aktion* thus strive for tangible political results through performance contexts—demonstrations, street theater productions, and working groups—that link art with action. In sum, Hahn defines "art" as a utopian project to unmask present conditions to make the future "recognizable" (1978, 202) and therefore promotes agitprop as engaging in a search for forms conceived for public delivery (1978, 61), although her analysis does not proceed much beyond identifying its categories and types.

True to its time, *Literatur in der Aktion* focuses on the women's movement only in a subsection devoted to "expansion of the material repertoire" (Hahn 1978, 167). Comments throughout the study hint at an emergent concern with gender dynamics, yet Hahn consistently frames discussions of power, politics, and art in gender-neutral terms. Describing poetry by Arno Reinfrank, for example, she concludes merely that Reinfrank "never reduces love to sex nor conceives of it as an isolated free space, but rather symbolically encodes the social problematic, just as in the nature poems" (1978, 31).

This rather oblique acknowledgment of feminism in *Literatur in der Aktion* confirms Dagmar Herzog's diagnosis of the complexity of German New Left attitudes toward sexuality and women's issues. Especially relevant to what we observe in Hahn's case is the evidence Herzog finds for both New Left hostility toward feminism and a preoccupation with "the relationship between the personal and the political, between sex and what had happened to the attempt to change the world," as she puts it in a related essay (1998, 429). Sexual liberation, according to Herzog's analysis, was embraced by the New Left as socially transformative (à la Herbert Marcuse and Susan Sontag),[5] while a commitment to feminist goals was forcibly contained. The restrained treatment of feminism coupled with insistence on the salience of a personal-political dichotomy in Hahn's *Literatur in der Aktion,* we can conclude, mirrors the general New Left paradox.

Where tensions about the personal-political nexus do, however, surface for Hahn is not in *Literatur in der Aktion,* but in her poetry. In interviews Hahn gave after she turned to the lyric genre, she voices relief at being able to reconnect with literature, free from academic constraints of impersonality and impartiality (1985c, 163). She emphasizes repeatedly that the personal entails the political: "Every love poem, however private it may appear, is always also a social poem. The more radically I speak about myself, the more directly I address social conditions. From the women's movement we know the slogan: The private is political and vice versa. I can only underscore that" (Schmitt 1986, 74). At the same time in what appears to be a reprise of Hamburger's theory of poetry, Hahn sets firm boundaries between her private self and the poetic *I*, explaining that "[an] 'I' in the poem is never identical with my person" (1988b, 59). By training an academic scholar familiar with the assumptions of interpretive objectivity, she expresses the distance between the represented speaker and the poet here in terms of writerly procedures. Hahn describes a composition process that begins with rhythms, rhymes, and materials collected over a period of several months (Schmitt 1986, 74), and texts written "with a clear head" rather than out of some naive outpouring of immediate feeling (Hahn 1984, 93).[6] But it is important to Hahn to show that rational thinking and the heightened state of awareness practiced by creative artists are not mutually exclusive. She formulates this position even more decisively in her 1994 Heidelberg lectures, "What comes from the outside must be transformed and handed back again. . . . Poems require time. Lifetime and life experience. They are condensations of lived life. Poetry cannot be had more cheaply" (Hahn 1994, 4). The private is political, and poetry is therefore both.

Ultimately, as Hahn's focus on gender issues in politics becomes more pronounced in the 1980s–1990s, her writings are stimulated by readings of Adrienne Rich, whose work was becoming known to German audiences. Even prior to this turn, however, Hahn has already revisited the activist art principles outlined in *Literatur in der Aktion*, progressively inching ever closer to an explicit engagement with feminism to account for the situation of women writers. Central to the terms of this engagement are Hahn's understanding of performance dynamics, her conviction that poetry and politics are inextricably connected, and her interest in women writers. Two interviews with Hahn in the 1980s describe poetic work as calculated performance. In the first, she likens poetry to ballet, in which the spectator sees only the perfection of the dance, not the laborious effort required to produce it (1985b, 165). The second compares the poet to a tightrope walker who maneuvers under the greatest of constraints, yet performs as if a god (1987b, 114–18).[7] Meantime, several poems from this period, including "Ihr Kampfgenossen all," draw on the conventions of political art adumbrated in *Literatur in der Aktion* by staging a public venue for acts of poetic performance. "Ars poetica," for example, evokes the seductive powers of Lorelei-like verse over listeners

(Reich-Ranicki 1998, 735), while "Annonce" ("Announcement") mocks the public format of newspaper personal ads when it proclaims the poet to be "zu alt um schön zu sein und / noch nicht interessant" ("Too old to be beautiful and / not yet interesting") (Hahn 1993, 118).

"Meine Damen und Herren" ("Ladies and Gentlemen"), from a later collection, positions the poet squarely in front of an audience to which she provocatively and wittily remarks: "Das Gedicht meine Dame ist kein Kölnisch Wasser / für kalte Kompressen auf Herzen / ist kein Deo gegen den Angstschweißgeruch" ("The poem, madame, is no eau de cologne / for cold compresses to the heart / is no deodorant against the sweat smell of angst") (Hahn 1988a, 64). Poetry, the poet continues with bravado, should neither aid in the conquest of women nor in the creation of weapons. Rather, she lectures, you, the audience, should be open to being changed by the poem. Hahn, of course, here reworks Rilke's famous lines about art changing one's life (expressed with the verb *ändern* in the poem "Archaïscher Torso Apollos" ["Archaic Torso of Apollo"]).[8] Revisiting this phrase in an interview, Hahn insists on poetry's interaction with readers: "For the poem cannot only change [*verändern*] the reader, first of all the reader changes the poem, or to formulate this another way, what can be read out of a poem is only whatever was put into it, by the author and sometimes even more by the reader, when the reader and poem come into conversation with each other" (1987b, 111). Subsequently she reiterates the importance of the reader's contribution, much in the spirit of the terms Domin envisioned in *Doppelinterpretationen*: "My poems write themselves to the end in the mind of the reader. Each reader understands them in his own way" (Hahn 1989b, 23).

Like Domin in *Wozu Lyrik heute* as well, Hahn emphasizes that poetry and politics have reciprocal functions. This reasoning links Hahn's early work with her later writing about women authors, and allows us to trace these themes to her 1981 and 1983 essays about Stefan Hermlin. Taking Hermlin as a model, Hahn emphasizes that his journalism is closely related to his poetry (1983b, 7).[9] She elaborates on this poetry-politics connection by noting that some readers have mistrusted Hermlin's poetic ambiguity as an ingenious masking of the unambiguously political (Hahn 1981b, 95). By 1988, Hahn programmatically asserts the need for poets to be politically committed: "The politician may be powerful. The poet is all-powerful. The politician makes the achievable possible. The poet, everything possible achievable" (Hahn 1988b, 64). In this aphoristic formula we recognize one of the most fundamental assumptions made about the lyric genre after 1945 in German-speaking countries: that all poetry must be engaged. The subtle expansion of that premise by Hahn evolves through seemingly disconnected parts of her work, as her concerns with social issues in the 1970s are translated into efforts to reevaluate women authors of the 1940s and 1950s.

Our observation of this evolutionary flow across Hahn's oeuvre, I think, problematizes the ways in which we conceive the history of women's writing, for in Hahn's case there are evidently multiple and sometimes contradictory affiliative relationships constantly at work as literary influences. Considering the situation of women writers after 1945 from the vantage of 2000, Karen Leeder points to a continuum in literary careers and literature production between the Third Reich and the immediate postwar years and attributes the style of some contemporary poets to these models created in the 1940s and 1950s, observing, "Inevitably, perhaps, the instability of recent years has provoked a return to traditional forms and the apolitical stance of the immediate postwar years. In part no doubt also as a reaction to the prosaic banality of the 1970s, writers like Ulla Hahn, Doris Runge, or Karin Kiwus have developed a highly wrought culture of form and feeling" (see Leeder 2000, 212). In light of Hahn's interest in Kolmar, Le Fort, Huch, and Domin in particular, I suggest that our understanding of what binds these two periods of literary production (the 1950s and the 1970s) should be refined by tracing the discourses Hahn uses to explain and validate poetic production.

In a series of widely dispersed texts published in the 1980s and 1990s, Hahn promotes the literary work of women: Else Lasker-Schüler, Gertrud Kolmar, Nelly Sachs, Ricarda Huch, Gertrud von Le Fort, Sarah Kirsch, Emily Dickinson, Hilde Domin, Marie Luise Kaschnitz, Sylvia Plath, Ingeborg Bachmann, Christa Reinig, Doris Runge, Annette von Droste-Hülshoff, and the poets anthologized in *Stechäpfel* (1992b).[10] The aesthetic program she works out in relation to women's writing and feminist theory proposes anew that literature can reshape society. Here Hahn focuses on the character of poetic texts (the precision of language, qualitative contributions of form, and nature of textuality) and is drawn to content involving the past, memory, and mortality. Rather than drawing on her familiarity with the contemporary literary scene as demonstrated in *Literatur in der Aktion,* Hahn consolidates her artistic agenda by looking beyond the present to women writers of earlier periods, including several whose careers bridged the division customarily marked by 1945. Meanwhile, her systematic references in *Stechäpfel* to feminist thinkers (especially Adrienne Rich) elucidate a relation to literary tradition and language that combines both an attraction to dominant models and a self-conscious conviction that women authors work against this grain. Hahn finds this combination empowering.

Hahn champions women authors by celebrating their struggles against political oppression, disparaging their public neglect, and admiring their resistance to linguistic constraints. Hahn's 1982 essay on Else Lasker-Schüler, for example, concluded that she was "certainly no political poet," but that she was interested in pure justice (1982, 213), and thus demonstrated general ethical concerns, which Hahn regards as a justification for rediscovering women writers. Soon, however, Hahn dispenses with the need for any sort of political justification of her topic beyond considering women's literature for its own sake. Asked about her interest in Gertrud Kolmar, Hahn stated, "I find that in the literary history a great many women poets have been grossly neglected. . . . I view it also as a certain duty to draw attention again and again to poets and women poets whom I consider to be important" (1985c, 167). While Hahn comments at length on the difficult circumstances in which Kolmar lived, poetic craft comes to the fore as the salient criterion for appreciating Kolmar. "In metaphor," she remarks, "words rebel against the logic of order if language is freed from the corset of abstraction; borders are abolished, oppositions linked" (1983a, 182).

In the case of Le Fort and Huch, who—unlike Lasker-Schüler, Kolmar, and Nelly Sachs—cannot readily be called oppositional writers, Hahn relies on a strategy of acknowledging their obscurity, praising their traditionalism, and yet discerning subtle social tensions in their work. Hahn concedes that she had long forgotten Le Fort's novels except for a vague sense of characters who "progressed through life as very noble, helpful and good figures, often unto death" (1985b, 95). Still, she insists on reading gender tensions in Le Fort's biography as seminal: "The world of male activism remained foreign to her," Hahn states, and "indeed the possibility of a feminine exercise of influence lies precisely in this alienness, in the fact that the woman recognizes the laws of this masculine world but does not accept them" (1985b, 109). Regarding Huch, Hahn displays respect for her use of tradition and dismay at her diminishing reputation (1985a). Hahn's discussion of "Uralter Worte kundig" ("Familiar with Ancient Words") focuses on Huch's reversal of traditional gender roles (that is, men as active, women as passive) (Reich-Ranicki 1998, 138–39) while her reading of "Mein Herz, mein Löwe" ("My Heart, My Lion") as an anti-fascist statement expresses admiration for Huch's boldness (2000, IV). Huch, too, is political for Hahn.

In comparison with Le Fort and Huch, Hahn views Hilde Domin as occupying a position of clear political engagement because she responds to the Holocaust in her poetry and at the same time negotiates a balance between personal subject matter and poetic expression in a way that

Hahn finds compelling and broadly political. Hahn emphasizes the distance between raw feelings and Domin's poems, in which "the rational, calculated interaction with the word only distills what is worth communicating out of the inner chaos" (1987c, n.p.).[11] On the occasion of Domin's eightieth birthday, Hahn likewise extolled her use of language and underscored her political engagement by emphasizing the difference between Domin's "poetics based on a social foundation" and the aesthetics of Gottfried Benn, who espoused an asocial, monologic poetry (1992a, 23).[12]

Whereas Kolmar, Lasker-Schüler, Le Fort, Huch, and Domin allow Hahn to explore public/private distinctions, historical events, and gender constructions in terms of discussions contemporary to her own work, Droste-Hülshoff, Dickinson, and Plath elicit focus on the status of poets who are de facto literary icons of the past. Her essays on these poets adumbrate subjects that are gaining prominence in Hahn's oeuvre in the 1990s: mortality, reputation, religion, and power. The socially determined limits, self-imposed constraints, and writerly problems that affected these women poets certainly resonate with Hahn, but it is first and foremost interest in broader questions about the significance of lyrical experience that motivates her concern with their work.

Hahn's 1987 review of new Dickinson translations, which appeared just before the publication of *Unerhörte Nähe,* highlights the innovative language of this early modernist, arguing that "in a masterly manner the poet brings into play the ambiguities of the words, forces out of them new meaning through unusual juxtapositions" (1987a, 9). Here Hahn celebrates poetry's lyrical qualities and appreciates Dickinson's unique modernism. That analysis broadens the application to historical texts of Hahn's assertion that the personal is political, with justification as current poetry scholarship suggests. Modernity, as Virginia Jackson observes in her trenchant analysis of Dickinson's work, has succeeded in making the lyric a preeminent form because the privacy it expresses "has become one way to understand public life" (2005, 204). "As the lyric has been taken to represent individual expression," Jackson continues, "it has also become representative of *our* individual expression—whoever we are" (2005, 204). Furthermore, Hahn's readings of historical texts through a lens of empathy remains constant with respect to her initial ideological commitments, even when explicit public connections seem to be made tenuous by her emphasis on the personal. The occasion of Droste-Hülshoff's 200th birthday demonstrates such a response. Hahn unapologetically calls forth the pathos of poems by Droste-Hülshoff, terming them an attempt to bridge the gap "between the longing for eternal security and a suspicion fed by contemporary, materialistic instinct" (1997b, 19). Similarly, in another essay that looks at Droste-Hülshoff's "Die Taxuswand" ("The Yew Hedge"), Hahn interprets it as an encounter with time's passage and changed relationships. There Hahn observes, "The yew hedge is a time wall that divides yesterday from today, youth from age" (Reich-Ranicki 1998, 95), evincing a keen preoccupation with mortality that surfaces in Hahn's own collections *Epikurs Garten* (1995) and *Galileo und die zwei Frauen* (1997), which bracket that publication.

The case of Sylvia Plath moves Hahn from a consideration of pathos and subjectivity toward deeper reflection about poet persona. Hahn vigorously critiques the way in which text dissemination and biographers' preconceptions shaped public awareness of Plath (see also Morris 2000). Two articles, "Kurzschluß aufs Leben: Wenn Biographen Moralisten werden" ("Short Circuted Life," 1990) and "'Ich habe dir nie einen Zitronenkuchen versprochen.' Gerichtstag über sich selbst: Sylvia Plath in ihren Tagebüchern" ("I Never Promised You a Lemon Cake," 1997c), compare Plath's lyrical and biographical identities: "Plath's inexorable circling around her own subjectivity in so many different forms makes clear above all that when we create ourselves through language, each utterance can only be regarded as a fragment" (1997c, L10). Given the absence of a German variant of American confessional poetry (represented by the work of Plath, Sexton, Lowell, Berryman, and others), the terms of her respect seem purposely chosen to deflect the suspicion that such "private" poetry is merely self-indulgent.[13] Moreover, Hahn is equally concerned with reputation, for she criticizes the presentation of Plath's work in German editions she terms unrepresentative and takes issue with critical characterizations of Plath as a pathological author. And parallel to these essays she protests against the distortion of words by individuals who twist them in the poet's mouth, the audiences who don't understand, "oder sie in einen Käfig am Kirchturm hängen / bis sie verdorren daß sie dir deine Wörter / biegen und brechen" ("Or hang them in a cage on the church tower / until they wither, that they your words / bend and break") (1997a, 56).[14]

Childhood experiences and domestic circumstances frequently become a focal point for these empathetic readings. Elaborating on the lives of the women writers she analyzes, Hahn inserts into her essays concrete elements of class or religion that mark political and gender divisions: a reference to Le Fort's Catholic heroines, the economically trying circumstances in which Lasker-Schüler worked, or the aristocratic yet circumscribed world in which Droste-Hülshoff moved. Indeed, in Hahn's own writings from the 1990s, comparable allusions to a working-class milieu, dialect, and her Catholic upbringing heighten the tensions between high and low art. "Fassade" ("Façade") contrasts the perfectly groomed exterior of its protagonist with the abuse by an alcoholic father whose blows mean that "hinter den Zähnen / stottert das Mädchen noch / immer am hochdeutschen Alphabet" ("behind her teeth / the girl still stutters / with the high German alphabet") (1995, 64). "Spartakus im Rheinland" ("Spartacus in the Rhineland") recapitulates the biographical path Hahn took. Calling herself an "Arbeiter / Kind" ("worker's / child"), the poet writes about finding her way from "dä Dom in Kölle / die Kirche im Dorf" ("the cathedral in Cologne / the church in the village") to receiving "Kommune statt / Kommunion Hammer und Sichel anstelle / von Brot und Wein" ("commune instead of / communion hammer and sickle instead of / bread and wine") (1997a, 14–15).

Abundant biblical phrases in Hahn's poems, rewritten parables in the afterword to *Stechäpfel,* and the stifling small-town Catholic atmosphere of her novel *Ein Mann im Haus* draw on these experiences of her youth as well. These references to religion are not parodically marked like those of Bertolt Brecht, but instead are deeply bound up with Hahn's fascination with words, which precedes a formal understanding of the lyric genre. Indeed, Hahn's 1986 Gandersheim award speech unconventionally traced her interest in poetry back to a devotional book she uncovered in her mother's attic, introducing her to ballads, dramas, and poems by Paul Gerhardt, Friedrich von Spee, and others: "I did not understand a word of the text, it probably didn't even dawn on me that it could have a meaning. Rather it kept me mesmerized by its syllables with the magic of a spell" (1986, 25).[15]

While the attention to issues of politics, gender, class, and religion broached in these texts is defused through their appearance in scattered, journalistic venues, the afterword to *Stechäpfel* (1992b) treats these matters directly and in concentrated form. Here Hahn focuses on the asymmetrical balance of power between the genders, the conditions under which women authors have created, and a programmatic vision for the future. In a departure from her usual practice of eschewing words that signify power—*Macht, Kraft, Stärke, Gewalt*—Hahn bluntly paraphrases sentiments about gender dynamics as voiced by the American poet Adrienne Rich in "When We Dead Awaken" (1971): "Im männlichen Universum nahm ich natürlich Vorstellungen über Frauen, Sexualität, Macht aus der subjektiven Sicht männlicher Dichter auf" (quoted in Hahn 1992b, 372).[16] Broader in conception than *The Other Voice* (Rich 1976), a comparable English-language anthology for which Rich wrote the introduction, *Stechäpfel* represents women's writing across historical and national boundaries. Describing selection criteria, translation quality, and thematic considerations that shaped the anthology, Hahn's afterword stresses the impetus brought to the feminist movement by the author Virginia Woolf, and French feminist theorists Hélène Cixous and Luce Irigaray, and reproves the general underrepresentation of women authors in print (Hahn 1992b, 365–66).

Hahn dismisses two possible frameworks for a project such as *Stechäpfel:* the "'Wir-Frauen'-Konzept" ("we-women concept") (1992b, 368) and the notion of rupture that Hugo Friedrich used to explain the rise of modernism in *Die Struktur der modernen Lyrik* (1956, 371). The abstract solidarity of the former, predicated on the sense that all women share similar experiences, is not plausible to Hahn due to the historical and geographical scope of her anthology. The latter, Hahn rightly observes, cannot explain women's writing since they were excluded in the first place from the tradition that modernism ostensibly rejected, "A *l'art pour l'art,* that art as an end in itself, can hardly be made out in poetry by women; hermetic poems are the exceptions" (1992b, 371). Instead Hahn emphasizes that women should depict their own realities (1992b, 371).

In Rich, Hahn finds a sympathetic model with biographical parallels since the American writer recounts how participation in 1950s and 1960s dissent movements prompted her to link women's experience and literary expression (compare Rich 1979, 44–45). Emphasizing the urgency of her cause, Hahn, for example, interjects a telegraphic statement attributed to Rich's essay "When We Dead Awaken" (Rich 1979), "Heute ist die Poesie von Frauen oftmals beladen mit Ärger" ("Today the poetry of women is often full of anger") (Hahn 1992b, 387). The cogent formulations of Rich provide Hahn with terms to break with power structures that, as Michel Foucault has observed, are perniciously entrenched. Indeed, through Rich, Hahn is able to more directly connect poetry with questions of power and at last refines the poetic agenda she had been gradually articulating in her writings about women poets since the 1980s.

Hahn uses Rich to frame programmatic statements, as when she cites a passage in which Rich describes learning one's poetic craft from men as an absorption of formal canon and subtly gendered "universalism" (Hahn 1992b, 369). A discussion of writing about the body and sensuality by Rich motivates Hahn to call for women writers to question "images of women and ways of behaving" (Hahn 1992b, 369). Likewise she celebrates language much in the same way as Rich did in her 1977 essay "Power as Danger: Works of a Common Woman" when asserting, "Poetry is above all a concentration of the *power* of language, which is the power of our ultimate relationship to everything in the universe. It is as if forces we can lay claim to in no other way, become present to us in sensuous form" (Rich 1979, 248). Thus Hahn defines writing as self-realization: "When women write, it is also a search for identity, for a place in the world, not for a new, this time feminine I-ideal in utopia" (Hahn 1992b, 369).

But while Hahn defines her own position via Rich, grounding her conclusions about the disjunctures between female experience and masculinist culture with quotations from the American's writings, she rewrites Rich in key respects. Unlike Rich, Hahn insists on universality as a touchstone: "The space of art is universal. Gender plays a role there among many other socio-cultural characteristics, such as heritage, race, and religious affiliation" (Hahn 1992b, 374). Further, she locates the emancipatory thrust of women's poetry in a "weiblich[e] Ästhetik" (feminine aesthetic) expressed on the level of subject matter and choice of perspective (Hahn 1992b, 374). This reference to "weibliche Ästhetik" engages with the discussion begun in Germany by Silvia Bovenschen's 1976 essay "Über die Frage: Gibt es eine 'weibliche' Aesthetik?" ("About the Question: Is There a Feminine Aesthetic?") (Bovenschen 1976), which continued in essays by Ursula Heukenkamp (1985) and Barbara Lersch (1988). Mindful of that debate, Hahn had herself penned a poem, "Gibt es eine weibliche Ästhetik," that carried out Virginia Woolf's ironic suggestion in *A Room of Her Own* that women authors should create a true picture of men by describing the male bald spot (Reich-Ranicki 1998, 759).[17] The poem mischievously admires the decrepit physiognomy of a middle-aged man, concluding after describing his shining head that he is the most beautiful of all men.

Hahn's insistence on the universalism of art, quite obviously, too, reactivates one of the chief legitimizing strategies for poetry in the postwar decades—the evocation of an international literary standard to validate the ethical intentions of German authors. Emulating international (especially American) trends, German literature after 1945 had, as we have seen in discussion of Domin's work, rather unquestioningly perpetuated modernism's cultural presumptions that such aesthetic concepts as originality and abstraction were gender-neutral. Alicia Suskin Ostriker observes in regarding the American literary scene that modernism prompted two distinct styles in women's poetry: "The first was an extension and refinement of the traditional lyric style which concentrated on intense personal feeling. The second, a more radical break from the immediate past, was formally innovative and intellectually assertive but avoided autobiography" (Ostriker 1986, 44).

For Hahn, the genesis of the feminist project aimed at breaking this mold resembles the awakening Rich describes in her own life: "I was writing very little, partly from fatigue ... partly from the discontinuity of female life with its attention to small chores, errands, work that others constantly undo, small children's constant needs" (Rich 1979, 43). Though at first discreet, women's frustration accomplishes a breakthrough via the discovery of the connection between poetry and power. In this spirit, Hahn's "Ballade von Galileo und zwei Frauen" ("The Ballad of Galileo and Two Women") of 1997 confesses "Der Job der Mann das Kind das Schreiben alles / Unter einen Hut—es geht nicht mehr" ("The job the husband the child the writing everything / under a single hat—it doesn't work anymore") (1997a, 78). As the title hints, the text posits that women's liberation parallels the Copernican revolution. Hahn questions whether a paradigmatic shift has really occurred in science or society. The two women despair, for they know they have paid in working toward such change with broken relationships, overwhelming tasks, and physical stress. Galileo provides them solace because even his genius yielded to torture. Meditating on the cancer that killed her mother and finding similarities in Inquisition torture, the poet imagines how the course of history might have changed had Galileo had the courage to state the truth that "Die Sonne nicht / Die Erde steht im Zentrum" ("The sun not / the earth stands at the center") (Hahn 1997a, 79). The stunning line break underscores the false recantation Galileo made of his theory. In the end, painfully aware that changes in the status quo come slowly, the poet seeks solace in the transcendent moon, so unaffected by human strife, "Ganz weich ganz / Wie eine runde Sache" ("Quite soft quite / like a round thing,") (Hahn 1997a, 80).

The clarity of science, however, eludes Hahn and her hopes for women writers. Hahn's poem "Befähigung" ("Aptitude") laments that once the muses aided writers as "Meisterinnen des Schmerzes und des Entzückens" ("Mistresses of pain and delight") (1995, 79). Today, poets struggle to find voice and to write from their own experience:

> Wer lehrt uns Wörter
> gewichtiger als das was weiß bleibt
> auf dem Papier. Und wer
> bringt uns ein Schweigen bei
> das die Welt nicht enger und leerer macht (1995, 79)

> Who teaches us words
> weightier than what remains white
> on the paper. And who
> teaches us a silence
> that does not make the world narrower and more empty.

Hahn's question is unpunctuated and rhetorical. In the absence of masters, and even gentle muses, the poet positions herself together with others trying to write—finding the sense of community suggested by the word *uns* (us). Although she embraces a conception of literature dedicated to altering power structures, Hahn acknowledges that it is difficult to break old paradigms. Her poetry employs subtle positionings of the lyrical *I* and highly crafted language to advance a feminist agenda, mapping a poiesis of rereading and of rewriting that is complex, and highly variable.

Tropes and Forms

Since the 1990s, Hahn's approaching to defining a new poetics has become more programmatic. Her lecture series "Poesie und Vergnügen—Poesie und Verantwortung" ("Poetry and Pleasure—Poetry and Responsibility," 1994) makes plain that she regards the historical position of the poet at the end of the twentieth century as more fraught with difficulties than at the century's beginning. The poet, Hahn observes, "must bear and use productively the tension between communicative and formal media" (Hahn 1994, 14). She thus dismisses the divide between *l'art pour l'art* and *literature engagée*. Hahn explains, "I can only continue my art when I place myself under the conditions of art, and those conditions are not only of an aesthetic but also of a social nature. . . . This idea of the poetic includes conceptions about social reality, and to these conceptions the poet answers, by refuting or transforming them" (1994, 14–15).

For Hahn, art today demands a careful formal structuring of language to reach its communicative, social goal. Hahn insists that "only . . . in formed language the supra-personal nature of what is said is ensured" (1994, 5), and aligns her work with that of modernists who turned the personal into a calculated artistic strategy. Citing Paul Valéry's rejection of art based on solipsistic values alone, she qualifies, "In this sense Gottfried Benn's definition is also to be understood: 'There is no other subject matter for poetry than the poet himself'" (1994, 5). The aesthetic language of this argument is further adumbrated in "Gedicht" ("Poem") from *Galileo und zwei Frauen* (1997a).

The generic title "Poem" is followed by the dedication "Für Proteus" ("For Proteus") and a six-line quotation from Ovid's *Metamorphosis* about a being capable of transforming into a man, lion, boar, serpent, steer, stone, or tree. Candidates for the role of Proteus might be the critic Marcel Reich-Ranicki (a longtime supporter of Hahn), or an aging poet with stylistic volatility and the stature of, say, Hans Magnus Enzensberger,

Günther Grass, or indeed Peter Rühmkorf, with whom Hahn compares herself in *Poesie und Vergnügen.* "Similarly to *Peter Rühmkorf* I like to write in tongues," Hahn comments, interjecting several additional references to his work (1994, 8). In "Gedicht," however, Hahn meditates not on one author, but instead on the relationship of poem to poet, exploring problems that can be generalized to all writerly craft:

> Schwer zu erklären daß ein Gedicht
> keinen Gegenstand hat wie ein Schiff
> seine Container eine Jahreszeit ihre Blumen
> Unteilbar wie eine Primzahl
> Daß es flieht wie du vor der Zeit
> und vorbei ist
> wenn du zu schreiben aufhörst zu
> lesen aufhörst wenn du dich nicht
> mehr erinnerst was du gerade noch
> warst in einem Aufblitzen
> einem Moment lang ein Wort lang
> Schilfrohr Flamme Staub Komet
> der vorbeizischt ein Schwarm
> kleiner Vögel zwitschernd über
> uns   alle hinweg   nichts Greifbares
> nicht einmal schwarz auf weiß
> Höchstens Kindermalkasten
> springendes Wasser an dieser
> Erde festbinden   Hostie
> unter der Zunge Vertrauen
> gelassen und blind   Gespielt
> auf Syringen   hart wie eine
> Brise   so wie an den Hut getippt
> Jetzt und Vorbei   Oh
> du Angst vor dem Ende endlose Angst
> daß alles vorbei ist bis alles vorbei ist
> solange wir schreiben
> solange wir lesen kann es
> kein alles geben   solange du schreibst
> solange du liest sind nur die anderen
> für dich gestorben wenn du es liest
> wenn es dich liest aus
> setzt unter wuchernden
> Himmeln Fallobst Septemberäpfel

das Rohe und das Gekochte
das Leere das Gestillte der Überfluß
Hand und Fuß mit Schuhen und ohne
Mann und Frau mit Sehnsucht
und ohne Brotsuppe mit Bier   Jetzt
und Hier   sag was du willst was
willst du   mehr als alles   zurück   und
Für   Immer Nichts hört auf
wenn du aufhörst zu
Sein   oder?   Nichtsein kann es nicht geben
im Gedicht nicht geben und nicht im Leben
Nimm das Holz aus der Glut Keiner
den Asche erfreut   Gib Namen Prämissen
Gib Namen   Kleine Unterkünfte über
dem Abgrund gegründet   All die Musik
auf der Stille in Beethovens Ohr.
Abgestellt endgültig abgestellt   Irgendwann wirklich
das letzte Gedicht   Darf keine Trauer sein
Fangzahnordnung für ein paar
Leichenteile kross schwimmend in Katastrophen
und frischer Wäsche
Rosen regnen herab keinerlei
Messerschneiden Ziegelsteine
Mag sein
          Gefaltete Hände von einem Fräulein
          die anno Nero schon
          Bravo Da capo Bravissimo rief. (1997a, 24–26)

Hard to explain that a poem
has no object like a ship
its container a season its flowers
Indivisible like a prime number
That it flees like you before time
and is past
when you cease to write to
read cease when you do not remember
any more what you just
were in a flash
a moment long a word long
reed flame dust comet
that whizzes past a swarm

of small birds twittering over
us   all past   nothing concrete
not even black on white
At most a child's paint box
springing water on this
earth binding firm   consecrated host
under the tongue trust
tranquil and blind   played
on lilacs   hard like a
breeze just like tipped on the hat
Now and past Oh
you fear of the end endless fear
that everything is past until all is past
as long as we write
as long as we read it can
give no all   as long as you write
as long as you read only the others are
dead for you and when you read it
when it reads you
abandons under rank
heaven windfall September apple
the raw and the cooked
the empty the stilled the excess
hand and foot with shoes and without
man and woman with longing
and without bread soup with beer   Now
and here   say what you want
do you want   more than everything back   and
For   Always Nothing ceases
when you cease
Be   right?   Not being cannot exist
in the poem and not in life
Take the wood from the fire   No one
delights in ashes   Give names premises
Give names   Small accommodations founded
over the abyss founded   All the music
to the stillness in Beethoven's ear.
Switched off finally switched off   Sometime really
the final Poem   Can be no mourning
Fang order for a few
body parts crisply swimming in catastrophes

and clean wash
roses rain down not any sort of
knife-cuts bricks
May be

> Folded hands of a young maiden
> who already anno Nero
> Cried Bravo Da capo Bravissimo.

Considering the importance Hahn attaches to form, we can see that the formal elements she deploys in the poem contribute strongly to its meaning. Hahn begins the 61-line text with a comparison mediated by the adverb *wie* (like) and two examples of what a poem is not. Neither a compartmentalized container ship (a familiar sight in the port city of Hamburg, where Hahn resides) nor a recurrent season with its predictable flowers, poems have dynamic properties that Hahn subsequently elaborates. Moreover, as the text moves beyond the careful repetition of *wie* in the opening lines, the poet shifts from the explanatory phrase "Schwer zu erklären, daß . . ." (the conjunction *daß* is repeated in lines 5 and 26 only) to metaphorical and more speculative descriptions of poetry. The poem is written in free verse that allows Hahn to play syntax off effectively against enjambment, using end stops and calculated breaks within the poetic line. Anaphora, assonance, and other rhetorical effects frame this poem as a work that dialogically reaches out to listeners (through the addressee of the text), rather than operating as an intimate piece or private monologue.

Equally important to the account of poetry that Hahn proffers is the tension the poem creates between reworked language and metaphors of inspiration. In the first sixteen lines, the text explains that poetry has occult properties—irreducibility (*Unteilbar wie eine Primzahl*), elusiveness (*nichts Greifbares*), and incendiarism (*Aufblitzen, Flamme, Komet*). However, its ephemeral nature (emphasized by the words *es fleiht, einem Moment lang, vorbeizischen*) rather than eternal value is emphasized and connected with the mortality of the poet (lines 7–8). Choosing words that describe categories of things or generic objects, rather than cultivating a language of specificity as she had done in her previous collection *Epikurs Garten*, Hahn deflects the poem away from tangible description. This turn disassociates poetry from mere representation and nudges it toward a particular type of abstraction that is a legacy of expressionist lyric. Indeed, the rhetorical register echoes work of Benn, Trakl, and other early modernists. The reference to a comet is reminiscent of expressionist poems prompted by Halley's comet in the early twentieth century (a phenomenon that proved less inspirational upon its return in 1986) and invokes expressionist millennialism (thoughts not far removed from broodings about the year 2000). The key word *Schilfrohr* refers back to the poem "Ihr Kampfgenossen all" from Hahn's first collection of poetry, reminding readers that she split with comrades-in-arms and planned to "schnitz mir aus Schilfrohr / eine helle Flöte" ("cut me from reed / a bright flute") (1981a, 69). Other words and phrases like *Himmel, Fallobst,* and *Septemberäpfel* stand outside of syntactic cohesion in chunks, a montage that evokes elements of traditional poetry (for German readers, works by Wilhelm Lehmann, Günter Eich, or Karl Krolow would come to mind).

At first rapidly citing examples of what does and does not make poetry, "Gedicht" modulates to a more leisurely tempo in the section treating the free play of the imagination (*Kindermalkasten, Gespielt / auf Syringen*). It slows dramatically to meditate on the act of writing in face of the finality of death, starting with the apostrophe *Oh,* placed at the end of line 24. Hahn conspicuously makes no claim that poetry has eternal status. Instead, she foregrounds the very transience of acts of writing—of the poet composing (*solange du schreibst*), reading (*solange du liest*), and abandoning materials. In the latter instance, she marks an unconventional break at the end of line 32 by manipulating where the verb *aussetzen* falls. Only as long as they last do these moments defy the constraints of temporality.

Not entirely temporal, poetic creation then unfolds in the space created by conceptual dichotomies (raw/cooked, emptiness/abundance, and man/woman). The latter category is indicated by the phrase *Mann und Frau mit Sehnsucht,* which gesturally points toward the title of Gottfried Benn's "Mann und Frau gehn durch die Krebsbaracke" ("Man and Woman Walk Through the Cancer Ward," 1970). Working the capacity of language to express the imagined possibility of the infinite through such symbolic pairings, the poet asserts that poetry creates its own vital here and now. Here Hahn rewrites the famous soliloquy from Shakespeare's *Hamlet* to cancel out nonexistence and death (lines 44–45), punctuating this declaration with the sole rhyme pair that occurs in the poem, *geben/ Leben.* The rhyme marks a turn toward different syntax and content, and assertion of the intersubjective relationship between the speaker and listener through which they give life to each other.

With the imperatives in the lines that follow, the poet admonishes the addressee of the poem to return to writing, to give names and premises. The phrase "Kleine Unterkünfte über dem Abgrund gegründet" evokes the poetic register of Rainer Marie Rilke, or Nietzsche's *Also sprach Zarathustra* (see Nietzsche 1982, 16). Imagining the potential scope of this project, Hahn now compares writing to music still alive in the mind of Beethoven after he had become deaf. This model points to a complex procedure to achieve creativity, for as Hahn comments in her Heidelberg lectures, "*Beethoven* wrote down fragments of individual themes in note-books, laid them aside, continued to work on them and developed them over the years," later incorporating these initial ideas into mature works (1994, 6).

Finally, however, the last poem will be written, lines 51–52 observe. Hahn appropriates the title of Gottfried Benn's last poem, "Kann keine Trauer sein" ("Can Be No Mourning"), as "Darf keine Trauer sein." Benn's poem muses with detachment, recalling the deathbeds of Annette von Droste-Hülshoff, Hölderlin, Rilke, and George. By contrast, Hahn's transformation of the modal verb *können* (can) into *dürfen* (permit, allow) alters the statement from an expression of cool acceptance to a gesture of social or self-control. It also mediates the transition to the closure presented in line 59 through the comment "Mag sein." After this comment, the delicate roses whose petals rain down return the reader to imagery of poetic beauty that recalls Hilde Domin's *Nur eine Rose als Stütze* and Rilke's famous grave inscription.[18] The rose's fragility seems more delicate against harsh critical dissection (*Messerscheiden*) and gravestone-like *Ziegelsteine*. The concluding salvo from the past (Nero's time) turns maiden-poet into a spectator with folded hands, making her a witness to art while adroitly invoking a simultaneous sense of the poetic present and of the past.

At work behind this poem are many of the same conflicting forces we have seen addressed in Hahn's prose writings about poetics. While terms like *Schiff, Blumen, Flamme,* and *Staub* evoke the vocabulary of the traditional poetic canon, Hahn's curt delivery of nouns and abruptly cut phrases (such as "Jetzt / und Hier" versus the conversational expression *hier und heute,* or "Sein oder? Nichtsein" in contrast to the expected "Sein oder Nichtsein") produce the same radical juxtaposition that she observed in the work of Emily Dickinson. Like the qualities Hahn admired in the work of Kolmar, a precarious balance between metaphor and abstract terms (for example, the leap from comparing poems to prime numbers to terming them "nichts Greifbares," nothing concrete) are calculated maneuvers. The shifting subjectivity and fragmentation that Hahn raised for consideration with respect to Plath resonates with the way in which Hahn breaks down the opening lines of "Gedicht" and appropriates the terminology of Gottfried Benn. Hahn's definition of poetry in "Gedicht," moreover, echoes Hilde Domin's conception of the poem as "der unverbrauchbare Gebrauchsgegenstand," the useless commodity (1988a, 57), or "magischer Gebrauchsgegenstand," magic commodity, the very formulation Hahn chooses to describe Domin's work on her eightieth birthday (1992a, 23).

Using ritual acts to structure and lend solemnity to events in "Gedicht," Hahn describes two qualities that make poetry unique—the unexpected immediacy of artistic inspiration and the variability of the positions occupied by its participants. The poet addressed as *du* (you) writes and ceases writing while paradoxically Hahn continues to write. The poem itself is compared with the act of granting forgiveness through last rites and that divine grace conferred with "Hostie unter der Zunge" (line 20). Carefully breaking apart formulaic utterances, "Gedicht" speculates about death using examples from mundane life—the daily sharing of meals establishes a broader dynamic of give-and-take that parallels the dynamics of performance and audience response. The dialogic character of the poem situates poetry within the interior perspective of the creative writer, yet breaks this solitude by insinuating the solidarity of writers who share a craft (*solange wir schreiben*). Tensions of proximity and distance are implied by pronouns (*du, wir*), and also by the third-person remove embodied in the line "Gefaltete Hände von einem Fräulein").

Hahn's calculated formalism used as a vehicle for expressing her poetics in "Gedicht" is inevitably bound up with gender through the interplay of female and male imagery woven into the poem. This gendering of subject matter exemplifies, I contend, what Rachel Blau DuPlessis, citing Nancy J. Vickers, terms the "foundational clusters" of poetry. "To talk about lyric," DuPlessis observes, "one must say something about beauty, something about love and sex, something about Woman and Man and their positionings, something about active agency versus malleability" (1994, 71). These fundamental poetic materials (tropes or notional clusters) are the essence of what makes poetry and they are, DuPlessis explains, by their very nature gender-inflected. For DuPlessis, these clusters involve a profound coming to terms with "voice (and silencing), power (appropriation and transcendence), nature (as opposed to formation and culture), gaze (framing, specularity, fragmentation), and sources of poetic matter—narratives of romance, of the sublime, scenes of inspiration, the muse as conduit" (1994, 71). In "Gedicht," we are not meant to encounter a confirmation of traditional gender roles. Rather, Hahn uses ritualized dialogue, formal structures, and reworked tropes to create a palimpsest intended as a new poetic discourse.

The New Formalism Reconsidered

Considering the near disappearance of poetry from the German literary scene after 1968 and repeated charges that New Subjectivity was nothing more than political resignation caving in to narcissistic, personal insight—or, as Erich Fried put it, the poem "saw less and less until it saw nothing" (1978)—it is not surprising that the type of new formalism Hahn practiced met with critical distaste. Even after the spectacular resurgence of the lyric genre as a medium with appeal for elite audiences occurred in the 1990s, Hahn's work remains anomalous, largely because it is not directed toward creating effete products, but rather, as her title *Gedichte fürs Gedächtnis* (*Poems for Memorizing*) suggests, toward generating a poetry that can be easily accessed by general readers who might well appreciate traditional rhyme, content, and rhetoric.[19]

Hahn argues for a constant transformation of the lyric genre in terms that make clear that the nature of her project is inextricably linked to social—and also personal—transformation, specifically of gender roles:

> If we look at the love poems of women, we find until after the war almost exclusively poems in which the woman subordinates herself to the man who is the object of her affections. . . . After the two major women's movements—at the turn of the century and in the sixties, seventies—this model was no longer possible. Women sought a new image of themselves, sought demarcation from traditional models and necessarily collided with these models. So painful, so unbearable were the contradictions between the head (which had grasped the necessity of independence) and the heart (which yearned for the relinquishing of self), that the love poems of women sounded at times like declarations of war. (1994, 15–16)

Though the unconventional alliance Hahn forges with lyric genre tradition complicates her contemporary reception, it allows her to appeal to universal values, even while she draws attention to the feminine subjective position she writes from and the postmodern fragmentation of experience. In Hahn's work, canon is embraced, but also overturned. Exaggeration, decontextualization, and demolition occur every step along the way. Using these distancing techniques as interventions to gain objectivity and authority on a provisional basis, Hahn sees herself as liberating women poets, even in the absence of clarity about poetry's influence on social transformation in the future. Never claiming to know where this process of aesthetic change will lead, Hahn treads an unusual path, one that continues to emerge as she moves forward.

Chapter Four

✦

Language as Experience: Making It Real

"Writing," Ursula Krechel observes at the opening of *In Zukunft schreiben* (*Writing into the Future*), "is an outstanding opportunity for sharpening thinking, bringing something into the reality of experience for oneself and others and preserving it" (2003, 7). In fact, the titles of her works provocatively signal this investment in critical apprehension. Between her first collection of poetry, *Nach Mainz* (*Toward Mainz*, 1977), and her fourth, *Vom Feuer lernen* (*Learning from Fire*, 1985), Krechel published essays that boldly headline the writerly quality of intellectual and ideological debates: "Leben in Anführungszeichen: Das Authentische in der gegenwärtigen Literatur" ("Life in Quotation Marks: The Authentic in Contemporary Literature," 1979), "Kulturzerstörung: Wird der Kuchen zerstört, indem man ihn teilt und ißt?" ("Cultural Destruction: Is the Cake Ruined When One Divides and Eats It?" 1983), and "Meine Sätze haben schon einen Bart: Abmahnung an die neue Weiblichkeit" ("My Sentences Already Have a Beard: Admonition Against the New Femininity," 1983). Later collections, such as the poetry volume *Technik des Erwachens* (*Technique of Awakening*, 1992), the essays in *Mit dem Körper des Vaters spielen* (*Playing with the Body of the Father*, 1992), and the writers' handbook *In Zukunft schreiben* (*Writing into the Future*) use similarly edgy titles to pique the reader's interest. These provocative titles display Krechel's fierce commitment to writing as heuristic exercise and they mirror her engagement with the shifting intellectual environment in Germany, especially discussions of feminism. Indeed, feminist impulses stimulate Krechel's work from the start of her career, providing leverage for her trenchant critiques of aesthetic representation and social dynamics.

The perspicacity of Krechel's political commitments and her sustained reflection on aesthetic topics make her work a particularly useful test case for how feminism does or does not serve as a means for renegotiating the terms under which the lyric genre operates after 1968. The relationship between her essays and her poetry collections is highly reciprocal.

In prose, Krechel comments boldly on authenticity, aesthetic value, and feminism, while in her poetical work she experiments with montage, cinematic technique, and long poem forms in a relentless search for modes of representation more adequate to contemporary realities. Over the course of more than three decades, these projects have explored the transformative capacities of modernist aesthetics and conceptually pushed in the direction of postmodern indeterminancy.

With Krechel, as with Domin or Hahn, we encounter the act of writing as a practice of self-assertion. While Domin was especially concerned with the ethical dimensions of literature and used the lens of gender obliquely to frame readership dynamics, and Hahn to date interrogates traditional assumptions about gender role subversively through the manipulation of discursive conventions, Krechel proceeds with a more open and consistent feminist agenda. Describing her craft for *In Zukunft schreiben,* Krechel is invested in the belief that language has transformative power. "In other words: it is a matter of a strong individualization in one's perspective on the world in dealing with language, in processing of what is perceived," Krechel writes (2003, 9). Furthermore, she continues, "Whoever begins to write opens a space that wants to be filled, not fully written" (2003, 9). This powerful insistence on the capacity of writing to be a conceptual intervention is compatible with the poetics of Domin and Hahn, and indeed, as I have argued elsewhere (Melin 1997, 220), Hahn and Krechel in important respects pursue complementary poetics, despite obvious differences in subject matter. Yet Krechel's emphasis on making space for what cannot be articulated signals a more radical poiesis than we have encountered so far, for it commits her not only to rewriting traditional content but also to grappling with poetic materials in terms of the fundamental representational issues that shape cognition.

This chapter begins with an examination of Krechel's early feminist commitments in *Selbsterfahrung und Fremdbestimmung (Self-Experience and Outsider Designation,* 1975) and her important essay "Leben in Anführungzeichen," which analyzes the critical nexus of authenticity and gender.[1] I then connect aesthetic positions defined in this early work with the essay collections *Lesarten (Ways of Reading,* 1982) and *Mit dem Körper des Vaters spielen* (1992), and the poetry cycle *Verbeugungen vor der Luft (Air Bows,* 1999), where Krechel further addresses representational problems. These works from the 1990s reveal that at a time when feminist concerns had apparently been eclipsed in the literary environment, Krechel continued to explore aesthetic and social questions in terms relevant to conceptualization of the woman writer's experience. The chapter concludes with a discussion of how Krechel conceptualizes poetry in her handbook for writers, *In Zukunft schreiben,* which has bearing on her more recent verse collections.

Like other women writers of the 1968 generation, Krechel confronted what Angelika Bammer has termed "the strategic difficulty of finding a new language in which to simultaneously write women as subject *into* literary discourse and free women *from* the constraints of gender" (2000, 231). Rising above the tendency of 1970s–1980s poetry to become mired in cliché and triviality (Leeder 2000, 208), Krechel has produced highly original work that in the estimation of many scholars and critics grew "more oblique and self-reflexive" (Leeder 2000, 212). Her high-profile essays and innovative verse express a poetics that deploys feminist thinking to reshape the lyric genre as it is practiced in Germany. Reappraisal of that work exposes the fluid interaction of gender issues and aesthetic criteria in the lyric genre, which has helped define the persistently transitional character of recent German verse as it has evolved since the 1990s.

Feminism and the Crisis of Authenticity

"The unreconcilability of what I do and that what I believe I am doing, the German idealistic contradiction par excellence, lives powerfully in the women's movement," Ursula Krechel writes in an issue of the New Left journal *Kursbuch* devoted to the topic of conservatism (1983b, 149). Krechel, who made her first forays into writing as a teenager in the early 1960s,[2] studied German literature, theater, and art history and worked briefly as a dramaturge before becoming a professional freelance writer. Her published work shows a broad command of literary genres, encompassing essays, prose fiction, drama, and poetry. Krechel's debut poetry collection *Nach Mainz* (1977) already reflected her search for tangible subject matter and transparent language capable of interpolating literary allusions, cinematic images, and references to contemporary politics. Subsequent publications included lyrical poetry, narrative verse, poem sequences, and montages that display impressive technical adeptness.[3]

As a poet, Krechel demonstrates a keen ear for dialogue, combined with a penchant for visual thinking (evident in her use of quotidian scenes, cinematic clips, and references to the visual arts), and a preference for texts composed of loosely connected segments.[4] Encompassing both long poetic forms and precise, lyrical observations, her work shows a breadth of voice in the poetry collections *Verwundbar wie in den besten Zeiten* (*Vulnerable as in the Best of Times,* 1979c), *Rohschnitt* (*Rough Cut,* 1983d), *Vom Feuer lernen* (*Learning from Fire,* 1985), *Kakaoblau*

(*Cocoa Blue*, 1989), *Technik des Erwachens* (*Technique of Awakening*, 1992), *Landläufiges Wunder* (*Commonplace Wonder*, 1995b), *Ungezürnt* (*Unangered*, 1997), *Stimmen aus dem harten Kern* (*Voices from the Bitter Core*, 2005), *Mittelwärts* (*Toward the Middle*, 2006), and *Jäh erhellte Dunkelheit* (*Suddenly Illuminated Darkness*, 2010a).[5]

Krechel's initial publications included the well-received theater piece "Erika" (1974), whose main character struggles against marital and professional conventions that hamper her efforts to become independent.[6] The early *Selbsterfahrung und Fremdbestimmung* (1975/1983), a well-researched project of scholarly dimensions, documents the major positions adopted by German postwar feminism. It addresses the topics of relationships among women, patriarchal control, feminism in the public sphere, reproductive issues, and femininity (*Weiblichkeit*).[7] Although she traces the women's movement back to the nineteenth century, Krechel is primarily concerned with the contemporary situation, and accordingly refers to Herbert Marcuse and Susan Sontag (Krechel 1975/1983, 85 and following and 10 and following).[8] Nonetheless, she diagnoses a significant difference of German feminism in relation to the women's movement elsewhere: "In the American women's movement, the differentiation from the left was stronger from the beginning than in the Federal Republic, although here as there a large portion of the participants came from the student movement" (1975/1983, 42), an observation that resonates with Hahn's similar background in political action.

By 1979 when she published her major essay on authenticity, "Leben in Anführungszeichen," Krechel's focus had turned in an aesthetic direction. In this work, she claims that a fundamental shift has occurred in how literature expresses connections between experience and knowledge, and her illustrations link this change directly to women's writing. Authenticity, of course, is a problematical concept, and Krechel quite consciously explores its various permutations primarily through examples that question whether literature represents life experience per se or filtered perception. At the start of the essays, Krechel registers the increasing identification of the narrative *I* with the *I* of the author in recent writing—as well as the firm division of the two in every introductory scholarly account to literature. Rather than rejecting this conflation out of hand as simplistic, Krechel contemplates why the attraction of "realistic" (that is, factual or verifiable) perspectives might have led to a merging of the two concepts. The obvious, yet questionable, dichotomy thus becomes the point of departure for examining the ways in which pressure to be "authentic" gradually alters practices of literary representation itself. Krechel's refusal to be limited by epistemological categories in this instance reminds us of Hamburger's acceptance of a coequal empirical *I* and lyrical *I,* but Krechel pushes beyond Hamburger's point of resolution in paradox as she reframes the theoretical problem for the contemporary context.

After citing a passage by the Dutch author Anja Meulenbelt that describes how difficult it is to write about reality, Krechel uses the example to diagnose an extant collapse of the traditional life-versus-art dichotomy that had long structured the representation of subjective experience. Evoking the Goethean dyad of *Dichtung und Wahrheit* (*Poetry and Truth*), Krechel observes the consequences of this new development: "The dichotomy assumes that writing, when it is the former, represents something that is not lived, the not-true or unreal. What has changed brings with it unforeseen consequences. Insofar as the building blocks of a subjective perception are pushed closer to each other, the relationship between experience and perception has radically changed" (1979b, 102).

This essay was certainly prompted by the emergence of New Subjectivity, which Krechel observes had given rise to texts where authors spoke apparently without constraint about themselves, thereby effacing the presumptive boundaries between text and author (1979b, 82). While postwar German writers were no strangers to debates about realism, discussions of authenticity had always been inflected with contextually specific ideological commitments. In 1947 Hans Werner Richter had already called for literature that would reflect the reality of experience in defining the early program of Gruppe 47 (Arnold 2004, 55–59). In a later iteration of what it meant to be authentic, Hans Magnus Enzensberger in 1963 aligned himself, Günter Grass, and Peter Rühmkorf with the poetic vocabulary of William Carlos Williams by virtue of these writers' ability to work "fragments of everyday life, scraps of slang, words from the world of consumer goods" into their poetry (1963, 49). The quotidian details and unaffected tone of Krechel's poetry prompted critics to situate her work within the evolving style of New Subjectivity, yet her theoretical treatment of authenticity is cautious about this trend. "Leben in Anführungszeichen" is substantially devoted to considering why women writers might want to embrace New Subjectivity, because the "authentic" seems to provide a better form of witness to reality. However, in the course of this discussion, Krechel points out that authenticity is no aesthetic panacea. Tackling an issue that had long been unresolved for contemporary German writers working in the lyric genre, namely the general problem of subjectivity, she questions both the construction of boundaries between the public and private spheres and the implications of vesting literature with a quasi-therapeutic, psychological function that casts it as the expression of the personal crisis of an author.

Krechel emphatically breaks with the aesthetic tradition when she values the fact that contemporary literature no longer insists that art be detached from quotidian life. This pragmatic grounding for art is not without hazards, though it clears the way for a greater range of subjective expression. Considering the emergence of authentic writing by women in particular, Krechel worries that patriarchal values might be unintentionally reinscribed through the production of highly mimetic or replicative texts:

> Woman as her own material, into which she inscribes herself, and in writing duplicates herself, duplicates the attribution of femininity in a patriarchal context. It is more difficult for her, according to the attributions, than for the man to produce distance from herself, which viewed positively means: she conceals herself (or whatever it is that she considers her discovered identity) less behind rhetorical models. She believes that she is her unadorned self and yet writes onto the image in the mirror in which she finds she reflects herself again and again. (1979b, 90)

This analysis clearly points in the direction of a psychoanalytic/poststructuralist conception of feminine writing, but with reservations, for Krechel acknowledges that the author who is striving to be "authentic" is potentially burdened with a false sense of originality or even narcissism.[9] Rhetoric and traditional literary models are likewise inimical to truly authentic expression, in her opinion, for they subordinate authenticity to linguistic conventions. Instead, an alternate aesthetic resolution is sought by Krechel, primarily in later publications, one that allows her to interrogate the notion of authenticity and ultimately reframe its role in women's writing in terms of the complex relation between contemporary texts and literary canon.

The relationship of Krechel's own poetry to traditional forms provides her with a starting point for subsequent analysis of these writerly practices in the 1983 issue of the leftist journal *Kursbuch*, which was devoted to the topic of conservatism. Krechel observes in her essay "Kulturzerstörung" ("Cultural Destruction"): "When I write a poem, I destroy the common perception, destroy a tradition of writing" (1983a, 140). Krechel's intent is certainly not simply to evoke principles of antagonistic destruction that grounded the explanation of modernism advanced in Hugo Friedrich's account of the lyric genre after symbolism (1956). Instead she advocates a postmodern paradigm of fragmented construction, a Derridean bricolage of radical intertextual relations.

Noting the penchant of contemporary writers for piecing together texts from autobiographical materials, bits of memories, and quotidian scraps, Krechel finds the roots of these techniques in montage, which was part of the stylistic legacy of modernism. This particular strain of modernism, as we have seen, was part and parcel of the literary environment for contemporary German poets, including Friederike Mayröcker and Helmut Heissenbüttel, who in exploiting the linguistically experimental capacities afforded by montage since the 1950s, had not shied from increasingly radical experiments.[10] Later decades, too, had witnessed expansion of fragmented forms across the lyric genre. From Friederike Mayröcker's *Tod durch Musen* (*Death by Muses,* 1966) to Jürgen Becker's *Das Ende der Landschaftsmalerei* (*The End of Landscape Painting,* 1974, a work reminiscent of Frank O'Hara's poetics of individualism) and the dense, documentary ballads in Hans Magnus Enzensberger's poem cycle *Mausoleum* (1975), pastiche figured increasingly in the late 1960s and early 1970s as a technique affiliated with ideological liberation. Krechel's distinct contribution to these developments occurs in a further essay, "Meine Sätze haben schon einen Bart," in which she reflects on what it means to be open to archaic and "found" materials. She remarks that the resurgence of texts modeled after premodern forms paradoxically coincides with the stylistic turn to pastiche. Yet in the postmodern context, deployment of conventional forms does not equate with an unquestioning acceptance of tradition. Rather, as Krechel asserts, this development signals the emergence of a writerly consciousness that was becoming detached from historicity: "From the debris pile of history it is above all the simple forms that survive: fairy tale, saga, legend, riddle, motherhood. They can always be invented anew—like the wheel and fire" (1983b, 149). Forms (and here Krechel means primarily genres, although she unexpectedly inserts the social category of "motherhood") become in essence generic containers for any individual poet's voice. The capacity to liberate an author from historical context through nonspecific, malleable simplicity is intrinsic to the use of these capacious foundational materials.

Fragmentation and the radical dissolution of coherence, as Krechel is aware, do not, however, remove the tensions that outsiders (here women) experience in relating to the cultural mainstream. Already her 1979 essay on authenticity, which noted the dangers of hiding behind rhetorical masks, recognized the persistent vulnerability of these "others," even when authentic, individual experience is viewed as culturally valuable. Now Krechel's interest lies in registering the tug-and-pull between the margins and the dominant center at a point when these categories already seem less clearly demarcated and their interrelation more complex.

The year in which the essay "Meine Sätze haben schon einen Bart" appears represents a turning point in terms of the status of German women's poetry when the backlash against feminism became clearly evident (1983b, 144). Reflecting on this change, Krechel notes, "The women who had learned to speak publicly at the end of the sixties fell silent, the farther along the seventies go, and that for good reason" (1983b, 145). Indeed, she cites the development of ideological rifts within feminism as a contributing factor and regrets the "burial of women's literature under the Argus eyes of feminist literary scholarship" (1983b, 154). Because the social issues that feminism addressed still persist, Krechel does not see a way to bridge the chasm between the public sphere career of a woman writer and her life: "And the few self-references, user codes of the auto-biographical materials, scraps of memory, traces of the day that go into writing leave life far behind them, for the writer that you meet while shopping, who says to you, yes, I'm still alive, is not the one who writes but instead her tiresome everyday wrapping, which doesn't tell you what her texts say" (1983b, 153). Here we see Krechel defining authenticity in terms of quotidian concreteness, aleatory structure, and parlando tone, and yet the closeness to "reality" that these desexualized poetic tools promise does not remove the gap between life and artistic representation. Thus in considering the quandaries of women writers from an aesthetic perspective, Krechel's writings from the 1980s and 1990s do not find a fully satisfactory solution for how best to represent experience because neutral "authenticity" does not turn out to be the answer for the question of how to create adequate self-representation.

Parallel to these efforts, however, Krechel in numerous essays examines the work of writing and its social context with greater focus on the psychological dimensions of literature. This approach leads her to fruitful insights into the status of women's writing within patriarchal culture. *Lesarten,* which pairs carefully selected poems from a wide range of historical periods with her own short interpretations of them, was initially published in 1982 and expanded for a 1991 edition. Krechel also delivered a series of lectures in Vienna, which were first published in *Wespennest* (1991) and later issued as part of *Mit dem Körper des Vaters spielen* (1992).[11] These collected works embrace, yet also intentionally reshape, the modernist literary canon by recuperating a forgotten history. In them, Krechel forcefully affirms the importance of literature, advocates the recovery of neglected writers, and describes the habits and practices of writers. The eponymous essay "Mit dem Körper des Vaters spielen" concludes programmatically that poetry must foster multiplicity and intellectual engagement with patriarchal culture if literature is to continue to be a tool for social transformation. Thus, to maintain the position it had held in the German literary context since 1945 (see Melin 1997, 232), Krechel argues that the lyric genre must adapt to contemporary realities.

Both *Lesarten* and *Mit dem Körper des Vaters spielen* reveal Krechel's copious knowledge of literature and a historically and geographically diverse taste for authors ranging from Quirinus Kuhlmann to Rolf Bossert, Karoline von Günderode to Nelly Sachs, and Anna Akhmatova to Frank O'Hara.[12] Her interrelated overarching projects in these two collections are the reappraisal of mid-century modernists once regarded as radically avant-garde and the rediscovery of neglected women authors. The essay "Mit dem Körper des Vaters spielen" makes plain that Krechel's agenda is not simply to produce a new canon, for it consolidates her insights into the writerly thought process by turning to explanations of creativity developed in feminist scholarship by Nancy Chodorow, Carol Gilligan, and Eva Meyer, who employ psychoanalytically based theories to clarify the intellectual relationship between women authors and their fathers.

Western culture, Krechel notes in consonance with post-structuralist psychological interpretations of creativity, has long privileged monolithic logos over feminine multiplicity (1992, 105), thus, the father figure sets the intellectual measure for the aspiring woman author. This circumstance, however, creates a particular dilemma for the woman writer, who in seeking to measure up to the father, finds she must struggle against her mother (1992, 91).[13] Indeed, she finds herself unlearning "adaptation, adjustment to other, close people, to be great in the small, solicitude instead of standing up for oneself" (1992, 92). Krechel observes that in so doing, "the future woman writer denies herself, camouflages her intention, in order to protect herself from injury. She speaks with a double tongue" (1992, 103–4). In place of these forms of subordination, an equality and interaction among texts placed on equal footing would instead make productive writerly work possible (1992, 118). On the cultural level, the individual woman's search for intellectual identification with the father mirrors for Krechel the crucial, problematical link between female writers and the "male" literary tradition.

The aesthetic possibilities imagined in Krechel's discussions of authenticity and creativity have far-reaching implications for her work in relation to this model of identification and influence. By distinguishing "authenticity" from literal mimetic representation, Krechel opens poetic work to radical expressive forms, while still accommodating the persuasive authority of realism. In exposing the patriarchal cultural basis of canon as a fundamental intellectual problem, Krechel addresses the general issue of how creativity originates and frees the woman writer from being merely the subject of self-representation. These deliberations go beyond the dyadic possibilities envisioned in Domin's conception of poet-reader dialogue, as well as Hahn's focus on female/male dynamics. Boldly, Krechel concludes the essay by elaborating qualities that women's writing in the lyric genre should display—a preference for multivocality, an intellectual engagement with "patriarchal" culture, and ultimately a belief that writing makes freedom possible—qualities she strives to achieve in her own work.

Writing Poetry, Writing About Women

A number of critics reviewing Krechel's lyric work in the 1990s chafed at an apparent mismatch between the technical innovations of her language and the traditional requirements of representation. Commenting on *Technik des Erwachens* (1992), Michael Braun observed that Krechel's montage technique becomes problematical when the language of the poem is so overwhelmed by such montage that it appears completely discharged from its communicative functions (1992, 102). Similarly, the "overly" poetic words and structures in *Verbeugungen vor der Luft* (1999) prompted reviewer Thomas Poiss to remark that there appeared to be a gap between theme and execution that made even the successful figures of speech merely seem stuck on (2000, v). Such reactions to new poetic techniques are by no means unique to German literature, for as Marjorie Perloff confirms for contemporary American poetry, "a frequent objection of mainstream poetry criticism is that, without some measure of representation—the mirror held to nature, to social custom and the 'march of events'—the poetic text becomes meaningless" (Perloff 1998, 239).

As Krechel's poetic work distances itself increasingly from conventional lyrical forms after 1990, her poems rely increasingly on fragmented language that dissolves expected cohesion. Yet, as we have already seen, Krechel's preoccupation with the representational technique of montage itself is invariably connected with broader concerns about the nature of creativity. In an essay that considers where and how writers work, Krechel observes, "Since the explosive technical development of writing systems, which demand the digital adroitness of a piano player, mechanical understanding, and the perseverance of a seamstress, writing has remained a masculine domain, but transcription has become feminized"

(1996, 12). This tension between *Schreiben* (writing) and *Abschreiben* (writing down, transcription) informs her collection *Verbeugungen vor der Luft* as a whole.

The emphasis scholarly critics of Krechel have placed on coherent communication as a measure of successful writing brings into focus a set of underlying assumptions about the lyric genre that have thickened around discussions of postwar German poetry. Put in schematic terms, the referentiality of mainstream modernism is highly prized even today, while postmodernism is still regarded skeptically, largely due to the privileging of aesthetic coherence and political intent, and trepidation about what happens when texts abandon representation. At stake in Krechel's aesthetic project, as we have seen, is a very purposeful engagement with problems of representation and gender issues, and the question of whether poets can legitimately rewrite modernist tenets through the process of poiesis that Threadgold has described as a path to creating new paradigms (see Threadgold 1997, 1–4). *Verbeugungen vor der Luft* offers one of Krechel's most ambitious attempts to negotiate these questions in the lyric genre itself, for its poems raise questions about authenticity, canon, gender, and the status of artifacts. When the cycle is read as an exercise in poiesis (the performative rewriting of the practices of poetry), we see that it is woven together through repeated moments of intense authorial self-reflection and that even when Krechel engages in fragmenting experimental techniques, she is continually drawn back to the modernist paradigm.

A second 1995 essay, "Auslassungen über das Weglassen" ("Letting Go About Leaving Out"), which appeared in the literary magazine *Zwischen den Zeilen,* heralds poetic practices that are realized in *Verbeugungen vor der Luft.*[14] In this commentary, Krechel reflects on how she constructs poems, focusing in particular in her account on the resonance of words, echoes of other literary texts, and aspects of the writing that make it a trial-and-error process. Emphasizing her own keen perception of the distance between the author as person and the created text, Krechel nonetheless recognizes that readers would find the notion of composition as constructive experimentation unsettling because they instinctively crave a clearly recognizable authorial voice (1995a, 71). Krechel's remarks are reminiscent of the attitudes of modernists like Edgar Allan Poe, T. S. Eliot, Ezra Pound, and Gottfried Benn, whose works were well known to German audiences. The poetic techniques she describes, on the other hand, correspond in large measure to the montage techniques inspired by cinematic splicing that Krechel had employed in previous collections of poetry. However, the author now sets a somewhat different course for her aesthetic program, noting, "The writing of poems is a continual production process; yet I am just as interested in the continual operation of cutting. At the margin of each line, the possibilities branch out into the endless, a continual, yet not regrettable, leaving out" (1995a, 65).

Referring to Eliot and Pound, Krechel observes that encounters with other languages and influences enlarge a writer's sense of words. "One's own language is a cosmos," Krechel notes, "dialectical impulses expand and irritate it; T. S. Eliot and Ezra Pound have shown how the boundaries of one's own language diffuse through foreign-language interspersions" (1995a, 66). For Pound, translation played a crucial role in mediating aesthetic expansion. With Krechel, the process depends on how intertextuality plays itself out in the creative mind of the poet:

> But I, the author, have a wealth of other texts in me, echoes thrown back by the love of certain poems, submerged spots, sunken reading treasure, children's rhymes, dramatic ballad endings, Bible verses, scraps of dialogue from the film seen yesterday. They are there, clog the writing pores, but no cosmetic treatment expunges them from memory. (1995a, 69)

Though this statement implies that no author is fully original, the notion of the inner library also liberates the individual writer. Krechel, indeed, describes her working practices as a poet with access to this creative source, comparing poetry to a laboratory where she can experiment with semantics, all the while carefully testing words for their reliability (1995a, 70). This scientific comparison, as well as Krechel's argument in favor of a pluralistic conception of authorship, are clearly meant to revive the formulations used by Gottfried Benn to describe poet creation as well, though Krechel is less clinical than Benn.

Throughout this essay, Krechel insists on the importance of process and the writerly manipulation of words. For her, even texts that arise through montage, heteroglossic language, and intertextual echoes—linguistic elements that have a preexistence before they are incorporated into the poem—show the hand of the author who reworks them. Comparing writing to the art of printmaking, she observes: "Just as the 'dirty thumbprint' of the etcher is often mentioned in graphic printing, I am really interested in the insertion, the reconstruction of a tiny irregularity that astonishes; for me it draws closer the flash of beauty, of something successful, gives it sharper contours" (1995a, 66). By identifying the physical trace as a sign of the artist's individuality, this comment emphasizes that it is not the perfection of the artwork per se, but rather the making of it that Krechel admires.[15] It also connects this essay with Krechel's aesthetic project in *Verbeugungen vor der Luft*. In this collection, Krechel explores the nature of art from multiple perspectives in reflections that are sequentially connected across poems. Moreover, the final part of the collection includes an extended sequence poem, "Goya, späte Jahre" ("Goya, Late Years"), that mediates on printmaking as an exemplary aesthetic model for creative work.

The fifty-nine poems of *Verbeugungen vor der Luft* are divided into four sections, each given a title that suggests an aspect of making poetry ("Das Material entzündet sich von selbst" ["The Material Ignites Spontaneously"], "Legierung und Legende" ["Alloying and Legends"], "Rotlichtphasen der Aufmerksamkeit" ["Red Light Phases of Attentiveness], and "Nachtarbeit, Nachtverlust, Schriftverlust" ["Night Work, Night Loss, Writing Loss"]). When the collection ends, it does so paradoxically with a text about a poem coming into existence. The strategic position given that text, "Ein Gedicht entsteht" ("A Poem Comes into Being"), registers Krechel's constant position since her debut with *Nach Mainz* that true poetry is to be understood as constructive process. Here again she celebrates the labor of poetic craft rather than enacting a display of reverence toward the poem as a finished, fetishized object.

By design, *Verbeugungen vor der Luft* promotes this open-ended, processual conception of writing from the outset. The book's four sections are subtitled to orient readers to the aesthetic issues that preoccupy Krechel in this work: claims that art makes about its own authenticity, the formative power of canon, the significance of aesthetic reflection, and the status of created artifacts. While Krechel's intense experimentation with language in *Verbeugungen vor der Luft* militates against syntactical clarity (as Poiss observes), the dense alliteration, literary allusions, and abrupt juxtaposition of montaged elements compellingly draw attention to how poetry is itself constructed. Reading the texts in relation to Krechel's essays, however, the reader comes face to face with a larger poetic project. My concern, accordingly, lies in drawing out aesthetic themes that emerge in this poetic cycle and relating these strands to Krechel's deliberations about art, particularly questions of representation and modernism.

Issues of authenticity, which as we have seen play a central role in Krechel's theoretical conception of writerly work, surface repeatedly in the first section of the collection. The opening poem, "Die Erde hat sich bewegt" ("The Earth Has Moved Itself"), much like Stefan George's famous "Komm in den totgesagten park und schau" ("Come into the Park That Has Been Pronounced Dead and Look," 1958), evocatively fuses landscape description with demarcation of a poetic program. It opens by setting the gears of pathetic fallacy in motion: "The human green lays itself on the trees / impresses onto the blood veins its control" (1999, 7). The first stanza maps a terrain marked by a poetically celebrated species (the linden), ravens, and a *Sonneblum* (sunflower) reminiscent of the sturdy *Helianthus* in William Blake's "Ah! Sun-Flower" (1972), Edward Mörike's "Im Frühling" ("In Spring," 1968), or Georg Trakl's "Die Sonnenblumen" ("The Sunflower," 1972).[16] Yet this landscape proves unfruitful. The stanza closes tersely, "Sow, reap not. *Nevermore*" (1999, 7).

The allusion to Edgar Allan Poe splits the poem in half and refers readers to the modernist aesthetic framework. Widely recognized as one of the originators of modern poetics, Poe is particularly important for postwar German verse because his "Philosophy of Composition" provided grounding for Gottfried Benn's influential series of talks "Probleme der Lyrik" (1951), Hugo Friedrich's seminar lectures "Die Struktur der modernen Lyrik" (1956), and later Hans Magnus Enzensberger's afterword to *Museum der modernen Poesie* (1960b). These programmatic statements about poetry from the late 1950s and 1960s made Poe a touchstone for discussion of the lyric genre by German writers.

But Krechel quickly moves beyond the constraints of modernism by providing a description of the head-hanging sunflower that is "far removed from the dull creatureliness" (1999, 7). The image conceptually bridges past divisions between art and life. The static, painterly scene delineated in the first stanza gives way to discourses that bubble up in the second stanza as "mutters and murmurs, screams and whispers" (1999, 7). The poet declares that it is time for planting work (spading and fertilizing) and not for harvest. "Then the human green / passed over into other hands," the poem comments, noting that now it is possible to see "a thumb as green relative / of the beautiful hand" (1999, 7). The sublation of the traditional dichotomy of work and beauty adumbrates a subtle tension between art-making and art objects. The poem concludes with a whimsical vision of an iron portal that theatrically frames a scene of cavorting twice-shorn poodles and wintery yew branches, effectively setting aside the convention that art simply reproduces nature by instead unabashedly displaying art as artifice. Subsequent poems in *Verbeugungen vor der Luft* further examine poetry's claims to mimesis, taking up again the aesthetic discussion initiated in Krechel's essay "Leben in Anführungszeichen."

Chief among the problems of literary mimesis is the separation of poetry from life, and Krechel, as we have seen, seeks to eliminate this division in the lyric genre by making quotidian experience central to poetics. Krechel's debut collection *Nach Mainz* had posed this problem primarily in relation to content. There, one poem mused that "Some days a poem lies right in the street" (Krechel 1983c, 39). Now in "Eine Methode, den Mai zu erleben" ("A Method for Experiencing May"), which concludes the first section of *Verbeugungen vor der Luft,* Krechel shifts the terms of this argument to a more abstract level, contrasting the high velocity of life with slow moments of quiet contemplation: "[I] do not have with mankind a peaceful stay / expelled by loud din, from the expressway, the excavator" (1999, 24).[17] Here nothing seems fixed. "Never is it still in the clammily undercooled night," the poet writes, introducing the vision of a tectonic upheaval that leaves the Rhine in flames after a natural rather than man-made disturbance (1999, 25). This earthquake, which shakes even the houses, causes the poet to rethink even her own work, for she concludes, "then it is time to think over the method / that is the painful mother of all" (1999, 25). This mode of ostensibly "raw" experience, which the "authentic" seeks to approximate, alters the poet's thinking, and yet produces tensions for her as well.

The collection's second section raises issues of canon against the backdrop of cataclysmic change and instability announced at the end of the first part. The key poem in this group, lengthily titled "Und da sie jetzt mehr dachten, litten sie auch mehr" ("And now that they thought more, they also suffered more"), registers the contingent status of canonical literature when it observes, "In the hierarchy of books, plunges. / In the book of nature, no unequivocalness of reading" (1999, 50). These thoughts, nonetheless, drive the poet to an optimistic conclusion: "The expansion of the library: / the diminution of the hierarchy" (1999, 51). Aphoristically, the generalized critique of canon continues the revisionist aesthetic project initiated by *Lesarten* and *Mit dem Körper des Vaters spielen.*

This foregrounding of canon is reinforced by two additional poems from the section that address problems of expression. In the one, the very title, "Überschuß des Lebens: Überlappender Ton" ("Surplus of Life: Overlapping Tone") mediates on the contemporary artist's dilemma of trying to make a genuine statement while trying to sort out the meaningful elements within a surfeit of quotidian details. The other, "Was verschweigst du, wenn du schweigst?" ("What Do You Silence When You Are Silent?"), broods about the difficulty of achieving expression at all. This poem tensely describes a buildup of "legends" through a holding back of expired words ("Lagerfrist der Wörter abgelaufen"), and injurious silence ("lähmend / das Schweigen"). These pent-up words are finally released through an intense physical act of producing speech: "Scattering effect of labials / the lips open themselves / feather-light condemned" (1999, 53).

Turning to the topic of aesthetic reflection, the next section, "Rotlicht-phasen der Aufmerksamkeit," picks up where the second section has left off, with another poem about speech and speech organs, "In der wortlosen Kaverne des Mundes" ("In the Wordless Cavern of the Mouth") (1999, 57). Whereas the first section of *Verbeugungen vor der Luft* introduced the question of authenticity and the second section grappled with the formative power of canon without special attention to questions of gender, the third part binds gender with language through the placement of the poem entitled "Quand les hommes parlent, les femmes ne se taisent pas" ("When men talk, women do not keep quiet") at the heart of the section. The physical imagery that surfaces in this section signals a turn from theoretical issues to poetic attention to concrete materials. The heightened, physical awareness that accompanies creative mental process culminates in the final poem in this section, "Berg- und Talpredigt" ("Mountain and Valley Sermon"), which charts the peregrinations of a restless poet.

The poem absorbs readers in perceptions of bodily discomforts, somnambulism, and transience experienced by the poet. Countering this drift of impression is a series of formulaic discourse akin to those mentioned in "Auslassungen über das Weglassen" that Krechel manipulates. Strikingly, Krechel uses repetitious phrases to prescribe writerly practices as a set of "beatitudes": "Blessed be the discipline of the disciplineless," "blessed be the expenditure of soberness," "blessed be the departure from laziness on the edge of diligence," "blessed be also the dash" (1999, 74). Elsewhere quasi-proverbial declarations and wordplays on their terms are interjected and repeated with minimal variation: "necessity teaches telephoning," "necessity teaches carrying, schlepping," "need for more manpower," and "necessity teaches pseudo-thanks" (1999, 74–77).

Out of such necessity—and apparent randomness—poetry arises. The poet registers the potential drive, however, to find some fixed form:

> die frühmorgendlichen Hopser ohne Ziel
> wie Predigten ziellos mäandrieren, wenn man sie nicht festnagelt
> (was nie geschieht zur Hochamtzeit) (1999, 77)

> the early morning hop-waltzes without destination
> like sermons aimlessly meandering, if one does not nail them down
> (which never happens at High Mass time)

The latent desire for more than wandering sermons is, however, coupled with an appreciation for what is gained by not putting things into words. The poet admonishes, "Respect the silence / early murdering in the early morning, when necessity does not yet give wings to the conspiracy theory" (1999, 77). Given this flux, the mock Christology of "Berg- und Talpredigt" (with its references to the Sermon on the Mount, the Beatitudes, the Crucifixion, and Judgment Day) lends an aura of ritualized authority to the poem's statements and generates a rhetorically somewhat more predictable structure.

Since for Krechel experience is perception, one of the conditions for the creation of poetry is openness to random elements and free-floating discourse exercised in "Berg- und Talpredigt." But while such postmodern text montage mimics fragmentary and intimate operations of the cognitive process, its fluidity is not intended to produce a coherent thesis. To interpret such fragmented work, we can profitably turn to the critical framework advocated by Susan S. Lanser. Lanser proposes that rather than regarding women's writing primarily in terms of palimpsestic discourses between a dominant text and oppositional subtext, readers should notice the complementary interactions of the two. According to Lanser, stylistic features, such as complex surface design and rhetoric, should be interpreted as a response to the dominant aesthetic (Lanser 1997, 682–86). This model, I am convinced, proves instructive for reading the poems in *Verbeugungen vor der Luft,* for it positions us to work past the surface linguistic complexity, which thwarts conventional readings of the poems as representational texts. Thick with references to other works, clichés, neologisms, and fleeting epiphanies, the poems continually refer back to the pivotal modernists. Indeed, in the fourth section of the collection, the allusions to the artist Francisco Goya and the poet Hugo von Hofmannsthal urge readers to contemplate the intricate relations that develop among works of art, and when we notice what these dynamics imply, in the way Lanser suggests, we arrive at a better understanding of Krechel's aesthetics.

Because the status of art as artifact is a problem central to the poetics Krechel propounds, she continually reminds readers that poetry depends on the primacy of language and physical materials. "The poem has no object, it is an object itself, yet one that blurs before unpoetic eyes, that constructs itself only with precise looking, reading, listening," Krechel writes (1995a, 61). Krechel's celebration of the poem as a special kind of *Gegenstand* (object, artifact) hinges on our ability to read the text both as a dynamic interaction of parts and as a coherent whole. The poem thus conceived compels the reader to reflect on and synthesize disparate elements through what it represents. Turning to the final section of *Verbeugungen vor der Luft,* "Nachtarbeit, Nachtverlust, Schriftverlust," we can now observe how Krechel's references to sight, sound, and reading serve this end. Here the poetic program Krechel outlined in her essays from the 1990s provides interpretive orientation for my reading, in particular of the poem "Goya, späte Jahre" ("Goya, Late Years"), which occupies a central position in the concluding section of *Verbeugungen vor der Luft.*

The poems that comprise the book's final part ("Nachtarbeit, Nachtverlust, Schriftverlust") oscillate between optical and acoustical modes of apprehension. The initial text in this group, "Meine Füße gingen lieber aus der Zeit" ("My Feet Preferred to Go Off Beat") muses about visual images boldly sketched as "gestures of thought, coloraturas of the glance / deep frozen dialogue" (1999, 81). Its lines describe the discovery of a young eagle that perished after straying into a vineyard. Associative splicing brings about a density of language that describes landscape contours, the demise of brilliant foliage, and a writerly attentiveness to details and positions. Three poems later, "Haben wir uns verstanden?" ("Have We Understood Each Other?") asks whether modes of perception and expression exist for an unusual array of sounds:

> Eine stabile Stakkatoliebe
> Trommelwirbel im Ohr, Regsamkeit und Pfropfen.
> Gibt es das? Gibt es das Präteritum? (1999, 84)

> A steady staccato love
> Drum roll in the ear, alertness and plugs.
> Does that exist? Does the simple past tense exist?

Krechel continues in this vein with another query, "Tinnitus, theses on the earthquakes / heartbeat register, register list for wordless half tones . . . did that exist?" (1999, 84). Ultimately the poem's second stanza responds to these questions indirectly: "What was there aside from the questions? / Tool for indulgence, night work, night loss, loss of writing" (1999, 84). Its conclusion exposes an absence of tools to achieve a complex understanding of these phenomena: "Perhaps only an error / but paid for dearly. Silence about it—just as: Stars stood around the house / with distant mouths, then it was still" (1999, 84).

Yet these verbal miscommunications are followed by the greater clarity about artistic process that is expressed in the next poem in the collection, "Goya, späte Jahre" ("Goya, Late Years"), an eighteen-part poem sequence that concentrates on visual phenomena. Now visual art functions as a trope for all creative art, including the poem, which unfolds with greater narrative cohesion as well:

> Bilder sind Schwarzpulver
> Kohlenstaubgefäße, kalte Verzweiflung.
> Keine Korrekturen mehr! (1999, 85)

> Pictures are gunpowder
> vessels of coal dust, cold despair.
> No more proof sheets!

The text confirms the shift made in *Verbeugungen vor der Luft* to the visual by stating that "the eyeballs replace hearing" (1999, 85). Indeed, the poem's second section carefully positions the artist in this mode of perception by declaring, "The stillness sits in my ears. / I sit behind my eyes" (1999, 85). Once visual thinking is established as the dominant mode of apprehension, the poem begins an evocative sketch of the historical Goya's life from his 1766 arrival in Madrid to his self-imposed exile in Bordeaux and death in 1828 (Janson 1991, 630–32). Salient factual details that receive mention include spies, the Inquisition, a female companion, an altar painting, and anonymous exiles (Krechel 1999, 86).

Throughout the poem, Krechel draws parallels between the work of artists and writers. Goya holds a *Pinsel,* which could be either a brush or pencil (1999, 85). The phrase "keine Korrekturen mehr!" ("no more proof sheets!"), which is repeated twice, applies equally to art print and book production. Evoking the black-and-white contrast fundamental to both bookmaking and printmaking, as well as to ethical choices, the poem relates how Goya's patrons and others perish:

> Schachfiguren der Geschichte
> Schwarz auf weiß
> doch Goyas Förderer (1999, 88)

> Pawns of history
> Black on white
> yet Goya's patrons

Finally, Goya leaves Spain for a place that is "neither white nor black," in other words a location seemingly free of ethical choices. There, in France, "seeing is understanding" (1999, 89), because Goya does not understand a word of French. Near Bordeaux, Goya finds, "the silvery light of the Atlantic water / the velvety black of the coal / album after album" (1999, 90). Thus in the poem, the drawings now become books.

All forms of artistic communication, however, carry with them possibilities of both representation and distortion, the concluding section of the poem reminds us. "From etching to lithography / from one curiosity to new curiosity," it begins, recording the invention of the lithography process during Goya's lifetime (1999, 90). Indeed, we might remember as well that this change in artistic technique is not just a matter of technological advance, but also of reproduction. Images are reversed when printed through the etching process while lithographs yield exact correspondences; likewise, written words are read as they appear, whereas typeset printing also operates on the principle of reversal. The final lines of the poem relate how Goya's print plates had been seized by the monarchy after Napoleon's defeat (compare Janson 1991, 632). To this loss, Goya responds tersely, "[I] recommend my new work" (1999, 90). At the end of Goya's life the poem concludes with a sense that the artist has left unfinished business:

> Kein Sterbenswörtchen dringt zu ihm
> kein Sterbenswort
> in den Sand gesetzt
> in den Sand gezeichnet (1999, 90)
>
> Not a single last word comes to him
> no last word
> set in the sand
> drawn in the sand

The fact that the artist can never make a final statement, however, brings this unspoken word closer to a state of pure art, for it is only the text itself that traces it by recording its absence.

Verbeugungen vor der Luft closes with a text that describes a similar moment in which the poem seems to have become completely wordless, only to miraculously constitute itself again: "Vanished was all notion of work / dictionary warm a sun stood high," it begins, reassuring the reader that a time will come when semantic clarity arrives (Krechel 1999, 97). Then the final lines echo and subtly challenge Hugo von Hofmannsthal's "Ballade des äussern Lebens" ("Ballade of the External Life") which famously answers its inquiries into human purpose by observing, "And yet the one who says 'Evening' says much, / A word from which profundity and sorrow runs / like thick honey from the hollow honeycomb" (Hofmannsthal 1952, 16). For a writer as resolutely committed to unpretentious authenticity as Krechel, such an utterance seems uncharacteristically poetic.

Krechel, however, interrupts this mood, declaring that no word is spoken, iterating that statement in both active and passive voice ("fiel / war fallengelassen worden," "fell / was allowed to fall") (1999, 97).

This unexpected twist allows the poem to end not with the meaningful words of an orphic poet, but with an act of reception that seems intent on absorbing the poem: "Good fortune was, remained / Honey sucking, bright eyes" (1999, 97). To be clear, the allusion in these lines to Hofmannsthal does not signal a return to abstract symbolism, but rather, I believe, a renewed affirmation of Krechel's appreciation of authenticity. Remembering Krechel's reflections on the ways authors internalize others' works, we must read this text as a palimpsestic reference to language that potentially transcends immediate experience. It is a potentially risky shift in subject matter since at face value the poem seems to reproduce nostalgically a kind of language and content that belong with an older conception of poetry as artifact, and yet Krechel's point is precisely that poems are always in the process of construction, for its title, "Ein Gedicht entsteht" ("A Poem Comes into Being"), pointedly contradicts that reading.

At the beginning of her career, Krechel made plain that her choice of subject matter arises from a deeply held sense of commitment: "I write about women, because I know the situation of women better than that of men. I write about women, because the objective situation of women stands in contradiction to this society's conception of itself. We can read its power relations from the situation of women" (1974b, 34). As we have seen, her poetological essays make abundantly clear that the underlying complications for this new writing is that the mode of representation depends on our definition of what is regarded as truly "authentic." Her essay on Irmgard Keun returns us to this paradox, for it identifies problematical aspects of taking an overly literal approach:

> The common wish of those women who suffer from the ahistoricity forced upon their gender is to represent with photographic accuracy those women who have emerged from that ahistoricity for a moment, in order to win them for themselves, at least in reproduction. This wish, however, tends to lead to a feminist neopositivism in which the joy of seeking and finding lost persons blurs the questions raised by the discovered texts and by the very process of searching itself. (1979a, 121)

Neopositivism, as Krechel recognizes in her theoretical essays, draws on the compelling power of realism. Questioning the practices of highly mimetic representation, Krechel does not resolve the quandary of how best to approach truth through artistic means of reproduction. Rather, through intense engagement in *Verbeugungen vor der Luft* with these aesthetic issues, she reconnects with poetological conventions in the lyric genre that have in the past been effective in asserting poetry's position as an exemplary artifact. These conventions enable symbolic language, and yet Krechel resolutely deconstructs their textual authority by interpolating them through montage in a way that reveals poetry to be processual. It is a characteristic poetic gesture for Krechel.

By the time Krechel published *Verbeugungen vor der Luft,* she had in fact moved well beyond thinking in fixed categories about aesthetic and social issues, and such thinking yields in her oeuvre more complex reflection on all aspects of the poet's work. In a 1995 essay on Ingeborg Bachmann she tells of revisiting places where Bachmann had lived, collecting impressions of the author's life, ethical convictions, and her frustrated attempts to come to terms with the postwar discontinuities. The reader encounters Krechel responding to this journey by commenting on how much boundaries blurred later in the twentieth century. In particular, she registers the collapse of binary hierarchies and labels like "insider" and "outsider" that had provided the developing feminist movement with enabling insights. In their place, Krechel discerns the evolution of more complex notions of social networks:

> The dichotomy exploiter-exploited, like that of perpetrator and victim, derived from the general political discourse of the sixties and used by the new women's movement for describing differences between the sexes, was replaced in the eighties by careful analysis of mutual complicity, which did not seek individual measure or guilt, but rather the interweaving of social dependencies of the sexes. (1995c, 15)

While Domin came to describe the interaction of male and female elements in creative work as a form of hermaphroditism, and thus approaches the sense of interconnectedness that Krechel advocates, Krechel adopts an approach that lies beyond the constraints of biological identity. Instead of ideologically dismantling gender positions or effacing the boundaries between insider and outsider, she relies on poetic work. The fluidity of discourses in *Verbeugungen vor der Luft* produces the sense of the interconnectedness of all the experience poetically expressed through the evocative fluidity of pastiche. The poetic techniques of montage itself become a vehicle for Krechel's exploration of the limits of authenticity, a means to experiment with the capacity poetry offers to push communication to its limits and to fuse experience with perception through lyrical representation.

In Zukunft schreiben and Poetic Voice

Domin and Hahn talk about poetry as an act of transformation, demonstration of personal fortitude, and declaration of social engagement; only Krechel talks about *voice*. By voice, Krechel means both the physical utterance of the speaker, but more importantly "voice and vision" in the sense of poetic identity as cultivated by American schools of creative writing (2003, 144). Voice as the heightened expression of personal choice plays an especially prominent role in postwar poetry, where, as Michael Clune observes in connection with the work of Frank O'Hara, it becomes "the guiding principle of liberal society" (2005, 182). Such poetry, Clune argues, "reverses the liberal dynamic, opening the taboo and utopian prospect of a collective national subject. The poems dramatize the particularity of personal experience slipping through the grip of liberal subjectivity and expanding into a collective subjectivity that functions as the master trope of the new poetic realism" (2005, 182). *Voice* for Krechel is similarly connected with artistic self-confidence and freedom. Admiring the creative writing program at Columbia University, Krechel briefly explains the concept of finding one's own voice in the American sense to her readers, but then immediately reinterprets *Stimme* (voice) in her own terms as a form of energy akin to singing, an activity that opens poetry to public performance (2003, 144). When we align the discussion of voice in Krechel's recent work with this type of public expression, it becomes apparent that what is at stake with *In Zukunft schreiben* (*Writing into the Future*) is not merely subjective individual speech, but most emphatically the future of collective identity.

What we encounter in this work is Krechel's rejection of a potentially enervating model of constrained, rationalized choice in order to embrace individual spontaneity. Hence, the matter of voice taken up by *In Zukunft schreiben* serves to foreground anew the flawed democracy of the public sphere by exposing the tendency of rationalism to level and restrain. To counter this suppressive power, Krechel offers the concept of "voice," not as an autonomous and private gesture, but as a practice that recognizes that it is possible to transform the subjectivity of self-expression into a valid force that operates in the public sphere. Voice because of its very idiosyncratic nature potentially instantiates the purest expression of democracy. For these reasons, *In Zukunft schreiben* casts the lyric genre as especially well equipped to respond to contemporary conditions. In pursuing this argument, I am interested in how Krechel's work as a whole might be read through the lens of recent lyric theory which, as Clune summarizes, argues "that personal poetry represents the prototype of progressive, micropolitical postmodern personhood" (2005, 182). I am particularly concerned with the discussions from *In Zukuft schreiben* about how writing functions as an activity outside or within culture because Krechel's treatment of such topics as communication, creative practices, tradition, and translation are a good indication of where postwar German poetry has sought to produce destabilizing insights for poets and readers alike.

In Zukunft schreiben announces itself as a "handbook for all who want to write," thus a fundamentally democratic project. While it adheres to handbook conventions by distinguishing the characteristic features of drama, narrative, and poetry, *In Zukunft schreiben* mostly addresses the creative process itself. Its purpose is part encouragement to new writers to engage in hands-on exercises, and part commentary on the materials, habits, and limits of writing. A slim volume, it explores such topics as beginnings, forms, the fundamentals of narrative, words and their sounds, and techniques of appropriation and resistance. It even includes a chapter on the sufferings of aspiring writers that frankly discusses inglorious subjects like writer's block, abandoned projects, and unoriginal repetition. The handbook begins with an acknowledgment that writers always work in a historical context governed by aesthetic values and taboos and the liberating assertion that against this historical background, above all "the change in the capacity to perceive, compared with earlier writers, is an important part of the work" (2003, 8–9).

Krechel emphasizes that only keen, individual perspective opens new conceptual space (2003, 9). Terming writing "Mitteilungen unter verschärften Bedingungen," or communication under extreme circumstances (2003, 11), she demonstrates how linguistic utterances shift in meaning by illustrating the impact changes in word order itself have on written communication (2003, 14–15). In this context, she again affiliates her conception of how writing works not with a prescriptive understanding of genre theory, but rather with a dynamic process of reader response. "Literary scholarship speaks about a [reader's] horizon of expectation, produced, changed, reshaped by reference to the genre," Krechel observes in affirmation of the principles of hermeneutic interpretation (2003, 20).[18] Moreover, she recognizes from the outset that writing involves fictions of distance and proximity that allow the author to use language to play with or close off expression (2003, 21–31). All writing, she thus concludes, is fundamentally construction, and as an experienced writer she seeks to give encouragement to novices to become continual innovators and individualistic manipulators of language.

The second chapter then introduces practical writing exercises (2003, 37), which Krechel sees as useful in expanding the repertoire of techniques available to a writer. She provides examples of how to conduct detailed observation, description, and narration (2003, 32–54).[19] These illustrations extend through the subsequent chapter via Krechel's passing remarks on the practices of working writers: Friederike Mayröcker's laundry baskets full of notes, the scribble-mania Walter Benjamin diagnosed, and experiments in suspended time performed in James Joyce's *Ulysses* and Virginia Woolf's *Mrs. Dalloway* (Krechel 2003, 60–64).

Having treated the representational constraints of various genres (including suitable content, thematic structure in long works, conventions of narrative time, and other matters), Krechel embarks on a detailed discussion of poetry in the fourth chapter. Her remarks foreground the capacity of words and sounds to function as "sinnlich wahrnehmbare Ereignisse," perceptible visible events (2003, 95). Krechel centers this discussion on matters of *voice,* describing with admiration the work of Kenneth Koch, who promoted one poetry project on Manhattan's Lower East Side and another in a nursing home. This example underscores Krechel's interest in promoting poetry not as an exclusive activity for the artistic elite, but as a collective, democratic enterprise in which creative energy can be obtained from common language (*Alltagssprache*), reading out loud, and compassionate teaching (2003, 98). Hence, while writing about what matters relevant to the *creation* of poetry, Krechel simultaneously and quite significantly describes modes of *reception* that dynamically shape the kind of poetry produced. At stake in her choices of examples is a new conception of the lyric genre as an anti-elitist, publicly shared, and nonprescriptive forum.

Further discussion of poetry in this chapter moves the reader even more firmly into areas where poetry is defined primarily through relationships. Krechel asserts that every poet in effect invites others to imitate his work, and she recommends that aspiring writers learn freely from other writers (2003, 100). She acknowledges that the experience of sharing one's writing is intimidating, but sees workshop interaction as critical for a writer's development, citing in particular the example of Hélène Cixous's writing courses for students (2003, 106). A section entitled "Die innere Bibliothek" ("The Inner Library") celebrates the beneficial effects of being well read to the point of having internalized good models.

This encouragement to novice writers to find internal and external sources to fuel creativity is an important counter to the stereotypical image of the marginalized, creatively driven writers. The discussion casts the writer as a meditative apprentice who acquires the vocation through intentional choices, a role that Krechel illustrates from a biographical perspective. Returning to Archibald MacLeish and Martin Opitz, who first sparked her interest in poetry (2003, 111–14), Krechel now devotes a generous nine pages to the sound of poems, which she sees as their initial attraction to readers. This excursus on her own beginnings recalls for readers Krechel's early contact with Opitz, the first author of a poetry handbook in German. Regarding Opitz, she notes that "his insistence on poiesis, the making of verses, impressed the girl, possibly she understood at the beginning only Opitz's triumphal insistence upon individual perspective, his strategy for avoiding senseless foreign words and learned puffery" (2003, 112). His concrete advice about what constitutes poetry engaged the teenager's imagination. From MacLeish, on the other hand, Krechel takes other lessons. Noting MacLeish's keen awareness of how poetry generates images and language, Krechel praises how clearly his undogmatic poetics ("undogmatische Poetologie") are articulated: "He teaches how in the poem one forces one's way through to things and from things to images in their reciprocal relation" (2003, 113). Expanding the view, Krechel traces from MacLeish an imagistic poetic line leading back to Pound, T. S. Eliot, William Carlos Williams, expressionism, baroque poetry, and even to Klopstock and Hölderlin (2003, 113).

What fascinates me about these musings is that Krechel so concretely locates the origins of poetry for herself. The site she describes is a real library that she visited regularly where German incunabula are housed close to works imported as part of the postwar reeducation programs of the Allies. That the works of American modernists occupy a prominent space in these stacks is no surprise, considering the rapid dissemination of Williams, Eliot, and Pound in German translation in the 1960s and the enthusiasm of authors like Enzensberger and Höllerer for them. It is significant for us that Krechel confirms the early influence of these authors on her understanding of the writerly craft, because the account reveals the unpredictably fluid nature of the literary environment. Showing readers her own discovery of poetry, Krechel depicts herself as a person too young to participate in postwar public intellectual discussions, yet as someone who was nonetheless drawn to writers who were strongly invested in linking poetry with the project of creating cultural identity. This fascination with Opitz and MacLeish ties Krechel's aesthetic origins to a time when the lyric genre and questions of individual, cultural, and national identity were linked, reminding us of the high stakes involved in postwar discussions of poetry.

In the chapter that follows, "Techniken der Aneignung" ("Techniques of Appropriation"), Krechel expands the focus on intercultural exchange by returning to the matter of voice and considering how writers relate to models, especially through work as translators. Here Krechel outlines heuristic practices that writers can use to enlarge their repertoire, ranging from scribbling, copying, imitating, and translating to freely adapting the works of others. Certainly she has in mind paradigms of influence explored by Harold Bloom, since she cites *The Anxiety of Influence* in a previous chapter (see Bloom 1973, 82, 202). While fully aware that these questions could be pursued in a scholarly manner (2003, 126), Krechel is nonetheless primarily concerned with how the physical qualities of the writing become realized through exercises of imitation. The sounds of words, effect of rhythm, and control of breath (*Atem* and *Atemwende*) (2003, 126–27), Krechel observes, are inseparable from the meaning of a text. Thus when Krechel discusses the problem of untranslatability, she does so in terms of ineffable qualities of language—*Sprachmusik, Sprachmelodie, Sprachmagie,* the music, melody, and magic of language—as well as matters of vocabulary, cultural specificity, and historical context (2003, 128–32).

Calling the author-translator a "secret agent" (*Geheimagent*) for her or his role in mediating between cultures and smuggling texts into another language, Krechel cites the work of poets as translators as having a productive influence on literary culture (2003, 132). The role of the author is not that of the technical translator in her view. The writer, Krechel observes, "cannot excuse himself for the degree of difficulty of the text. He cannot excuse himself at all. The text has no space for apologetic bows" (2003, 133). The writer-translator, however, may revolutionize the poetic repertoire like Hölderlin with his Pindar translations, choose to ignore the original as Brecht did in his translations from Chinese, or create a wholly separate poetic language as Celan did through his extensive translations (Krechel 2003, 134–38). Since Krechel herself has not taken on creative translation projects, the point she makes bears further examination in the context of her oeuvre. Montage, of course, brings the creative writer into intimate contact with the appropriated text, but it does not demand the kind of sustained projection of poetic voice that is required for translation. Krechel, as we have seen, variously employs montaged elements in her poems, and she is thoroughly aware of the profound effects of poetic influence. It is my contention that we must, thus, conclude that her preoccupation with questions of voice in *In Zukunft schreiben* should be interpreted as a maneuver to redirect attention from the qualities of an individual poet's oeuvre to the performance context of literature—in effect an admonishment to comprehend voice as a crucial instantiation of subjectivity and to realize the potential of creative acts in the public sphere.

Voice, Krechel reminds us, shows the proximity of poetry to song (2003, 144). She relates it to public verbal expression (including poets screaming through a microphone) and rhetorically implies that successful marketing for writers depends on fabricating the individual personality of the author (2003, 145–46). True literary style, Krechel continues, cannot be developed by simple imitation (2003, 146–47). For that reason, she advocates teaching aesthetic work—philological attention to words, keen hearing and listening, and appreciation of how texts are understood (2003, 148–49). While the pragmatic and creative objectives of the handbook seem somewhat at odds with each other in this discussion, the larger theoretical trajectory of Krechel's concern with influence emerges in the end. The two concluding chapters of *In Zukunft schreiben* turn to examples of how writers resist feedback, struggle with impediments to writing, and overcome difficulties, arguing cogently that absorbing poetic influence does not mean following lockstep in the footsteps of the past.

The conclusion of *In Zukunft schreiben* is rhetorical, not unlike the final poem in *Verbeugungen vor der Luft,* a mirror of the feeling of postpartum depression that Krechel confesses always comes at the end of a project (2003, 194). Still, Krechel rouses to proclaim that each book becomes "eine neue Realität" (a new reality) and a "*fait social*" or social act (2003, 195–96). "Whoever writes poems always has the end ahead of him," Krechel writes (2003, 196). Thus, the cycle of authorship becomes continuous.

Compared with her more theoretical works, such as "Leben in Anführungszeichen," *Mit dem Körper des Vaters Spielen,* and *Lesarten, In Zukunft schreiben* is refreshingly pragmatic. The extensive treatment it gives to the materiality of language even appears at times theory-adverse. Writing for a general audience, Krechel opts for journalistic clarity. Through abundant examples, she establishes elective affinities with many authors, consistently reaching back into the German canon, but also reaching out internationally to modernist and feminist sources, especially Anglo-American works. The emphasis she places on the individual practice of writing exercises, reader response theory, workshop dynamics, creative translation, and non-hierarchical paradigms of influence speaks to her egalitarian values. Here we find a fresh iteration of the liberalism that had been sought throughout the postwar era in German discourses about aesthetic, political, and social issues. For Krechel, this transformative potential of culture is, however, definitively linked to a feminist agenda. The autonomy she claims for the lyric genre is inseparable from the right to self-assertion for women.

After 1945, the lyric genre was prized in German-speaking countries for its ostensibly transformative capacities. Poetry was proclaimed to be in search of a new language—literary expression that would marry modernist stylistic innovations with postwar democratic values. Skeptical that such a literary agenda of social transformation can be realized through ideology, yet hopeful that the lyric genre might achieve such ends, Krechel emphasizes the powerful formative capacities of poetic language itself. In her work, writing functions as a heuristic practice that involves self-reflection and acute awareness of the polysemantic capacities of language. Rather than rhetorically bemoaning the marginalized status of the lyric genre today, Krechel negotiates the interface of modern and postmodern conditions by drawing attention to her own position as a writer and our positions as readers. Embracing principles of voice and authenticity, the material that for Krechel constitutes "the building blocks of subjective perception" (1979, 102), she has developed her oeuvre through intense reflection on the nature of women's writing. Krechel's poems inhabit language in an especially complex way—as montage that simultaneously evokes and disrupts meaning and as poetic cycles that push for new modes of interpretation that go beyond a focus on expression. Her work invites the reading of poems not as ideological documents, but rather as dynamic texts in which we as readers continually rediscover the ways in which language comes to signify.

Chapter Five

✦

Writing Differently Through Poetry Anthologies

Women's poetry anthologies make large claims. One of the earliest aims grandly "not just [to] present prime examples for a chapter in a modern literary history, but rather be a part of human history itself" (Virginia 1907, n.p.).[1] Another, published almost a hundred years later, views itself extravagantly as "above all a plea for the poetry of women—and not although, but rather because they write differently" (Reich-Ranicki 1998, 27). Such claims reinforce conceptions of the lyric genre's specialness and resonate with positions that we have previously encountered in the foregoing case studies: Domin's argument that poetry constitutes courageous intervention, Hahn's that its heightened expression opens the possibility for reimagining the world, and Krechel's that its "authentic" materials have transformative power. All three poets assert, like the anthologists whose work will occupy us now, that poetry is a crucial, collective project that expresses our humanity. Yet despite these appeals to universal values, these positions are, as we have seen, complexly informed by aesthetic, social, and theoretical debates that are at once particular to the German literary environment and inflected by historically specific transnational currents. With startling unanimity, Domin, Hahn, and Krechel have explored the performative aspects of poetry, only to show that to make it possible for the lyric genre to relate to its audiences by representing itself as in dialogue with readers, a great deal of effort is required on the part of the poet.

Clearly it is difficult for individual writers, however bold, to transform the nature of that poet/reader exchange because this presumptive dialogue is embedded in the larger context of literary conventions. Modern anthologies—more so than individual poets—have been responsible for those reshaping literary values, functioning as tools for dynamic cultural production. For reasons that will become apparent, this predicament has had an especially pronounced impact on women writers. By focusing on anthologies, I thus want to consider how this publication form played several different roles in constituting the literary environment in Germany after 1945, some more supportive of women authors than others.

Despite the century dividing the publication of *Frauenlyrik unserer Zeit* (*Women's Poetry of Our Time*, 1907) and *Frauen dichten anders* (*Women Write Differently*, 1998), the two anthologies quoted at this chapter's outset, they idealize poetry in similarly heightened terms. Both argue that women's poetry deserves greater attention because it embodies especially valuable, though by society overlooked qualities. This argument shapes other anthologies from the latter twentieth century with consistency as well, surfacing in prefaces and afterwords that poignantly recount the obscure status of women writers. Just as consistently, the qualities purported to make women's poetry different remain ineffable. The question this chapter pursues is why from the institutional perspective of anthologies this uncertainty about "feminine" writing is entrenched. The answer, I contend, has to do with the mechanisms of canon formation that pertain to these anthologies and with the general re-lyricization of poetry. Thus to analyze this evolution, we must take into account both the dynamics of canon and the relation of anthologies to poetic style.

Anne Ferry in her insightful analysis of English poetry anthologies, *Tradition and the Individual Poem: An Inquiry into Anthologies* (2001), points out that the special institutional function of anthologies derives from their relationship to readers:

> The wide social audiences more explicitly drawn into anthologies as distinct from other books of poetry, along with the anthology reader's awareness of the company of other readers—past, present, or to come—have the effect of making all entries in anthologies seem in some more special sense than other printed poems to be public, like works of art displayed in a museum. (2001, 127)

The synchronic and diachronic dimensions of how anthologies work with poets, readerships, and canons are, as Ferry explains, highly complex. For Ferry's model of the anthology as museum, it must be assumed that as Pierre Bourdieu asserts, poems as aesthetic objects embody cultural worth that can be exploited by the poet and others (1993, 76–77). John Guillory, following Bourdieu in his seminal study of these issues, *Cultural Capital: The Problem of Literary Canon Formation*, demonstrates that canon is not established merely through the application of evaluative judgments, but rather ultimately through historical-linguistic processes that determine which works become favored and persist (1993, 85–92).

Among the most important determinants in this process, as Alan Golding contends in *From Outlaw to Classic: Canons in American Poetry,* are the factor of whether the anthology is envisioned as a revisionist project or as an instrument of established canon (1995, 40). But each of these models of canon formation only partially addresses the role of the individual poem in this system, which Ferry finds so crucial to explore.

Recently Virginia Jackson has argued that we need to pay closer attention to what we consider to be the lyric genre, because in the gradual shedding of the widest variety of texts, she finds that "when the stipulative functions of particular genres are collapsed into one big idea of poems as lyrics, then the only function poems can perform in our culture is to become individual or communal ideals" (2008, 183). Nowhere, I believe, are the dynamics of this concentration more evident than in postwar Germany. Lyricization emerges as one of the poem's chief survival strategies, moving writers and anthologists alike to embrace such fragile qualities as individual voice, condensed expression, and transformative aspirations in ways that validate the unique properties of poetry at the very moment when the lyric genre is deeply questioned as a viable artistic form.

The present analysis focuses on six anthologies and considers the essays that adumbrate the projects envisioned by their editors. Their programmatically stated engagement with feminism echoes the positions previously encountered relative to the work of Hilde Domin, Ulla Hahn, and Ursula Krechel. At the same time, each anthology exhibits various nonpolemical forms of identity creation through paratext material that surrounds the poetry texts. These materials—dust-jacket copy, sequencing criteria, biographical notes, and source references—enhance the programmatic narrative advanced by each anthologist.

To appreciate the significance of these collections, we need to bear in mind the exemplary role such projects have played in the literary environment. Poetry anthologies that appeared in Germany in the latter half of the twentieth century often represent a heady convergence of political and aesthetic currents. After 1945, collections like *Tausend Gramm* (*Thousand Gram,* 1949), *Ergriffenes Dasein* (*Moved Existence,* 1953), and *Widerspiel* (*Counterplay,* 1962) described themselves as programs of a postwar cultural reform. Many later German anthologies, from Hans Bender's *In diesem Lande Leben Wir* (*In This Land We Live,* 1978) to *Berührung ist nur eine Randerscheinung* (*Feeling Touched Is Only a Peripheral Manifestation,* 1985), which captured the Greenwich Village–type flavor of East Berlin's Prenzlauer Berg right before the fall of the Wall, and Jörg Drews's *Das bleibt* (*That Remains,* 1995) also operate in this way. Given the expectation that poetry anthologies would make

formative artistic and political statements, it is hardly surprising that prolific editors like Bender and Drews depict their projects as more than
simple collections of texts.[2] Such ambitions position these publications to
be instruments for creating the dual cultural/national identity of a *Kulturnation* (a well-established role for art in the German literary context),
long after the early postwar political motivations for establishing such a
program had waned.

In fact, the postwar literary scene can be mapped by the cultural politics that play out in poetry anthologies. German audiences, including
young authors who became leading intellectuals, had had ample opportunity to read Louis Untermeyer's anthologies and similar publications,
since the books were imported as part of the Allies' cultural reeducation program.[3] Consequently, German translation anthologies like Hans
Magnus Enzensberger's *Museum der Modernen Poesie* (*Museum of
Modern Poetry*, 1960b), Karl O. Paetel's *Beat: Eine Anthologie* (*Beat:
An Anthology*, 1962), and Rolf Dieter Brinkmann's *Silverscreen: Neue
amerikanische Lyrik* (*Silverscreen: New American Poetry*, 1969), which
were inspired in part by American models, became privileged vehicles for
declaring new artistic directions.

Anthologies of poetry by women authors, which only appeared after
the wave of German feminism of the 1970s, cannot claim the same level
of influence. This minor status, which is regrettable, reflects the fact that
beyond issues of gender equity in publishing, the lyric genre seemed in
general decline in Germany, as elsewhere. Considering these factors, it
is especially important to examine which aesthetic discourses surface in
anthologies with regard to value, canon, aesthetics, readership practices,
national identity, and social context, for despite their salutary effects,
these strains perpetuated the outsider status of women's poetry, exercis-
ing prescriptive force in determining how women's writing is received or
excluded.

Anthologies of poetry by women give new life to long-standing postwar debates about the need for exemplary forms of cultural and ethical
expression at a point when these discourses were beginning to lose their
oppositional verve. Reaching two or more decades back to postwar ideological and aesthetic debates, women's poetry anthologies in the 1970s
begin to argue the legitimacy of their enterprise in favored rhetorical terms.
Indeed, they refuse the rigid aesthetic ideology of the late 1960s (including the insistence on politicized content and loose documentary forms),
and strategically put pressure on the cultural status quo by privileging the
use of apparently apolitical private expression. In effect, they challenge

the validity of binary categories of high versus low culture, private versus public spheres, and aesthetic tradition versus radical innovation.

By the 1980s and 1990s, anthologies of German poetry by women authors had become an important site for the reassertion of the individual agency of writers, but they also turned into a venue for the consolidation of canon. The anthologies cultivate empathetic readers and typically represent themselves as affirmations of women's collective identity. Though the programmatic statements they make occasionally border on stereotypical essentialism, the collections themselves work to direct attention to the individual talents of poets. At their best, these anthologies serve as a locus for the interpellation of identity politics and form a provisional canon of authors who are consistently included.

The anthologies I have chosen for analysis describe the literary environment for contemporary German women poets in clearly partisan terms. While Domin, Hahn, and Krechel each edit various types of literary collections, only Hahn compiled a women's poetry anthology, *Stechäpfel.* For this reason, we turn to a new group of texts to consider the institutional issues of women's writing related to canon formation through poetry anthologies. In keeping with the unifying context of this study, my analysis focuses on anthologies published in West Germany that reveal that these projects have a robust capacity for constructing cultural and social identity within the West German literary system.

Two of the anthologies date from the early 1980s, *Gezeiten: Neue Frauenlyrik aus der BRD* (*Tides: New Poetry by Women from the FRG* [Federal Republic of Germany]), edited by Elisabeth Thieß (1981), and *Mörikes Lüfte sind vergiftet* (*Mörike's Skies Are Poisoned*), edited by Christel Göbelsmann (1982). *Wenn wir den Königen schreiben: Lyrikerinnen aus der DDR* (*When We Write to the Kings: Women Poets from the GDR* [German Democratic Republic]), edited by Jutta Rosenkranz with the assistance of Hanne Castein, presents work by East German writers and was published in the West (1988). The three remaining anthologies were designed as comprehensive projects and appeared in the 1990s: Ulla Hahn's *Stechäpfel: Gedichte von Frauen aus drei Jahrtausenden* (*Thorn Apples: Poems by Women from Three Centuries,* 1992b), Elizabeth Borchers's *Gedichte berühmter Frauen* (*Poems by Famous Women,* 1996), and Marcel Reich-Ranicki's *Frauen dichten anders* (*Women Write Differently,* 1998). Produced, with the exception of *Frauen dichten anders,* by women authors (Göbelsmann, Rosenkranz, Hahn, and Borchers are also themselves poets), these collections demonstrate particular flair for connecting poetic practice with theoretical observations.

Raising Consciousness or Changing Readers?
Anthologies of the 1980s

In many respects, German poetry anthologies after 1945 reinvent productions from the golden age of Anglo-American anthologies in the
early twentieth century. Explaining the densely packed components like
prefaces, footnotes, and appendixes that often appear in anthologies during the heyday of English-language poetry collections, John G. Nichols
observes that "the task of creating anthologies for dual academic and
general readerships became especially arduous given the nature of the
modernist writing that was being anthologized for the first time" (2006,
170). According to Nichols, the preeminent anthologist Ezra Pound envisioned these books as a means for educating readers, providing them with
the tools to evaluate and interpret the new literature (2006, 182–84). For
German authors (and despite doubts about modernism's odd dual connection to fascism and democracy), Pound and his generation's anthologies
seemed a promising way to realize dreams for the massive reconstruction
of the publishing industry and literary life.[4]

When German writers reached to international modernism as an ideo-
logical model, they envisioned themselves as educating (or reeducating)
audiences. Programmatic collections of the postwar era, like *Deine Söhne,
Europa (Your Sons, Europe,* 1947), ed. Hans Werner Richter; *Transit:
Lyrik der Jahrhundertmitte (Transit: Poetry at Midcentury,* 1956), ed.
Walter Höllerer; or *Expeditionen: Deutsche Lyrik seit 1945 (Expeditions:
German Poetry Since 1945,* 1959), ed. Wolfgang Weyrauch), and heavily
annotated anthologies, especially Enzensberger's *Museum der modernen
Poesie* (1960b), espoused international aspirations to assert their own
legitimacy. Poet-anthologists who had been academically trained, like
Enzensberger, adroitly blended the model of copiously footnoted and
laboriously documented German scholarship with formats intended for
general readers. The collections counted on a well-educated audience, yet
were designed to be didactic.[5] The front and back matter of anthologies
advertised them as worthy of worldwide attention, promoted avant-garde
practices as a form of resistance to fascism, and boasted progressive thinking. Successful anthologists acted as public intellectuals, rather than effete
academics. Immediacy, clear language, and quotidian subject matter were
frequently elevated as worthy goals for aspiring writers (see Enzensberger
1963, 49). Anthologies, in short, positioned themselves as tools to mold a
new society of readers, and they began to alter poetic craft.

In so doing, they formed an unconventional and yet highly controlled
canon. In *Cultural Capital,* Guillory convincingly argues that "there can

be no *general* theory of canon formation that would predict or account for the canonization of any particular work, without specifying first the unique historical conditions of that work's production and reception" (1993, 85). Guillory points out that economic activity related to literary culture (including reproduction and dissemination) depends on factors like social networks and unspoken institutional protocols about the creation of canon (1993, vii). The weight of these extraliterary factors was very significant for German literary culture after 1945, for along with everything else in the country, literature underwent reconstruction. That rebuilding effort occurred very much as a public and uniquely restrictive process—through writers' meetings (especially Gruppe 47), publication paths guarded by the oversight of censors, licensed presses, and the controlled distribution of officially approved print material.

Documenting the marked asymmetry of status that affected the position of women authors relative to their male counterparts in the immediate postwar period (1945–50), Marianne Vogel observes that in those years women rarely were involved in the editing of anthologies, which had rapidly become one of the most influential categories of publication. Vogel also finds that women played only a limited role in the production of cultural-literary journals (2002, 226–27). Still, as Vogel points out, women authors were consistently involved in the cultural scene, especially the poets Elisabeth Langgässer, Marie Luise Kaschnitz, and Ricarda Huch, who were even active in writers' congresses (2002, 226). Considering that poetry anthologies such as *Tausend Gramm* (1949) and *Ergriffenes Dasein* (1953), and poetological essay collections like Hans Bender's *Mein Gedicht ist mein Messer* (*My Poem Is My Knife,* 1955), played a decisive dual role in setting the political-cultural agenda, however, the treatment of women poets in these collections is not incidental. Included in only a limited way—and sometimes grouped together with Jewish or experimental authors whose work seemed difficult for anthologists to subsume under other categories—women authors were literally placed on the margins.[6] Yet even with these marginalizing tendencies, I want to propose, postwar anthologies indirectly paved the way for women's writing, for they succeeded in making a compelling case for valuing the autonomous work of poets.[7]

Analyzing circumstances in American poetry that in many respects mirror the dynamics of the German literary environment, Golding in *From Outlaw to Classic: Canons in American Poetry* considers what qualities make anthologies robust tools for alternative poetic programs (1995, 22). Golding demonstrates that such anthology projects variously advance a political or literary program, propose the canonization of outsider poets, or work to undermine the institutional status quo (1995, 30, 36, 145). But the group synergy of poets (which he finds in the case of language poetry) exerts particularly strong pressure on canon, in his assessment: "The poet-centered approach to canon formation is important for restoring some sense of individual agency to the canonizing process, and it can remind academic critics to take poets' views on these matters as seriously as their own" (1995, 47). The reason this occurs is that the collective self-assertion of poets forces new modes of reading that enable audiences to come to terms with unconventional modes of writing, thus powerfully altering literary culture.

German postwar poetry anthologies, many poet-created, similarly worked to shift aesthetic values, and their success both advantaged and disadvantaged later anthologies of German women's poetry. Though the editors of the anthologies to be considered here repeatedly allude to commonalities in women's experience, their claims concerning the special status for women artists as a group did not lead to a significantly revised canon, in part due to an unraveling of that collective identity. Likewise, when these anthologies argue for poetic autonomy, they successfully appropriate the discourses of modernism that had been heavily trafficked in post-1945 literary debates. But because the postwar ethos, which valorized individualism as the foundation for social tolerance, was highly inflected with gendered assumptions (compare Leeder 2000, 200), it was not ultimately a satisfactory model. Remembering Jackson's contention that a narrowed conception of the lyric genre means that poems are constrained to exist either as individual or as communal ideals (2008, 183), the option that might have seemed more viable for German women writers—poetry rooted in subjectivity—was still at least theoretically suspect, while the route of common values was closed off because it was already occupied.

These factors make us aware that the poetological function of the anthologies to be considered here is highly complex. How a poem topically treats individual experience and argues personally for principles of human fairness is in part a measure of its suitability as an anthology piece, since the anthologies act as advocates for women writers. While the six editors applaud linguistic innovation, they ultimately make their case for poetry by women by idealizing subjective expression. Given the ideological commitments of women's liberation, however, there is a perceptible ambivalence about defining art as self-contained, using the discourse of German romanticism in which artistic production was troped as feminine passivity withdrawn from the public sphere (compare Helfer 2005, 299). This tension introduces a challenging paradox, for many of the individual authors in the anthologies in fact continue to work with the foundational thematic content, formal conventions, and gender positions that had evolved through the feminine troping of the lyric genre by men. Strategically, the anthologists are faced with the dilemma of how to reconcile apparently traditional texts with the argument that women's writing is new. The argument that frequently justifies these claims is that women only recently acquired the means to express their experience, which we may recognize as a reworking of avant-garde modernism's claim to breaking with the past. However, this discourse of newness actually has a long history in accounts of women's writing, as we can see by returning to Julia Virginia's early-twentieth-century anthology as a point of comparison.

Frauenlyrik unserer Zeit, a collection that sought to engage a broader readership for women's writing in the early twentieth century (Werner-Birkenbach 2000, 130), is a compact book graced by eight pictures of poets with their autographs and short biographies before their work.[8] It presents poetry by women authors born in the mid- to late-nineteenth century ranging from Johanna Ambrosius to Carolina Woerner. Paula Dehmel (wife of Richard Dehmel), Marie von Ebner-Eschenbach, Ricarda Huch, and the young Agnes Miegel are among the writers included.[9] A little more than a page in length, the introduction refrains from providing the reader with the kind of elaborate theoretical and documentary apparatus that became commonplace in later twentieth-century anthologies.

While its poems about the loneliness of women writers and the travails of love may not persuade contemporary readers that exceptional talent has been overlooked, Virginia makes a plausible argument for her project by suggesting that women are finally revealing themselves in poetry here. She attributes the past obscurity of women poets not to social constraints but to supposedly "natural" reticence. "Indeed even in earlier times poetesses came to the fore," Virginia explains, "yet no matter how significant their creative work, no matter how great their ability was—a peculiar shyness held the woman back from articulating in her poetry her deepest feminine experience" (1907, n.p.). Accordingly, the emergence of women authors is represented as a kind of Enlightenment emergence into maturity:

> Only in our days did first just a few, and then more "to whom a god has given the power to say what they suffer," dare to reveal their specifically feminine experience in their poems without holding back. Yes, one could daringly term recent women's poetry the unveiling of the feminine psyche, which for centuries had kept itself concealed. (Virginia 1907)[10]

Virginia's appeal is made more poignant by this reference to the female psyche, and indeed, a preoccupation with subjective experience motivates many of the poems.

Decades later, and against the background of postwar programmatic writing, anthologies born of mid-century feminist consciousness-raising groups return to discussions of women's poetry in surprisingly similar terms. *Gezeiten: Neue Frauenlyrik aus der BRD,* edited by Elisabeth Theiß (a slim, 61-page presentation of eight poets born after the war, 1948 to 1960),[11] is bound in creamy white paper that advertises the femininity of the project. The front cover is illustrated with an oval-shaped abstract line drawing that shows a seated nude woman with dark hair, seen from behind, with arms crossed over her left knee. Theiß, explaining her collection methods, states that she solicited submissions for the collection through the prominent feminist journals *Emma* and *Courage,* but she notes that the poems' subject matter did not follow the expected feminist agenda (1981, 61).

Written in unrhymed free verse, most of the poems offer personal reflections on daily life, travel, or relationships, occasionally with social or political commentary.[12] "Rapunzel" by Birgit Welz is characteristic of the oblique, almost gentle critique of society exercised by these texts. Its protagonist has sequestered herself from the world: "I sit here aloft / in my tower. / But I don't let down / my hair" (1981, 47). This anti-Rapunzel has isolated herself by locking doors, closing windows, discontinuing newspaper subscriptions, and turning off television and radio. When she takes a rare glance out the window, she finds that "what I see / prompts me to quickly / —for added security— / shove the chair under the doorknob" (1981, 47). The reader witnesses the speaker's withdrawal from the world, but is left to speculate about conditions in society that motivate her desire for isolation.

A brief afterword by Theiß explains that she started the project in 1980 through "intense engagement with so-called 'women's literature'" (1981, 61). Comments indicate that Theiß struggled with the book's focus and quickly changed its purpose as a result: "Although I had originally thought of a more feminist-orientated book, during perusal and selection of the extremely diverse material that was submitted I soon had to give up this conception" (1981, 61). Mindful of the individual women behind the texts, Theiß emphasizes her efforts to give submissions careful consideration. She concludes by telling readers that her own project, too, is subjective (*subjektiv*) and that the chosen poems "stand in as representative of among other things, the many thousand others that somewhere 'out there' secretly assist women like us in getting past the difficult hours and days and give us courage to go on" (1981, 61).

While Theiß frames her rather limited project as an endeavor that will be read almost exclusively by women, her effort to reclaim the subjective bears comparison with the other collections. *Gezeiten* uncritically accepts the notion that poetry has a quasi-therapeutic function, a rationale absent from academic treatments of the lyric genre and rejected in Domin's *Wozu Lyrik heute* (1968, 14). Furthermore, the remarks Theiß makes about her selection process also seem to imply, perhaps inadvertently, that little individual significance is attached to the individual poems. Instead, Theiß asserts that their real importance consists in their collective value in representing a larger, hidden body of work by women. Having begun the project with intentions of creating an openly feminist anthology, Theiß signals abandonment of political motivations in favor of personal expression, thus reinforcing a division of the public and private spheres through this turn to subjectivity. In sharp contrast to anthologies in the 1990s, especially Ulla Hahn's *Stechäpfel,* we see that Theiß also attaches no special import to formal experimentation or relation to the larger cultural environment. Nonetheless, as a historical document, the project is an extremely interesting example of canon in transition. The poems in *Gezeiten* are consistent with the style of New Subjectivity verse, even though the anthology does not challenge the status quo.

Published just a year later than *Gezeiten, Mörikes Lüfte sind vergiftet* constitutes a more sustained effort to advance women's writing, and it presents itself as a project confidently built on the foundation of a decade's work by the new women's movement (Göbelsmann 1982, 3). Editor Christel Göbelsmann, in fact, uses a quotation from a 1977 essay by Adrienne Rich to introduce the collection with a strong assertion of the power of poetic language:

> The necessity of poetry has to be stated over and over, but only to those who have reason to fear its power, or those who still believe that language is "only words" and that an old language is good enough for our descriptions of the world we are trying to transform. (Göbelsmann 1982, 3; compare Rich 1979, 247)

With this epigraph, gleaned from a Rich essay on power and danger, Göbelsmann paints an optimistic picture of social transformation as women become liberated from patriarchal ways of thinking. Obstacles removed, she predicts that creative women will "develop more comprehensive means of apprehending the world, our own means of thinking and of living" (1982, 3). Consciousness-raising groups that generate awareness of women's common history are one example that Göbelsmann sees as significant for women authors. Citing Virginia Woolf's observation in "A Room of One's Own" that poetry depends on intellectual freedom, which in turn depends on material conditions, Göbelsmann points to the marginal role women still play in literary life, and especially their inability to support themselves through writing (1982, 3–4). In terms that resonate with Rich's important 1971 account of her writing experience in "When We Dead Awaken" (1979, 44), Göbelsmann recounts how women expend energies in jobs unrelated to their creative works, writing late at night, early in the morning, or in between taking care of children. "We are compelled," Göbelsmann laments, "to find individual solutions that make it possible to combine relationships, motherhood, material survival, and the need to write with each other because collective social solutions are not available" (1982, 4). These circumstances explain for Göbelsmann the abundance of poetry by women relative to work in other genres, since short forms are better suited to working conditions where interruption occurs. Göbelsmann finds that the ability of women to write is compromised by insecurities about their own talents and the patriarchal literary system, which controls values, norms, and professional recognition (1982, 4).

As evidence of how women's literature has gained recognition, Göbelsmann mentions two anthologies, *Deutsche Dichterinnen vom 16. Jahrhundert bis zur Gegenwart* (*German Women Poets from the 16th Century to the Present*, 1978), edited by Gisela Brinker-Gabler, and *The World Split Open: Four Centuries of Women Poets in England and America, 1552–1950* (1974), edited by Louise Bernikow, as well as the *Handbuch der deutschsprachigen alternativen Literatur* (*Handbook of Alternative Literature in the German Language*, 1980) as landmark projects (Brinker-Gabler 1978; Bernikow 1974; Engel, Rheinsberg, and Schubert 1980). Lamenting that outside of feminist presses little has truly changed for women writers, she charges, "Political censorship presents itself as aesthetic criticism" (Göbelsmann 1982, 4). Describing her own project, which presents relatively unknown authors, Göbelsmann prides herself on incorporating a diversity of voices.

In Göbelsmann's preoccupation with establishing a women's literary tradition through citation of Rich, Woolf, and academic anthologies, we can see canon-building impulses at work, but in her discussion of poetics we can also recognize the difficulty of trying to align ideology with aesthetics. Göbelsmann remarks that she wanted to select poems that reflected self-assertion (*Selbstbestimmung*) and an openness to change (*Veränderungsbereitschaft*), and she notes that these categories leave out work that "can be opened up by the unique qualities of feminine aesthetic and the development of new contents and forms" (1982, 5). She justifies this omission by explaining that to free writing from the prescriptions of conventional literature, much imaginative work (*Phantasie*) is necessary. Resisting the call within the women's movement to create feminist poetry, Göbelsmann asserts that ideological conformity becomes a constraint:

> Consciousness of repression does not necessarily lead to a corresponding style of writing. We should have the courage to experiment with language. It must be capable of working through all subjects that are important to us. To enter into the language of poems, to ask, what story do they tell me, what does that mean to me, this seems more important to me than the question of whether it's feminist lyric. (1982, 6)

In suggesting that individual voice plays a more central role in writerly identity than ideological solidarity, Göbelsmann's remarks return us to Jackson's insight into the dichotomization of the individual and communal aspects of poetry, and to the shifting dynamics of feminism in the literary environment of the early 1980s that we observed in connection with Hahn. These quandaries are resolved by Göbelsmann through the anthology's design, which organizes texts by author, a conventional structure that emphasizes individual accomplishment. Concluding her remarks, Göbelsmann asserts that increasingly female poets are giving voice to the experiences of women and working to oppose oppression and marginalization, characterizing these efforts as *zornig* (angry), a term consonant with the poetics of Adrienne Rich (Göbelsmann 1982, 6), which, as we will see, are subsequently taken up by Hahn.

Such formal resolution is only provisional. For the collection, in which each set of poems is introduced by a short autobiographical text and author photograph, the cover art, an illustration by artist Heidemarie Hagen, is a black-and-white collage depicting in the foreground two cherub-like figures playing in a field of daisies split by a dark stream. In the background, the left-hand image of a woman who is nude from the waist up and seen from the back is balanced by step-like blocks and dark forms of trees and rocks on the right. The title's reference to the nineteenth-century poet Eduard Mörike, which is taken from a poem in the collection, seems to shed doubt on the viability of lyrical poetry. The violence of the disrupted idyll that visually confronts readers even before they open the book is also matched in intensity by Göbelsmann's passionate statements. *Mörikes Lüfte*, given these indications of conflicted intellectual and aesthetic commitments, ultimately must be read as a polemical work, with an intended instrumental function that is quite distinct from those of either poets' or academics' anthologies, for its primary purpose lies in advancing social change. Using polemical means to refine and consolidate the discourse about women's poetry, it raises issues that other anthologies will eventually need to address more critically.

Wenn wir den Königen schreiben: Lyrikerinnen aus der DDR, edited by Jutta Rosenkranz, represents such a first step in establishing a new canon of German women's poetry for a general readership. This slim yet rewarding collection of work by twelve authors identifies two motivating factors for the anthology. First, Rosenkranz pragmatically assesses the underrepresentation of women authors in poetry anthologies at the level of a mere 5–10 percent in most collections (1988, 133). Secondly, Rosenkranz critically notes that the discussion of "weibliches Schreiben" (feminine writing) sparked in German-speaking countries by Christa Wolf had been directed almost exclusively toward prose (1988, 133). Additionally, Rosenkranz mentions that "the poetry of GDR authors is barely or in only a limited way known to us" (1988, 133).

Though brief, Rosenkranz's three-page introduction mentions the somewhat predictable justification for the collection that it led to the rediscovery (*Wiederentdeckung*) of familiar authors and discovery (*Neuentdecken*) of new ones (1988, 133). Christa Reinig, Helga M. Novak, Inge Müller, and Sarah Kirsch are classified as well-known, established figures, while Eva Strittmatter, Elke Erb, Brigitte Struzyk, Sonja Schüler, and Christiane Grosz are accurately identified as writers who emerged in the 1970s. Kersten Hensel, the youngest of the authors and one who went on to receive much acclaim, is singled out in the afterword as an emerging writer, whereas the lesser-known Annerose Kirchner and Elisabeth Wesuls receive no special treatment.

Rosenkranz's project, which has a different scope from the previously discussed anthologies, intends to represent individual authors as completely as possible by displaying the spectrum of each poet's work (1988, 133). Qualitatively more discriminating in its selections, the anthology displays the thematic and formal diversity of contemporary poetry. Müller's lament about the gas chambers in "Europa" (Rosenkranz 1988, 10) contrasts with Kirsch's "Landaufenthalt" ("Stay in the Country"), a pastoral poem (Rosenkranz 1988, 38–39). The tightly controlled formal rhyme of Schüler's tender love poem "Für W." (Rosenkranz 1988, 116) sets it apart from Erb's montaged texts (Rosenkranz 1988, 55–60).

Citing Christa Wolf's remarks in the introduction to Maxie Wander's documentary collection *Guten Morgen, du Schöne* (*Good Morning, Pretty Woman*), Rosenkranz confirms the growing self-confidence and empowerment of women writers in East Germany (1988, 133). Unlike the ontological appeals to a common feminine identity that we have previously encountered, Rosenkranz follows up on Wolf's suggestion that self-definition itself leads to creativity and the independent capacity to make sober assessments (*jenen nüchternen Blick*). "Women do not want to be pinned down to specifically feminine themes any longer," Rosenkranz insists, "and they often go markedly farther than male authors when they deal with the conditions of family, profession, political context, and individual self-realization" (1988, 134). In innovative ballade, hymn, and sonnet forms, Rosenkranz finds evidence that authors are *eigenwillig* (a term that can be translated as self-willed, individual, or original) and she articulates an instrumental connection between individual autonomy and artistic experimentation. Accordingly, the *Eigenständigkeit* (independence) of East German women poets is seen as empowering to assertive social critique and even self-irony (1988, 134). Rosenkranz also takes up the question of how the *Kriegsvergangenheit* (the war past) is treated by the collection's authors, dividing them into two groups. Poets who lived through the war, she explains, continue to write about it and to perceive a continuing threat to humanity. "Among the younger poets," Rosenkranz explains, "the 'mastery of the past' gradually is moving into the background in favor of [treatment of] current problems" (1988, 134). This gesture meaningfully connects memory politics with discussion of contemporary social issues of interest to women by equating the two. Rosenkranz furthermore implies the broader applicability of this model by pointing out that three of the authors (Reinig, Novak, and Kirsch) resided in West Germany (1988, 135).

The common strain in *Gezeiten, Mörikes Lüfte sind vergiftet,* and *Wenn wir den Königen schreiben* is their acknowledgement of the difficulties that beset women authors, and all three anthologies share optimism about the potential for creative women to effect social change through literature. Differences among women (social status, sexual orientation, racial background) are, however, overlooked in the editors' appeals to women readers. The connection of the projects to a feminist agenda remains somewhat ambiguous. Whereas *Gezeiten* is more focused on providing an open venue for women's poetry and *Mörikes Lüfte sind vergiftet* showed polemical intent, *Wenn wir den Königen schreiben* demonstrates more sophisticated integration of literary context and contemporary poetics. Its nuanced engagement with concepts of feminine writing and openness to stylistic diversity makes plain that contemporary poetry is unlikely to conform to one ideological or aesthetic agenda, and we see that trend intensified in anthologies of the 1990s.

Toward Canon? Anthologies of the 1990s

Anthologies of German women's poetry in the last decade of the twentieth century move beyond the model of consciousness-raising we have encountered in *Gezeiten, Mörikes Lüfte sind vergiftet,* and *Wenn wir den Königen schreiben* and embrace canon-forming ambitions. In doing so they emphasize literary traditions over ephemeral works by contemporaries. Elizabeth Borchers's *Gedichte berühmter Frauen,* originally published by Suhrkamp Verlag in 1987, shares this focus with the anthologies edited by Hahn and Reich-Ranicki. Striving to represent the work of women poets of historical significance, Borchers presents authors with curatorial reverence, setting each poem on a separate page and adding a set of biographies austerely formatted in the same way. Here beyond comments about the education and work of the subjects, remarks about literary relations are added. Thus the profile of Bettina von Arnim notes her relationship to Goethe (Borchers 1996, 271), while the one on Emmy Hennings links her to her husband, Hugo Ball, and to other founders of the Dada movement (1996, 277).[13] Such editorial choices emphasize the proximity of women authors to the literary mainstream and enhance their stature.

To preempt questions about quality, Borchers explains that even when books are constructed according to the gender of authors, quality can also be assessed specifically, although she admits that division by "merit" is artificial to the practice of literature. Noting the abundance and quality of works written by men, Borchers points to the small number of women known for their writing and the fact that it was taken for granted that they would occupy a marginal position in literary life, which made them dependent on the benevolence of others. "This dependency," Borchers concludes, "led to forms of disregard that from time immemorial had been practiced in ways as much taken for granted and playful as intentional" (1996, 267).

The restrained tone relative to the more polemical anthologies previously encountered, is tempered in the account of women's writing that Borchers then constructs, beginning with Roswitha von Gandersheim, the first known female writer in Germany. Conceptually this swift treatment leaves Borchers little space to dispel stereotypes. The piety and demureness of Hildegard von Bingen is contrasted with a quotation from Gottfried Benn about the patriarchal canonization of "a few great men and they suffered deeply" (quoted in Borchers 1996, 268). Borchers leaps from quoting Heinrich von Meissen's thirteenth-century praise of women to the conclusion that women's poetry needs to be appreciated from new perspectives rather than merely subjected to old doubts about quality (1996, 268). Noting that many of the selections are in essence love poems (*Liebesgedichte*) (1996, 269), Borchers explains that everything from religious poetry to highly intellectual or sensuous works can be seen as an expression of passion. Finally, she concludes that the anthology reveals that the twentieth century, which is most fully represented in the collection, is "tatsächlich ein Jahrhundert der Frau," "truly a century of the woman" (1996, 270).

Despite these abrupt conceptual shifts, Borchers displays a high degree of critical sensitivity about what makes a good anthology piece. Citing the inclusion of several signature works, she announces departures too:

> What would a selection of poems by Droste be without her "Tower," or Ricarda Huch without "Fairly Tale of Heaven," or Else Lasker-Schüler without "Prayer," or Ingeborg Bachmann without her "Explain to Me, Love." . . . Thus this selection includes pieces subjectively and objectively expected, desired, unexpected; it takes the risk of passing over names at one time considered indispensable, and who may still be for their epoch, whose absence from a selection like this one, however, seems justifiable. (1996, 269)

Yet even with this claim about the canonical stature of certain poems, the sole text included in all three of the anthologies we are considering is "Am Turme" by Annette von Droste-Hülshoff. Moreover, the choice of authors in the three collections is by no means uniform and hardly daring, either. Borchers's selection shares thirteen authors with Hahn's—Mechthild von Magdeburg, Anna Louisa Karsch, Sophie Mereau, Karoline von Günderode, Annette von Droste-Hülshoff, Ricarda Huch, Else Lasker-Schüler, Nelly Sachs, Gertrud Kolmar, Elisabeth Langgässer, Marie Luise Kaschnitz, Hertha Kräftner, and Ingeborg Bachmann. To the core list Reich-Ranicki adds (in agreement with Borchers) only Catharina Regina von Greifenberg, Christine Lavant, Gertrud von Le Fort, Paula Ludwig, and Marianne von Willemer, who are absent from Hahn's selection.[14] The discontinuities in this canon point to two theoretical problems for women writers: since recognized authors like Droste-Hülshoff or Lasker-Schüler struggle alone and create no schools they are treated, much like Emily Dickinson, as idiosyncratic individuals and topical. Generic categories, even love poetry, which Borchers claims for women poets, also prove restrictive.

Ulla Hahn in editing *Stechäpfel: Gedichte von Frauen aus drei Jahrtausenden* skirts these potential restrictions by focusing on a diverse, emerging modern canon:

The majority of texts in this anthology date from this century [twentieth], as there are quite simply more poems by women from the last hundred years. That may be because they've not yet been definitively rejected from the aesthetic canon. However, the fact that such an abundance could even come into being is in any case a consequence of the women's movement, which created decisive social preconditions for the writing of women, the profession of the woman author. (1992b, 370)

Rather than presenting the selected poems as a historically sequential canon, however, *Stechäpfel* is arranged topically into eight categories, and an appendix documents authors' biographies. An ambitious after-word outlines selection criteria and offers a detailed rationale for the collection. Here, instead of embracing the hope espoused by Julia Virginia that an anthology voices *ein Stück Menschheitsgeschichte,* that is, a part of human history (Virginia 1907, n.p.), Hahn declares that every woman who takes herself seriously and does not wish to have her gender subsumed "im Abstraktum des Menschseins" ("under the abstraction of being human") must encounter a moment of experiencing herself as an outsider (1992b, 365).

For Hahn, the outsider position of women poets is evidenced in their status in other anthologies, and, as we have seen in her work as a poet. Having tried background reading in anthologies of Swedish, French, Mexican, English, Hungarian, Japanese, and Italian poetry published since the 1970s, Hahn expresses disbelief that so few women authors are included and concludes that women still have not been well integrated into the literature industry (1992b, 365). "As representatives of a nation," Hahn observes, "in anthologies of so-called national literature, women authors are barely present anymore" (1992b, 366). Hahn's choice words for the relegation of women authors to a general category of "others" or "miscellaneous" (*Sonstige*) ironically points to the construction of a Western canon in terms of outsiders and insiders (1992b, 366).

Since Hahn herself relied on previously published work rather than new translations and undiscovered texts, this predetermined, potentially Euro-centric canon presents a difficulty for *Stechäpfel.* "It would be revealing, for example, to have an international project in which specialists would select, and if possible translate the works of women authors they consider important," Hahn observes, pointing to Rilke's translations of Elizabeth Barrett Browning's *Sonnets from the Portuguese* as a shining example of how one poet's work can become part of the canon (1992b, 367). Hahn may well also have another example in mind with this statement, namely Hans Magnus Enzensberger's influential anthology *Museum der modernen Poesie.*

International in scope, like *Stechäpfel, Museum der modernen Poesie* was a uniquely successful project built on brilliant translations, many by contemporary poets. Enzensberger had invited readers to think of this "museum" as a workplace, an "annex to the atelier" that would prompt poets and readers alike to reenvision poetry (1960b, 766–67). Coming at a time when German poetry was open to transformation, *Museum der modernen Poesie* had a broad impact on its intended audience of poets. Hahn is well aware of this work. In fact, when she seeks to define her own project through references to Hugo Friedrich's *Die Struktur der modernen Lyrik,* she asserts the authority of her collection in the same way Enzensberger did in *Museum der modernen Poesie,* by making Friedrich's arguments central to the aesthetic paradigm of *Stechäpfel.*

Friedrich had charted the development of modern poetry through Charles Baudelaire, Arthur Rimbaud, and Mallarmé to the contemporary avant-garde, emphasizing the dissonant qualities of their work (1956). Following Friedrich's oppositional categories, Enzensberger provided readers with a means for interpreting modern poetry by cataloging the types of dissonances Friedrich had found and implying that the antagonism toward tradition that they express defined aesthetic quality. Hahn takes this argument in a different direction. A Germanist by academic training, Hahn in *Stechäpfel* likewise traces the development of modern poetry to French symbolists and cites Friedrich's seminal study. Writing at a very different historical juncture when such categorical thinking seems less persuasive, however, she departs from the model provided by Friedrich and Enzensberger and rejects their oppositional explanation of the lyric genre. Considering the transformation of poetry that began with the advent of modernism in the mid-nineteenth century, Hahn asks rhetorically what this change meant for the writing of women. "Certainly," she concludes, "not in break with the poetic tradition. One can only destroy what one possesses, and women had been barred for hundreds of years from access to education" (1992b, 371). Women poets, in this view, must envision entirely different modes of expression in order to be heard.

As an anthologist, Hahn addresses this problem both by organizing the text thematically and focusing her afterword on problems of translation. Regarding translation, Hahn finds the loss of linguistic richness to be a major problem for anthologists and points out that translated poems often provide a crude rendering of images and thoughts, justifying her preference for interlinear versions (1992b, 367). In grounding her decision to organize texts thematically,[15] Hahn reasons that chronological presentation simply results in a mishmash of different voices (1992b, 368), following the structure of Enzensberger's *Museum der modernen Poesie* in making this choice.

The aesthetic positions represented by these editorial decisions make *Stechäpfel* more of a poet's canon than is Borchers's anthology. Indeed, while Hahn demonstrates depth in her cognizance of discussions of feminine writing by Cixous, Irigaray, Bovenschen, and other theorists, she is more strongly drawn to authors' accounts of women's writing (especially those of Virginia Woolf and Adrienne Rich) than to theory. This attraction turns Hahn's attention to celebrating the transformative power of poetic language, in a segment that weaves in the previously discussed engagement with the poetics of Adrienne Rich.

What interests me about the shift in argument that occurs through the insertion of other writers' perspectives is Hahn's oscillation between moments of asserting collective unity (or at least shared experience) among women poets and of questioning their purportedly "universal" value. On the one hand, Hahn imagines a transnational sweep of women's poetry across centuries—from Sappho to Adrienne Rich, Louise Labé to Alta, and Li Tsching-dschau to Ingeborg Bachmann (1992b, 369). From this continuum Hahn envisions that progressive changes in human rights and emancipation will arise that will alter gender relations. Yet her specific examples, based in her own writerly praxis, focus on individual subjectivity. "If writing also means discovering one's self, making one's self visible," Hahn observes, "then this anthology can also be read as a growing interrogation of women's images and modes of behavior" (1992b, 369). Applauding self-discovery, Hahn thus ultimately identifies writing not as a utopian project, but as an exercise with concrete, real-life goals. "When women write, it is a search for identity, for a place in the world, not for a new—this time feminine—ideal *I* in utopia" (1992b, 369). Similarly, when justifying the thematic organization of poems, she explains to readers that it is intended to extend openness. Non-closure, Hahn argues, is a fundamental principle of art that she finds expressed in the Hungarian poet Agnes Nagy's admonishment "Dennoch schauen!" or "And yet, look!" (1992b, 370). This "and yet," Hahn explains, "is the basis for every work of art, every poem, even for those that express nothing but doubt, hate, pain, 'for every work made is a refusal of ruin and destruction'" (1992b, 370).

Though Hahn attributes the end of the sentence (and the concept of *Dennoch*) to Gottfried Benn, her references to him and repeated citation of Hugo Friedrich's *Struktur der modernen Lyrik* and Peter Bürger's *Theorie der Avant-Garde* (*Theory of the Avant-Garde*) seem quite calculated to position *Stechäpfel* for the reception accorded *Museum der modernen Poesie*. Hahn's conception of poetry, however, is in fact better aligned with that of Hilde Domin, who, it will be remembered, offered her own conception of "*Dennoch*" to describe the ineffable power of poetry. In *Stechäpfel* Hahn, too, emphasizes the emancipatory power of art or *befreiender Impuls* and rejects the view that poetry is *l'art pour l'art*, insisting instead on its communicative motivation (1992b, 371–74). Moreover, she finds that dialogic impulse strongly connected to real experience, concluding that "usually the communicative and poetic possibilities of language permeate each other, the lyrical reality remains bound to experienced reality" (1992b, 371). Foregrounding the dynamics of power that constrain women writers, Hahn, like Domin, insists that art operates in a universal space, is gender-neutral, and makes *Spiel* (play) central to its creation and reception (1992b, 373–75).

To explain that the diversity of forms and perspectives in *Stechäpfel* reflects the broad range of human experience that underlies the collection, Hahn devotes considerable attention to the subject of love poetry and poetry of relationships.[16] Echoing Domin, Marcuse, and Enzensberger's writings on the erotics of art (which, as we have seen, offered an alternate conception of poetry in the 1960s), Hahn informs her readers that a sense of *jouissance* is well represented in *Stechäpfel* (1992b, 377). Furthermore, she connects this sensuality with a new self-confidence in the desire for communication, "a communication that comes from the consciousness of being everything and complete, of possession of oneself in beauty and in pleasure" (1992b, 379). Hahn herself is bold in assuming what Georgina Paul terms in an analysis of younger German women poets "an overtly dramatized femininity, which both displays and contravenes its habitual silencing in the public sphere" (Paul 2007, 434).

Searching for a way to explain the history of women's writing and the broad parameters of *Stechäpfel,* Hahn launches into a declaration that women writers, regardless of geographical location or societal status, have similar experiences (1992b, 380). Ultimately, Hahn finds closure for her arguments by appealing to the commonalities among women writers. Looking back to Adrienne Rich's essay "When We Dead Awaken" and its comments about the struggles of Virginia Woolf and other women authors, Hahn (like Göbelsmann) observes that the years since Rich's publication have perhaps dimmed awareness of their difficulties:

> Many women authors, many women readers may have forgotten their "labor pains," many never felt them, many still have them ahead. But if writing means making oneself visible, then the process

of woman's becoming visible is in full swing. Not only in literature
and art, but in all areas of social life. (1992b, 387)

Strikingly, Hahn fears that feminism's contributions will be forgotten
as women become full participants in all arenas—social, political, and
cultural, "and in anthologies" (1992b, 388). This dramatic rhetorical gesture, and the altered literary environment that stands behind it, help set
the stage for the portrayal of women's poetry mediated in *Frauen dichten
anders*, edited by Marcel Reich-Ranicki.

Frauen dichten anders presents 181 poems together with short interpretations (two to four pages in length). Its very presentation seductively
invites spectators. A creamy white dust jacket sets off the sensuous white-
on-black illustration of a woman with long, flowing hair and an arm
bracelet by Henri Matisse (*Pasiphaé*, 1944). Red lettering on the spine and
front cover echoes the red binding of the book and matches a bound-in
red ribbon that offers a convenient bookmark for readers. The collection originated as columns in the *Frankfurter Allgemeine Zeitung*, and
the inside jacket confirms the reputability of the work of 54 authors and
91 interpreters who are themselves writers, critics, historians, journalists,
and poets. Acknowledging that no interpretation is exhaustive, it claims
that many of the ones included in this volume represent a particularly for-
tunate combination of "scientific analysis, literary opinion and personal
creed" (1998, 26). It also advertises the ability of each poem to impact
readers through "the feelings and the thoughts that aroused it and that it
arouses" (1998, 26). With much bravado it promises stimulating reading
intended to popularize women's poetry. Still, this hefty, chronologically
arranged anthology offers only a small expansion of canon.

Reich-Ranicki's introduction often stumbles over stereotypes in its
attempts to define *Frauenliteratur* (women's literature). Asking whether
it is literature about women (like Gustave Flaubert's *Madame Bovary* or
Henrik Ibsen's *Hedda Gabler*), Reich-Ranicki decides that the number of
such works is so extensive "that it is unnecessary—whether women like
these works or not—to devise a special category for them" (1998, 19).
Summarily setting this definition aside, he wonders rhetorically whether
women's literature is work written for women readers, then dismisses this
categorization on the basis of quality, commenting, "There may be such
books, but they belong rather to the realm of popular literature" (1998,
19). Casually he adds that he has never actually met an author of either
gender who writes for only one audience, thus he reasons that *Frauenliteratur* is any text written by a woman author, a notion oddly followed by
dismissive remarks about feminine writing (1998, 19).

Reich-Ranicki initiates this discussion by dismissively referring to Ruth Klüger's *Frauen lesen anders* (*Women Read Differently,* 1996). Yet his own analysis proceeds in a disappointingly literal way, taking Romeo and Juliet as examples of the different genders' temperaments and extrapolating that difference to writing (1998, 20):

> Because women feel and grasp the world differently, they must also read differently than men, and take in literature differently than they do. If women read differently, however, then it is self-evident that they also write differently. That is more or less true for all genres of literature, but probably is the most true for the one that is the most personal and intimate—the lyric. (1998, 20)

This assertion that the lyric genre is the site where feminine writing possibly finds clearest expression culminates in the rather trivializing comment that "Kurz und gut: Frauen dichten anders," "short and sweet: women write differently" (1998, 20).[17]

Happily for readers, Reich-Ranicki at this point launches into an excursus on women writers in relation to German literary history that proves more rewarding. Adopting a revisionist perspective and citing even the Bible (specifically Paul's letters to the Corinthians prescribing a subordinate role for women), Reich-Ranicki recognizes social constraints on their productivity. He maintains that although literature is not a masculine domain per se, it had been dominated by men until the eighteenth century (1998, 21). In social advances during the Enlightenment and French Revolution he finds support for the emergence of writers like Caroline von Schelling, Bettina von Arnim, Rahel Varnhagen, and Dorothea Schlegel. Their social world becomes a point of contrast for Reich-Ranicki's presentation of Annette von Droste-Hülshoff as "eine einsame Poetin" (a lonely poetess), whom he sees as an isolated exception of preeminent stature in the literary canon (1998, 23).

Here we can begin to observe the ways in which stereotypes persist in such nonacademic discussions of canon, precisely because they make an ostensibly compelling narrative. Turning to the early twentieth century, Reich-Ranicki recounts the slow transformation of the German literary climate. The expressionist Else Lasker-Schüler is represented as a poetess as "highly exalted as she was extravagant" (1998, 24), yet Reich-Ranicki comments, "It is not intellectual qualities, therefore, that stand in the foreground of her [Lasker-Schüler's] books, but rather the emotional, the temperament. And their foundation is usually the metaphysical world view" (1998, 24). He therefore concludes that all women's writing is extravagant, emotional, cryptic, and metaphysical. Even Ingeborg Bachmann, termed "the lyrical spokesperson of her entire generation," is subsumed under this framework, with her work termed "cerebral" (1998, 25). The "shy" Ilse Aichinger is contrasted with the "solidly grounded" Huch and Kaschnitz; Hilde Domin's tendency toward "Widerspruch und Widerstand" (contradiction and resistance) is juxtaposed against the pan-eroticism built on "Selbstbekenntnis und Selbstdarstellung" (self-confession and self-portrayal) found in the work of Sarah Kirsch (1998, 25). It seems rather ironic, therefore, that Reich-Ranicki concludes, "One should be wary of pinning the poetry of women down to certain types and tendencies" (1998, 25).

Reich-Ranicki is more discerning in advocating divergent interpretations of women's poetry.[18] Still, readers might wonder whether the anthology's construction actually advances new literary tastes. Set off individually on pages, the poems in *Frauen dichten anders* are a typographical stand for individuality, but they in fact occupy less space than the interpretations and, curiously, of the 91 interpreters, only 19 are women. The back matter of the book also reinforces an implied intellectual hierarchy in which interpreters seem to have the upper hand over poets, for it presents paragraph-length biographies for the interpreters while only the biographical dates and publications appear for the poets.

The interpretations, however, for the most part are more vigilant about avoiding pat categorizations of women's poetry and they approach the texts from fresh perspectives, in part because the brevity of the essays forces the interpreters to break with dispassionate academic discourse to keep the original *Frankfurter Allgemeine Zeitung* readership in mind. Many are voiced rhetorically, thus conveying a heightened sense of the immediacy of the reading and the impression of the interpreters' own personal investment in an encounter with the text. In terms of canon construction, the first and last interpretations in *Frauen dichten anders* clearly establish the collection's revisionist aspirations. Peter Wapnewski, writing in the opening text about the anonymous poem "Dû bist mîn" ("You Are Mine"), ably steers readers away from the assumption that women's poetry is artlessly sentimental by pointing to examples in the text of constructed subjectivity and emphasizing new scholarly perspectives on the ways in which seemingly marginal texts like this poem function as practice pieces for learning artistic style (Reich-Ranicki 1998, 30–31). At the end, Hermann Kurzke in his concluding commentary on Ulrike Draesner's "Schnabelheim" (a word that in this poem refers to the pelican's beak and home) depicts the poet as rummaging through language: "What others no longer need, the poet loves," Kurzke explains

(Reich-Ranicki 1998, 824). Draesner, he finds, innovatively "wants to make the knowledge hidden in language to speak" (Reich-Ranicki 1998, 824). Women's poetry is thus recognized to exhibit keen awareness of linguistic conventions. Wapnewski, Kurzke, and other interpreters reveal how texts in this collection engage in semiotic play and willful manipulation of language, arguing that while on the surface the poems may seem to conform to tradition, they in fact break—sometimes violently—with that tradition, crossing over into such textual modes as imitation, parody, and montage.

Throughout the anthology the interpreters sophisticatedly explain how readers can more productively understand poetry in relation to the authors' personal history. Frequently these readings indicate where the interpretive horizon needs to be expanded for women's poetry, and the individual pieces operate in counterpoint with each other in this effort. One of the major threads of the anthology is the work of Jewish poets. Nobel Prize winner Nelly Sachs is described by Ruth Klüger as an author who wrote poems about the victims of the Holocaust and about illness and the anticipation of death (Reich-Ranicki 1998, 218). Mentioning Adorno's famous proclamation about poetry after Auschwitz, Klüger hopefully asks whether the fundamental qualities of the lyric genre transcend history: "What is art? I suspect: not deep meaning and whispering secret. Art is play" (Reich-Ranicki 1998, 336).

Similarly, Friedrich Christian Delius reads in Else Lasker-Schüler's love poem "Hingabe" ("Devotion") the possibility of "what a great poet can make out of a trivial situation" (Reich-Ranicki 1998, 168). Twice repeating the term *Originalität* (originality), Delius emphasizes that Lasker-Schüler's particular originality "lies in [her] shyness, in renunciation of any wonder-filled chumminess with the cosmos" (Reich-Ranicki 1998, 168). This assessment is strikingly complemented by Klüger's assertion in a separate reading that "the lyric poet Else Lasker-Schüler should be taken seriously precisely where she costumes herself as the master of the unserious" (Reich-Ranicki 1998, 178).

Gertrud Kolmar's poems are powerfully connected by interpreters with her biographical experience as well. Jürgen Theobaldy confesses in his piece on Kolmar's "Abschied" ("Farewell"): "It is difficult for me to read the poem as if I knew nothing about the fate of its author" (Reich-Ranicki 1998, 231). This sense of foreboding is reinforced by Klaus Jeziorkowski's sense of loss: "Her poems have not become for us much more than ash" (Reich-Ranicki 1998, 246). However, he reaches the conclusion that "such a poem transcends the Jewish horizon" (Reich-Ranicki 1998, 247), a critical gesture that removes Kolmar's work from a position of marginalization. Likewise emphasizing universal qualities, Ulla Hahn's discussion of "Die Verlassene" ("The One Left Behind") concludes that while Kolmar's love poems therapeutically derive from her private life, they maintain a distance between poetry and experience (Reich-Ranicki 1998, 258).

A second important thematic strand in the anthology has to do with the nature of women's writing. Many of the interpreters emphasize the effect of its intentional construction, particularly in the case of Ingeborg Bachmann, to whom the anthology is in fact dedicated. In a perceptive interpretation of Bachmann's "Alle Tage" ("Every Day"), Thomas Anz argues that "the author wrote repeatedly from behind the masks of 'male' perspectives and manners of speech" (Reich-Ranicki 1998, 485). Writing about "Aria I," Helmut Koopmann applauds the opacity of Bachmann's verse: "There were times when one expected from a poem instruction and enlightenment, knowledge, insight. From this poem by Ingeborg Bachmann one cannot even demand comprehensibility" (Reich-Ranicki 1998, 500). Crypticness is the very essence of what the poem is about, Koopmann concludes, and to be valued for its own sake.

The two postwar poets with the largest representation apart from Bachmann in *Frauen dichten anders,* Sarah Kirsch and Ulla Hahn, receive perspicacious treatment from interpreters who read their texts as intentional constructions rather than naive emotional outpourings. Hahn self-reflexively emphasizes her own visceral response to reading Kirsch's "Bei den Stiefmütterchen" ("By the Pansies"), commenting that the poem "gripped me like no other" (Reich-Ranicki 1998, 628). Then Hahn seeks to instruct the reader who might be tempted to interpret the poem as personal expression by extricating it from private context. "Anyone who can love so selflessly," Hahn comments, "must be very self-aware" (Reich-Ranicki 1998, 629). Klüger's essay on "Die Verdammung" ("The Damnation") foregrounds Kirsch's radical use of enjambment to produce intentional ambiguities by opening up multiple syntactical linkages within a poem (Reich-Ranicki 1998, 646).[19]

The procedures for valuing Hahn's work, too, emphasize their artistry. Walter Hinderer terms one of her texts a *Kunststück* (magic trick) made of "calculated form and erotic content" (Reich-Ranicki 1998, 732). In an interpretation titled "Dissonanz ist schön" ("Dissonance Is Beautiful"), Werner Ross credits Hahn's calculated audacity with earning her a place in the impressive (*imponierend*) pantheon of women poets that includes Sachs, Kaschnitz, Ausländer, and Bachmann (Reich-Ranicki 1998, 744). Hermann Burger sees Hahn as making the task of the poem (*Aufgabe des Gedichts*) the project of ferreting out archaic relations and opposing "the insult of the moderated life" (Reich-Ranicki 1998, 750). Peter Demetz discovers Hahn's "hidden irony" (Reich-Ranicki 1998, 756), and Karl Krolow, a venerable practitioner of rhymed verse himself, declares that "Der neue Reim" (the new rhyme or formalism) represented by Hahn's work departs radically from traditional rhyme conventions by being more calculated (Reich-Ranicki 1998, 785).

On balance, Reich-Ranicki's intention of providing divergent readings of women's poetry in *Frauen dichten anders* is well sustained by the interpretive essays. The eclectic backgrounds of the interpreters contribute to this result, and the insights of fellow poets like Delius, Theobaldy, and Hahn are particularly instructive in the way they negotiate the complex, reciprocal relationships of readers and texts. The perspective of the poet-interpreters is also largely responsible for advancing an understanding of women's writing that is focused on language construction, rather than stereotypical qualities like empathy. "In the lyric genre greatness can also mean: a poet, a poetess has expanded our vocabulary," Peter Maiwald writes about Christa Reinig (Reich-Ranicki 1998, 586). Collectively the interpretations in *Frauen dichten anders* argue that women poets have accomplished just such transformations of the lyric genre.

The Problem with Anthologies

What do these anthologies tell us about the situation of poetry and of women authors? Guillory rightly cautions that "it is always a mistake . . . to read the history of canon formation as though individual acts of revaluation had specific and determinable ideological effects" (1993, 135). Indeed, the discourses of consensus, legitimation, and experimentation found in the anthologies we have considered do not lift the tentative self-assertions of individual authors to an apotheosis in canon. Instead, it becomes clear by comparing the six collections that the postwar German cultural environment has been continually reshaped by broad competing ideological and aesthetic demands.

Largely excluded from nonspecialized anthologies, women authors became emblematic of the institutionally precarious situation of poetry. By the 1990s anthologies began to serve a particularly crucial culture function, moving German women's poetry away from the identity politics of the 1980s and into an aesthetic space that needs to be reclaimed by the lyric genre. Their rather predictable canon tends to confirm that the commercial machinery of cultural production is not especially adaptable to innovative works, yet to their credit they use the marginalized status of women poets to illuminate the paradoxical cultural status of the lyric genre in general. Pragmatically speaking, the "comprehensive" anthologies edited by Borchers, Hahn, and Reich-Ranicki define only a slender common canon, particularly when they are measured against an enterprise like Raoul Schrott's expansive collection *Die Erfundung der Poesie: Gedichte aus den ersten viertausend Jahren* (1997). Furthermore, though much admired, the "canonical" women authors they promote remain isolated as creative artists. Unlike Gottfried Benn or Bertolt Brecht (pillars of the postwar poetic revival), they are not represented, nor do they appeal, as figures suitable for imitation.[20]

Rather than producing a radically new canon, these anthologies work toward defining qualities that make texts worthy of being considered canonical. They idealize poetry—poetry by women—in rather traditional terms, as intense, personal, brief, and sometimes sentimental or nostalgic. Because this aesthetic agenda is in many respects conservative, and despite the anthologists' claims, they are not really engaged in rediscovering overlooked authors, styles, or works. What they do accomplish is a lyricization of poetry that restores the intimate reader engagement with texts, making poetry once again an aesthetic experience. In the case of *Frauen dichten anders,* as we have seen, even the lush publication format of anthologies mediates this transformation of the experience of reading.

The rhetoric of shyness, masking of voice, and withdrawal depicted by the anthologies as characteristic of women's poetry also model postures that demand an intimacy with texts, forcing the more individual appreciation of qualities of poems and confirming Guillory's hypothesis that "the typical valorization of the noncanonical author's experience as a marginalized social identity necessarily reasserts the transparency of the text to the experience it represents" (1993, 10). Best understood as individual works, as the anthologists argue, the poems themselves increasingly become signifiers of the marginalization of poetic discourse in the private sphere. If the new, more intimate way of reading that the anthologies promote does not resolve the problematical aspects of subjective expression associated with the lyric genre, it does open new discussions. To contradict the perception that women's poetry is merely personal, the editors of the anthologies considered here continually need to point out that all literary representation is constructed artifice. Yet they also paradoxically insist that feminine writing is rooted in "experience" and "subjectivity," drawing on categories of poetry readily aligned with emotion and "authenticity," such as love poetry represents, even as they claim that subjectivity transcends the purely personal.

Apart from anthologies, poetry is rarely found on the shelves of commercial bookstores today, though in Germany it does regularly appear in a special section of the *Frankfurter Allgemeine Zeitung*. This lack of market presence has produced an inverse relation between the proliferation of German poetry anthologies at the end of the twentieth century and the exclusion of poetry. That equation, however, guarantees that the lyric genre retains its special aesthetic status as art artifact ostensibly appreciated only by the select few. For women writers, this absence of public outlets and literary models is not trivial. As Ursula Krechel observes in *In Zukunft schreiben*, there is an important relationship between possessing an inner library of models (*innere Bibliothek*) and developing the capacity to write. Reflecting on how to teach creative writing, she remarks on the critical connection between literacy and writerly thinking:

> Anyone who teaches writing cannot assume that students are widely read. If one insisted on that, reading would become an agony from the beginning. You can't sue for literacy any more than you can sue for spontaneity. It is the result of the seeking and finding of historicity and the present. But if one is not well read, writing atrophies in the narrowness of the authentic and what one has experienced oneself, made oneself, knitted oneself. (2003, 107)

In Krechel's view, reading and internalizing language are an important part of writing; experience alone does not suffice. Canon is in the end essential, but not necessarily for reasons given by literary historians, at least from the perspective of writers.

One of the most intractable dilemmas of postwar German culture is the question of the extent to which contemporary poetry in dialogue with canon can be used to define social as well as individual identity. At the heart of this quandary lies the debate about the relationship of contemporary culture to the past. In his essay "Valéry Proust Museum," Theodor W. Adorno described two attitudes toward cultural artifacts. For artists like Valéry, museums are dead space where art has lost its vital association with life and thus, according to Adorno, a working atelier where the past is destroyed becomes preferable (1955b, 222). Proust, adopting a much more passive stance vis-à-vis the museum, relishes art as conducive to the contemplation and reflection of the observer (1955b, 223–24).

The comprehensive anthologies of women's poetry that we have considered seem to mesh with this latter conservative attitude, presenting an aesthetic space respectful of established canon. But, to the extent they seek to redefine readership, these anthologies claim a generative function, both for poets and for readers, that aligns them subtly with the model of Valéry. In particular, by importing concepts from Virginia Woolf and Adrienne Rich to provide affirmation of women's writing, the more important anthologies seek to replace discourses associated with the historical avant-garde with a more refined subjective poetics, however individual those poetics might be. Although this strategy shifts attention away from feminist ideology, it arguably makes possible the reassertion of a poet-generated poetics, one more firmly grounded in individual subjectivity.

Anthologies of German women's poetry began to thrive in a literary environment marked by the marginalization of poetry itself, and in recent decades they have become a vehicle for representing a diversity of styles and ways of reading. Remarking that the most dynamic poetry today is not an expression of feeling but rather rhetorical energy, Harald Hartung proclaims in 1999, "The lyric genre is dead, but the poem lives" (1999, 330). With these changes has come a greater skepticism about theory. "You should not," poet Brigitte Oleschinski observes, "force any poem, to anything. You should not mislead it into fitting into your intellectual inclination. You should neither burden it with your diagnoses of the time nor with your aesthetics, nor your politics. You should not place it on a stage" (1999, 390). The anthologies of German women's poetry that evolved out of consciousness-raising projects in the 1980s were among the first to participate in such a refusal—of the modernist paradigm, stipulative aesthetics, and premature assumptions about women's commonalities. From this surprising maneuver what is gained is the possibility of an intimate appreciation of poetic texts and—for poets—a new relationship with readers.

Conclusion

✦

Observations on Belatedness

Discussions of modernism, the avant-garde, and postmodernism have found it persistently difficult to engage in a meaningful treatment of both feminism and the lyric genre, yet the aesthetic positions and ideological contradictions surrounding twentieth-century artistic movements become sharply apparent when viewed through the double lens of feminine writing and poetry. Nowhere are those contradictions more evident than in postwar Germany, where the intellectual environment was shaped by the concentrated engagement with international modernism that ensued with the end to cultural isolation in 1945 following the political collapse of the Third Reich. In this singular context, such fundamental literary matters as representation, authorial identity, reader practices, canon, and connoisseurship became inextricably bound up in broad cultural debates about the political, social, and cultural value of literature.

German women's poetry and poetics have dynamically related to this climate in large part through practices of textual rewriting, notional clusters, and performativity, which we have seen evidenced in the work of Domin, Hahn, and Krechel. Beyond the work of individual poets, poetological theory (Hamburger) and institutional structures (anthologies) have powerfully conditioned assumptions about the status of the lyric genre as well. As I have argued, during the postwar period there is a pronounced evolution toward the construction of a new reader/poet relationship that reflects underlying feminist assumptions and an awareness of the aesthetic potential of constructed performativity. Further manifestation of this development, I believe, can be seen by examining the occurrence of the trope of belatedness and, on a related poetological level, by contrasting Hamburger's notion of the lyrical *I* with Butler's concept of performativity.

In *The Logic of Literature,* as will be remembered, we encountered Hamburger's paradoxical definition of the lyric genre as a mode of expression rooted in subjective experience, which persuasively instructed readers to distinguish between the empirical *I* of the biographical poet and the constructed lyrical *I* of the writer (1973, 286). Coupled with this forceful assertion of objectivity in the exercise of aesthetic perception was, however, Hamburger's admission that readers cannot, ultimately, untangle these two identities (1973, 272). At its heart, this theoretical conundrum hinges on the assumption that poetry is fundamentally about the possibility of "genuine" individual subjective expressivity, for if it were not, we would have no access to the kind of Platonic essence that Hamburger implies is embodied in the poem. Without this structure of expressivity (which assumes an empathetic relationship between poet and audience), we would not need to distinguish these perspectives. Yet Hamburger's resolution of the paradox points in the direction of a deeper philosophical problem, too, for the fact that she is willing to allow the two possibilities to coexist in the aesthetic realm still constitutes an idealization of the lyric genre as a form having mystical properties that cannot be rationally obtained.

Leaving aside the many factors of historical-scholarly dispositions that account for the differences between Hamburger's position and Butler's concept of performativity, I want to focus on what it means to think of poetry as performative rather than expressive. Assuming a philosophical perspective, Butler's concern lies chiefly with the constraints posed by assuming a common epistemological standpoint in feminist debates:

> My suggestion is that the presumed universality and unity of the subject of feminism is effectively undermined by the constraints of the representational discourse in which it functions. Indeed, the premature insistence on a stable subject of feminism, understood as a seamless category of women, inevitably generates multiple refusals to accept the category. (Butler 1990, 4)

Certainly, since performativity poses one possible solution to these difficulties, we can understand its potential attraction to postwar German women poets, who, as we have seen, in any case have highly variable ways of relating to feminist commitments.[1] But if we take seriously Butler's assertion that the gendered self is constituted by "repeated acts that seek to approximate the ideal of a substantial ground of identity, but which, in their occasional *dis*continuity, reveal the temporal and contingent groundlessness of this 'ground'" (1990, 141), a new understanding of the lyric genre must also be found, for an altered dynamic of subjectivity is assumed.

This difference is a fine distinction, as we find confirmed in Butler, for in her words, "If gender attributes, however, are not expressive but performative, then these attributes effectively constitute the identity they are said to express or reveal" (1990, 141). Even though that change potentially alters the idealization of the lyric genre that concerns us here, Butler's philosophy insists that such developments are ultimately positive, since "construction is not opposed to agency; it is the necessary scene of agency, the very terms in which agency is articulated and becomes culturally intelligible" (1990, 147). Indeed, Butler finds evidence of the ways in which the consistency of laws or identity can be built incrementally through repeated acts in the construction of belatedness. In belatedness, which exists as a performed construction, Butler asserts that we encounter the fact that "the story of origins is thus a strategic tactic within a narrative that, by telling a single authoritative account about an irrecoverable past, makes the constitution of the law appear as a historical inevitability" (1990, 36).

Such an insight, I think, profoundly calls into question the ways in which we have assumed that the lyric genre operates. It reinforces DuPlessis's contention that poetry needs to be carefully read with an eye to tropes as they work as notional clusters (1994, 71–72), for the way in which a trope like belatedness performs now reveals in a different way the patterns of influence and flux of modes of consciousness within the lyric genre. Using this lens, we now find that belatedness as it saturates poetry calls to be interpreted as both an assumed nostalgia and as the symptom of a critical attitude involved when authors look to past literary models. Since it is impossible to read far in German women's poetry without encountering sentiments of belatedness repeatedly, it becomes all the more important to attend to the nuances of meanings behind the apparently emotive surface of this trope. Belatedness is a discursive formulation widely embedded in the work of women poets, whether expressed purely as longing for another time or as a coming-to-terms with the heavy influence of traditional canon. It surfaces in the abundance of poems that depict the woman poet finding language. Masked as naive reflection or artless ramblings, it still gives voice to the attenuated relations of poet, language, and culture.

Belatedness is certainly not a unified concept, nor is it confined to the lyric genre. For Michael G. Levine, writing about the poetics of Paul Celan, the term references the word *Nachträglichkeit,* used by Sigmund Freud as well as by Jacques Lacan to explain "psychical temporality and causality," but it also indicates the reflexivity of poetic contemplation that shapes Celan's poems (2004, 151–52). Analyzing modern fiction, Christopher Ames, on the other hand, concludes that belatedness operates as self-dramatizing artistic crisis, literary anxiety about tradition, or the transformative drive for newness at a time when literature is para-doxically becoming increasingly marginal for intellectual culture (1992, 39–43).[2] Indeed, belatedness is one form for negotiating the complexi-ties of influence recognized in Harold Bloom's *The Anxiety of Influence* or Judith Ryan's reading of the poetry of Rainer Maria Rilke (Bloom 1973; Ryan 1992), as when a poet evokes a distant voice to forge more powerful language. In these interpretations we can see a range of critical perspectives on it—some that read belatedness primarily as a matter of expression (in the case of Celan) and others that attend more closely to its larger signifying/performative function (compare Ames 1992; Bloom 1973; Ryan 1992).

In postwar German women's poetry, where we frequently find invo-cations of reflections on the past and intense childhood perspectives, belatedness can potentially signal different things. It is clear that since poems individually exhibit a range of expressive and performative quali-ties (and variable balance between the two would be most apparent in a close reading of a specific text), it is theoretically possible to read belat-edness as primarily a mode of expression. However, by tracing the trope of belatedness thematically across a number of poems, we observe the writerly effort needed to gain control over poetic voice, which appears when the trope of belatedness is deployed as a vehicle to explore the ori-gins of poetic language. In many instances, obvious political and social tensions mingle with agonizing subjective reflection and argue for a read-ing of the texts as response to history. Thus, Ingeborg Bachmann writes from inside the logic of Cold War antagonisms in "Hinter der Wand" ("Behind the Wall"), "I am the child of the great world fear, / that hangs in the peace and the joy" (Reich-Ranicki 1998a, 527). Likewise, Hilde Domin in "Herbzeitlosen" ("Colchichum") contemplates the meaning of her wartime exile from Germany and the loss of her own personal history, writing that "the door post is burned, / on which the years of childhood / were recorded / centimeter by centimeter" (Domin 1987c, 17). In the same way, Ilse Tielsch in "Ich gehe durch die alte Schule" ("I Walk Through the Old School") revisits a building with broken windows where doors are slammed by the wind, an institution whose director com-mitted suicide. Entering the principal's office, the poet allows the reader to experience her dramatic break with the past when she depicts altering grade reports. "I dip the pen into red ink, / cross out a life / and in my best calligraphy write / under it / Not satisfactory," Tielsch concludes (Melin 1999, 175). With harmonic resonance, the pain of loss from war and the Holocaust echoes in these poems as the sense of a profound longing for the irremediable past, that is, as belatedness.

In other instances, the connection between childhood and writerly creativity opens up a more personal space in which sensory impressions are allowed to mix with magic. Thus, Christine Busta in "Biblische Kindheit" ("Biblical Childhood") connects with the comforting presence conjured up by the name Habakkuk (in fact a brand name of a heater) in a time of scarcity.[3] Here the poet recalls that "Always bees around you buzzed / and your sack crammed with almonds, raisins, leaven / biscuits only baked in heaven" (Melin 1999, 117). Similarly, Rose Ausländer in "Alice in Wonderland" casts the lyrical *I* as an enchanted figure who is led off into a pine gorge. There, after drinking mushroom milk, she finds that "beetle small I scale a grass blade / Plainly the conversations of bee of bird ripple / my mother tongues" (Melin 1999, 157). In the poetic cycle "Death Valley," Sarah Kirsch transposes the lyrical *I* into an utterly strange landscape by describing her with language that makes her an Alice in Wonderland leading the way through an eerie Pompeii. After this maiden voyage over the Atlantic, the sequence safely returns the poet to home as Kirsch writes, "And later in Germany / She has forgotten the look behind / The mirrors, she would again lead / Her nice small life" (Melin 1999, 249).[4]

Such escapes from culture and society do not, however, always sooth, as Helga Novak reveals in "Ach, ich stand an der Quelle" ("Oh, I stood by the spring"). Here the poet, leaving a deep natural retreat, sinks ever deeper into a fox hole and brambles, as the poem rues sorrowfully, "oh I stood by the spring / and did not drink" (Melin 1999, 253). Novak's poem, which is strongly reminiscent of the sense of isolation voiced in Annette von Droste-Hülshoff's "Die Mergelgrube" ("The Marl-Pit") or "Der Knabe im Moor" ("The Lad on the Moor") and hence evocative of literary tradition, is painfully bereft of the consolation from nature derived by either Droste-Hülshoff or Kirsch. The profound source of renewal that the spring represents is lost to the poet.

Clearly, the way in which we experience these poems forces us to conceive of them in terms of subjective expression instantiated through the trope of belatedness, but the subtle temporal framing and shifts in perspective signal that performativity is at work in the texts as well. All these poets, I think, skillfully evoke belatedness in the interest of gaining *voice*. The uncanny conjunction between the unfolding of poetic language and the sensation of nostalgia, synesthesia, and reverie in the poems enhances the effect of the performance of finding words. Thus, Swiss author Erika Burkart in the collection *Ich lebe* (*I Live*, 1964) re-creates the magical years of childhood retrospectively, only to dramatically separate them from maturity as she brings the poem to closure with language. Deploying a complex synesthesia of visual, kinesthetic, audible, and tactile details,

Burkart evokes a childhood in which intense experience of the world surrounds the lyrical *I*. Burkart begins rhapsodically with the phrase "Als ich
ein Kind war" ("When I was a child"). However, she ends this expansive
reminiscence with a reversal, writing that when she lost childhood:

> die Erde sich drehte,
> die Herzen sich drehten,
> das Kreuz vom Baum,
> der Baum sich vom Wald,
> die Liebe sich trennte
> in ich du er sie,
> die Sonne im Kind,
> das Kind in der Sonne verschwand.

> the earth turned,
> hearts turned,
> the cross detached itself from the tree,
> the tree from the woods,
> and love separated
> into I you he she,
> the sun disappeared in the child,
> the child in the sun. (Melin 1999, 116–19)

With this gestural conclusion, the idyll is broken. No longer a child, the
poet loses unmediated relation to the natural world as her experience
fragments into disconnected objects and conflicting emotions, and is
parsed as parts of speech. Yet without precisely such mature and performed retrospective reflection, the poem could not express the subtlety
of human emotions and longings that it does.

One of the most frequently anthologized German poems by a woman
author, Else Lasker-Schüler's "Mein blaues Klavier" ("My Blue Piano"),
crystallizes the sense of belatedness in especially poignant terms, but
also exhibits the subtle crossover from expression to performativity that
occurs in poetry. Dating from 1936, the text opens in a lament over the
experience of exile:

> Ich habe zu Hause ein blaues Klavier
> Und kenne doch keine Note.

> Es steht im Dunkel der Kellertür,
> Seitdem die Welt verrohte. (Reich-Ranicki 1998, 187)

I have at home a blue piano
And yet do not know a note.

It stands in the dark of the cellar door,
Since the world turned brutal.

This blue toy piano, as Ruth Klüger incisively discerns in her interpretation of the poem for *Frauen dichten anders,* is a biographical detail that can be confirmed through a reference to the object in Lasker-Schüler's diary. The image has nonetheless been so transformed that, in Klüger's reading, readers find that "out of a childhood memory has evolved a symbolic instrument for the starry hands above and the rat feet below" (Klüger 1998, 188–89). Klüger persuasively interprets this instantiated childhood memory as the background for the loss felt by the poet when she was exiled during the Nazi era. Comparing the poem with Bertolt Brecht's famous poem "An die Nachgeborenen" ("To Those Born Later") (Brecht 1967, 724–25), and mindful of the special role that has been accorded poetry as the vehicle for making impassioned moral statements, Klüger concludes that "Mein blaues Klavier" is in fact a work best understood as delivered "from the speaker's podium to the public" (Klüger 1998, 190), despite its apparently private origins. While I agree with Klüger's reading, one unexplored aspect that troubles me about this poem, and many more by women poets after 1945, is the curious way the lyrical *I* is depicted as a child on the cusp of adulthood. The poet becomes a child again and is at the same time overwhelmed by a sense of having realized too late what that innocent and unreflected state embodied. This gesture is an instantiation of belatedness.

That sense of belatedness, which is frequently attached to the subjective position of the child, is used as a multifaceted trope by contemporary German women poets. Similar feelings of longing for the past ostensibly give rise as well to "Im Alten Land" ("In the Old Country") by Karin Kiwus, which appeared in *Von beiden Seiten der Gegenwart* (*From Both Sides of the Present,* 1976). Beginning nostalgically with a journey back in time, Kiwus writes that "not for a long time have I gone / as always in December / in the Old Country" (Melin 1999, 258–59). Drawn by this past, she concludes with a palpable sense of loss:

Die Nachmittage waren voll
selbstverständlicher Versprechen
der Himmel schneehell
wie eine Märzbecherwiese

und die Zukunft dahinter
ein sicherer Schimmer über dem Tau
so leicht und groß und griffbereit

The afternoons were full
of unquestioned promises
the skies snow bright
like a meadow of snowdrops
and the future beyond that
a lasting shimmer over the dew
so light and large and ready to be taken (Melin 1999, 260–61)

The empathetic response called forth in readers through these lines moves them to feel the deep longing that Kiwus strives to evoke. The phrase "lange bin ich nicht mehr" ("not for a long time") has the impact of a deep emotional sigh. The rich detail of the poem—the slow walk into the North German fields, the feel of a passing breeze, the fruity smells, and gentle touch—give the illusion that we move palpably into the space of the past. Yet as Hamburger argued in *The Logic of Literature,* the point of poetry is to create a work of art out of language that is its own reality, not simply to paint a picture of a fictional world. That, after all, is the purpose of performativity as well—to generate in another way a palpable aesthetic reality. The final lines of "Im alten Land" carry out this imperative by translating the description of the remembering lyrical *I* into a claim about the future. The closing scene is itself *griffbereit* (ready to be taken) in literal and metaphorical terms. Inscribing this world in text, the poem enacts just this capture.

"Whoever writes poems always has the ending before her/him," Ursula Krechel wrote in the concluding paragraph of *In Zukunft schreiben* (2003, 196). While poems intrinsically have the formal capacity for closure, poetry depends on the illusion of remaining open. Both expressiveness and performativity mediate that possibility, though in very different ways. Common to both is the concession that poetry is meant to be open—to further writing, to interpretation, and indeed to change in literature.

As I have argued, the discursive relationship between gender and the lyric genre has been, and continues to be, especially important for the evolution of German poetry through theory, poems, and anthologies. The trope of belatedness raises for our attention central problems of voice and subjectivity, for it intrinsically models the reader/poet relationship that Domin, Hahn, and Krechel sought by producing empathy. Through it (and other tropes), feminist commitments to literary transformation have been poetically translated into a way of reading and appreciating the lyric genre, a process that ultimately and continuously opens fresh creative possibilities. In this way troping as an essential poetic gesture confirms what Krechel aptly observes to be the generative capacity of writing: "The end is the imponderable condition after which the fortune of the beginning can follow anew" (2003, 196).

Introduction

1. The translations given are my own, unless otherwise cited. "Improved Version" appears in Charlotte Melin, ed., *German Poetry in Transition 1945–1990* (Hanover, N.H.: University Press of New England, 1999), 280–83.

2. It must be kept in mind that these theories did not necessarily align with practice. Although many younger writers who felt a kinship with Adorno's views resisted the artificial harmony projected by traditional verse during the postwar period, conventional poetry continued to speak with great success to the general public. Hillebrand describes how Rudolf Alexander Schröder read from church pulpits, with impressive results, and comments bemusedly that anyone who went to school after the war still can recall the names and poems of writers like Schröder, Hans Carossa, Georg von der Vring, Werner Bergengruen, Georg Britting, Reinhold Schneider, Gertrud von Le Fort, Ricarda Huch, Elisabeth Langgässer, and Ina Seidel. See Bruno Hillebrand, "Ende des Orphischen Gesangs—Gedanken zur Tonlosigkeit der deutschen Lyrik nach 1945," in *Traditionen der Lyrik,* ed. Wolfgang Düsing (Tübingen, Ger.: Max Niemeyer Verlag, 1997), 229.

3. Concerning trends and developments in German poetry after 1945 see Peter Rühmkorf, "Das lyrische Weltbild der Nachkriegsdeutschen," in *Bestandsaufnahme: Eine deutsche Bilanz 1962,* ed. Hans Werner Richter (Munich: Kurt Desch, 1962); Friedrich Wilhelm Wodtke, "Die Entwicklung der deutschen Lyrik seit 1945," in *Wissenschaftliches Jahrbuch der Philosophischen Fakultät der Universität* (Athens: Athinai, 1968); Peter Demetz, *Postwar German Literature: A Critical Introduction* (New York: Pegasus, 1970); Jürgen Theobaldy and Gustav Zürcher, *Veränderung der Lyrik: Über westdeutsche Gedichte seit 1965* (Munich: Edition Text und Kritik, 1976); Otto Knörrich, *Die deutsche Lyrik seit 1945* (Stuttgart, Ger.: Alfred Kröner, 1978); Jörg Drews, *Vom "Kahlschlag" zu "Movens": Über das langsame Auftauchen experimenteller Schreibweisen in der westdeutschen Literatur der fünfziger Jahre* (Munich: Edition Text und Kritik, 1980); Wolfgang Emmerich, *Kleine Literaturgeschichte der DDR* (Darmstadt, Ger.: Luchterhand, 1981); Hans Dieter Schäfer, "Zusammenhänge der deutschen Gegenwartslyrik," in *Deutsche Gegenwartsliteratur: Ausgangspositionen und aktuelle Entwicklungen,* ed. Manfred Durzak (Stuttgart, Ger.: Reclam, 1981); Horst Schumacher, "Entwicklungsphasen moderner deutscher Lyrik seit 1945," *Universitas* 36, no. 7 (1981); Klaus Weissenberger, ed., *Die deutsche Lyrik 1945–1975* (Düsseldorf: August Bagel, 1981); Judith Ryan, "'Your Life Jacket Is Under Your Skin': Reflections on German Poetry of the Seventies," *German Quarterly* 55, no. 3 (1982); Gerhart Pickerodt, "Zur

Lyrik der frühen achtziger Jahre," in *Tendenzen der deutschen Gegenwartslite-ratur,* ed. Thomas Koebner (Stuttgart, Ger.: Alfred Kröner, 1984); Peter Demetz, *After the Fires* (San Diego: Harcourt Brace Jovanovich, 1986); Uwe Wittstock, *Von der Stalinallee zum Prenzlauer Berg: Wege der DDR-Literatur 1949–1989* (Munich: Piper, 1989); and Hermann Korte, *Geschichte der deutschen Lyrik seit 1945* (Stuttgart, Ger.: Metzler, 1989).

4. On relational thinking, see Mary Field Belenky et al., *Women's Ways of Knowing* (New York: Basic Books, 1986).

5. In this sense the situation of postwar women authors has similarities to that of late-nineteenth-century authors, as discussed by Howe, who observes that "whereas the romantic movement valued qualities traditionally deemed feminine, such as the imaginative, the irrational and the poetic, this period, marked by a rapid expansion in women's writing, retreated from what it per-ceived as the dangerous formlessness of the romantic period, dwelling instead on the moral. The achievements of women writers, then, owed more to in-dividual talent than a general raising of female consciousness or to political developments." See Patricia Howe, "Women's Writing 1830–1890," in *A His-tory of Women's Writing in Germany, Austria and Switzerland,* ed. Jo Catling (Cambridge, Eng.: Cambridge University Press, 2000), 88.

6. Other factors that lie outside the consideration of the current analysis include the conflation of femininity with other stigmas (for example, labeling of Jews, immigrants, and other minorities), which can be linked to the problema-tized reception given to such authors as Rose Ausländer, Elisabeth Langgässer, and Nelly Sachs. For example, in one important postwar anthology, the work of women and Jewish authors is without explanation placed in a separate sec-tion. See Hans Bender, ed., *Widerspiel* (Munich: Hanser 1962). See further Gert Mattenklott, "Käte Hamburger im Kontext ihrer jüdischen Verhältnisse," in *Käte Hamburger: Zur Aktualität einer Klassikerin,* ed. Johanna Bossinade and Angelika Schaser (Göttingen, Ger.: Wallstein Verlag, 2003), 82.

7. The impact of these scholarly endeavors is noted by Puknus, who ap-plauds the move away from regarding qualities of subjectivity and emotion as compensatory, but he expresses reservations that definitions of feminine writ-ing run the risk of confining writing by women to a kind of neo-romantic irrationalism. See Heinz Puknus, ed., *Neue Literatur der Frauen* (Munich: C. H. Beck, 1980), 264.

8. Riley concludes that variability is a natural part of this process, arguing that "both a concentration on and a refusal of the identity of 'women' are es-sential to feminism. This its history makes plain." See Denise Riley, *"Am I That Name?": Feminism and the Category of "Women" in History* (Minneapolis: University of Minnesota Press, 1988), 1.

9. For accounts of "New Subjectivity" and discussion of the "death of literature," see Hans Magnus Enzensberger, "Gemeinplätze, die Neueste Lit-eratur Betreffend," *Kursbuch* 15 (1968); Charlotte Melin, *Poetic Maneuvers: Hans Magnus Enzensberger and the Lyric Genre* (Evanston, Ill.: Northwest-ern University Press, 2003), 97–100; Stuart Parkes, "Neue Subjektivität," in *Encyclopedia of German Literature,* ed. Matthias Konzett (Chicago: Fitzroy

Dearborn, 2000); and Cettina Rapisarda, "Women's Writing, 1968–1980," in *Post-War Women's Writing in German: Feminist Critical Approaches,* ed. Chris Weedon (Providence, R.I.: Berghahn, 1997).

10. Yet in the 1990s many younger women poets shied away from identification with feminist concerns, and indeed from theory in general.

11. It is worth noting that this work was published as part of the artists' program of the Deutscher Akademischer Austauschdienst (German Academic Exchange), a distinction that points to the presumptive institutional status of such a text.

12. Clearly Falkner does not refer here simply to aspects of canon formation, as does American poet Alice Notley when she observes: "What a poem is, how good—what it looks and sounds like overall, the kinds of subjects it's concerned with—all of this since when? since shortly after known history began, has, world-wide, been addressed by men with some input from women. A poem, looked at this way, is 'male,' most ways of composing and setting down lines of poetry, of grouping them into poems on the page, seem 'male'—the choices to be made are largely from among male solutions to male-generated formal problems." See Alice Notley, *Coming After: Essays on Poetry* (Ann Arbor: University of Michigan Press, 2005), 167.

13. See Lynn Keller and Cristanne Miller, eds., *Feminist Measures: Soundings in Poetry and Theory* (Ann Arbor: University of Michigan Press, 1994); Terry Threadgold, *Feminist Poetics: Poiesis, Performance, Histories* (London: Routledge, 1997); Julia Kristeva, *Revolution in Poetic Language,* trans. Margaret Waller (New York: Columbia University Press, 1984); Gisela Ecker, ed., *Feminist Aesthetics* (Boston: Beacon 1985); Naomi Schor, *Reading in Detail: Aesthetics and the Feminine* (New York: Methuen, 1987); and Molly McQuade, ed., *By Herself: Women Reclaim Poetry* (St. Paul, Minn.: Graywolf, 2000).

14. *Fräuleinwunder* could be literally translated as "miracle of the Super Girl," but it also echoes the term *Wirtschaftswunder* or "economic miracle" used to describe the German economy's postwar boom. Comparison of the "zero hour" and post-1989 developments foregrounds important consistencies in German cultural and intellectual life, as demonstrated in Stephen Brockmann, *German Literary Culture at the Zero Hour* (Rochester, N.Y.: Camden House, 2004), 252–58.

15. The currency this notion achieves is evidenced in the title of the anthology by Volker Hage, *Lyrik für Leser: Deutsche Gedichte der siebziger Jahre* (Stuttgart, Ger.: Reclam, 1980).

16. See Ursula Krechel, *In Zukunft schreiben* (Salzburg, Austria: Jung und Jung, 2003).

17. For example, anthologies were even used to devise poem-codes; see Alice Brittan, "War and the Book: The Diarist, the Cryptographer, and *The English Patient,*" *PMLA* 121, no. 1 (2006): 204.

18. This assessment is based on a survey of holdings at the Deutsches Literaturarchiv in Marbach am Neckar.

19. These findings agree with Guillory's conclusions about the treatment of noncanonical authors in anthologies. See John Guillory, *Cultural Capital: The*

Problem of Literary Canon Formation (Chicago: University of Chicago Press, 1993), 10.

Chapter One

1. In German letters, the publication credited with first articulating the notion of the lyrical *I* (*lyrisches Ich*) is Margarete Susman, *Das Wesen der modernen deutschen Lyrik* (Stuttgart, Ger.: Strecker und Schröder, 1910). See further Rolf Tarot, "Käte Hamburgers Lyriktheorie—eine Revision," in *Traditionen der Lyrik,* ed. Wolfgang Düsing (Tübingen, Ger.: Max Niemeyer Verlag, 1997), 265–66; and Paul Hoffmann, *Das erneute Gedicht* (Frankfurt am Main: Suhrkamp, 2001).

2. For a discussion of definitions, see Donald E. Hall, *Subjectivity* (New York: Routledge, 2004), 2–15. Though postwar German poetry is not known for ebullient self-expression, it is certainly characterized by preoccupations with the agency of writers, the autonomy of aesthetic works, and the tension between private and public expression, all of which are bound up with problems of subjectivity. Regarding Hamburger's treatment of subjectivity, individuality, and particularity as concepts, see also Renate Schlesier, "Was ist Interpretation in den Kulturwissenschaften?" in *Käte Hamburger: Zur Aktualität einer Klassikerin,* ed. Johanna Bossinade and Angelika Schaser, *Querelles: Jahrbuch für Frauen- und Geschlechterforschung* (Göttingen, Ger.: Wallstein Verlag, 2003), 48.

3. Hinderer in a schematic, yet quite useful overview of postwar literary trends concludes that by 1972 German poetry had passed through four main phases or styles characterized to varying degrees by abstraction (traditional verse, reception of modernism, cultivation of *Gebrauchslyrik* or occasional poetry, and in the 1960s a politicization of literature). He argues that these transformations led to the "paradoxical situation" of poetry withdrawing from reality only to be forced to discover new realities, a problem linked to questions of voice and authenticity. See Walter Hinderer, "Verlust der Wirklichkeit: Eine Ortsbestimmung der westdeutschen Lyrik von 1945 bis 1975," in *Arbeit an der Gegenwart: Zur deutschen Literatur nach 1945* (Würzburg, Ger.: Königshausen und Neumann, 1994), 29.

4. Poets who have sought to explain German poetry to American and English audiences, and vice versa, have been particularly insistent about this point. Enzensberger observed in 1963 that Fascist disfiguration of the German language was so complete that "how to write poetry in a language thus distorted was a question every German poet has had to answer since 1945"; see Hans Magnus Enzensberger, "In Search of the Lost Language," *Encounter* 21, no. 3 (1963): 45. In the 1990s, Sartorius continued this explanation with rhetorical flourish when he observed that aesthetic problems were always on the minds of German poets who were first and foremost preoccupied with postwar ethical dilemmas to the extent that "every new poem until the early Eighties had to pass a moral litmus test"; see Joachim Sartorius, "'Language, Foreign: Saying You and Being Heard': On Poetry in German, 1986–1996," in "Contemporary German Poetry," special issue, *Poetry* 173, no. 1 (1998): 122–23.

5. Hillebrand diagnoses a progressive loss of the register of the stylized aesthetic of orphic poetic voice in Germany, marking the onset of its demise by

1960 at the latest; Bruno Hillebrand, "Ende des orphischen Gesangs—Gedan-ken zur Tonlosigkeit der deutschen Lyrik nach 1945," in *Traditionen der Lyrik,* ed. Wolfgang Düsing (Tübingen, Ger.: Max Niemeyer Verlag, 1997), 235.

6. For the comments that sparked this debate about the "Tod der Literatur," see Hans Magnus Enzensberger, "Gemeinplätze, die Neueste Literatur betref-fend," *Kursbuch* 15 (1968).

7. Although *Neue Subjektivität* or New Subjectivity is primarily associated with writing in the 1970s, Hartung's study rightly suggests that the groundwork for this trend was laid in the 1960s and that it evolved without major interruption into literature of the 1980s and is in general compatibility with postmodernism. Terming New Subjectivity a paradigm shift, Stuart Parkes identifies its key com-ponents as the turn from sociocritical literature to writing about personal and identity issues. See Stuart Parkes, "Neue Subjektivität," in *Encyclopedia of Ger-man Literature,* ed. Matthias Konzett (Chicago: Fitzroy Dearborn, 2000), 757. In contrast to Hartung, Korte marks the end of New Subjectivity more explicitly with the return of conventional poetic forms in the 1980s. See also Ralf Schnell, *Geschichte der deutschsprachigen Literatur seit 1945* (Stuttgart, Ger.: Metzler, 1993), 392–440; and Hermann Korte, *Geschichte der deutschen Lyrik seit 1945* (Stuttgart, Ger.: Metzler, 1989), 157–66, 85–95.

8. A critique of these aesthetic priorities is launched in Jörg Drews, "Selbst-erfahrung und Neue Subjektivität in der Lyrik," *Akzente* 24, no. 1 (1977). See further Helmut Kreutzer, "Neue Subjektivität: Zur Literatur der siebziger Jahre in der Bundesrepublik Deutschland," in *Deutsche Gegenwartsliteratur: Aus-gangspositionen und aktuelle Entwicklungen,* ed. Manfred Durzak (Stuttgart, Ger.: Reclam, 1981); and Hans Dieter Schäfer, "Zusammenhänge der deutschen Gegenwartslyrik," in *Deutsche Gegenwartsliteratur: Ausgangspositionen und aktuelle Entwicklungen,* ed. Manfred Durzak (Stuttgart, Ger.: Reclam, 1981). Favorable appraisal of New Subjectivity is offered by Jürgen Theobaldy and Gustav Zürcher, *Veränderung der Lyrik: Über westdeutsche Gedichte seit 1965* (Munich: Edition Text und Kritik, 1976).

9. Scholarly discussion of *Die Logik der Dichtung* has focused primarily on its analysis of narrative forms. In centering on Hamburger's treatment of the lyric genre, the present study seeks to address issues raised by Hamburger concerning representation and interpretation that have been previously over-looked. Damerau contends that the underlying preoccupation in Hamburger's intellectual project as a scholar is a critique of the conception of truth, a con-cern that will again be articulated by Hilde Domin as a particular issue for poetry. See also Burghard Damerau, "Pro und Contra: Zu Käte Hamburgers Kritik der ästhetischen Wahrheit," in *Käte Hamburger: Zur Aktualität einer Klassikerin,* ed. Johanna Bossinade and Angelika Schaser, *Querelles: Jahrbuch für Frauen- und Geschlechterforschung* (Göttingen, Ger.: Wallstein Verlag, 2003), 120. In his account of Hamburger's theory, which perceptively focuses on the conception of the lyric genre, Tarot observes that Hamburger unchar-acteristically departs from the logic she uses to define other text categories when she makes the claim that poetry is in some way a genuine expression of reality. Tarot objects to this apparent reliance on an anthropomorphized

notion of poetry and thus proposes a solution to this impasse in Hamburger's genre typology by describing an alternate division of literature into two genres based on principles of imitation and mimesis. While I agree with Tarot that Hamburger's discussion of the lyrical *I* stands out as a contradictory element within *Die Logik der Dichtung* and requires other resolution in relation to genre theory, it is my contention that it is important to appreciate Hamburger's presentation of the lyric on its own terms—in full paradox because her observations are critical to our historical understanding of the tensions exhibited in postwar German poetry. See Tarot, "Käte Hamburgers Lyriktheorie."

10. Threadgold's title does not refer to the traditional poetics of rhetoric and hermeneutics that were developed for poetry, but rather to "feminist work on and with texts." See Terry Threadgold, *Feminist Poetics: Poiesis, Performance, Histories* (London: Routledge, 1997), 1. She is thus not concerned per se with lyric genre texts, but rather with practices of writing.

11. Threadgold makes clear her intent of questioning linguistic and structuralist approaches. German poetic theory is more indebted to traditions of hermeneutic interpretation, which receives limited mention in her study, and then only in passing in the context of a critique of Habermas's discourse theory; see Threadgold, *Feminist Poetics*, 111–14.

12. Hahn convincingly demonstrates that Hamburger's work was received by scholars as a "book by a woman" (*Buch einer Frau*), rather than on its own terms. See Barbara Hahn, "Erratischer Block oder von der Schwierigkeit, Käte Hamburgers *Logik der Dichtung* zu lesen," in *Käte Hamburger: Zur Aktualität einer Klassikerin*, ed. Johanna Bossinade and Angelika Schaser, *Querelles: Jahrbuch für Frauen- und Geschlechterforschung* (Göttingen, Ger.: Wallstein Verlag, 2003), 129. On the reception history of *Die Logik der Dichtung* see Dorrit Cohn, "Käte Hamburger, *Die Logik der Dichtung*," *Germanic Review* 45, no. 1 (1970); Geir Farner, "Käte Hamburger und das Problem des fiktiven Erzählers," *Orbis Litterarum* 33, no. 2 (1978): 113–15; Johanna Bossinade and Angelika Schaser, "Von der Außenseiterin zur Klassikerin: Käte Hamburger," in *Käte Hamburger: Zur Aktualität einer Klassikerin*, ed. Johanna Bossinade and Angelika Schaser, *Querelles: Jahrbuch für Frauen- und Geschlechterforschung* (Göttingen, Ger.: Wallstein Verlag, 2003), 9–10; and Michael Scheffel, "Käte Hamburgers *Logik der Dichtung*—ein 'Grundbuch' der Fiktionalitäts- und Erzähltheorie? Versuch einer Re-Lektüre," in *Käte Hamburger: Zur Aktualität einer Klassikerin*, ed. Johanna Bossinade and Angelika Schaser, *Querelles: Jahrbuch für Frauen- und Geschlechterforschung* (Göttingen, Ger.: Wallstein Verlag, 2003), 145–49. For responses to the second edition of *Die Logik der Dichtung*, see in particular Klaus Weimar, "Kritische Bemerkungen zur *Logik der Dichtung*," *Deutsche Vierteljahrsschrift für Literaturwissenschaft und Geistesgeschichte* 48 (1974); and Farner, "Käte Hamburger und das Problem des fiktiven Erzählers."

13. It should be noted that discussions of poetry by scholars-theorists, critics, poets, and others operated with quite fluid boundaries in the postwar German literary environment, as evidenced in the frequency with which the various participants in literary debates reference each other's positions.

14. A notable exception is Enzensberger's polemical critique of the avant-garde, which cites as a defining principle an exclusionary definition of the collective as "an exclusive band of men" (*Männerbund*); Hans Magnus Enzensberger, "Die Aporien der Avantgarde," in *Einzelheiten II: Poesie und Politik* (Frankfurt am Main: Suhrkamp, 1976), 64.

15. See Peter Bürger, *Theorie der Avantgarde* (Frankfurt am Main: Suhrkamp, 1974), 22. Schulte-Sasse traces Bürger's theory to Renato Poggioli's characterization of the avant-garde. See Jochen Schulte-Sasse, "Foreword: Theory of Modernism Versus Theory of the Avant-Garde," in *Theory of the Avant-Garde* (Minneapolis: University of Minnesota Press, 1984), vii–xv. Historically viewed, the avant-garde paradigm that privileged radical deconstruction became a foundational concept in the writings of "modernist" postwar German poets and was not clearly distinguished from notions of modernism throughout the early 1960s. This historical blurring of categories, Schulte-Sasse points out, occurs in Poggioli's theory and corresponds to Anglo-American tradition (xiv). With respect to the current consideration of German poetry, it is very important to recognize this elision of the avant-garde/modernism distinction. Dissonance and rupture are, in fact, elevated as fundamental to modern poetry in the 1956 study by Hugo Friedrich, *The Structure of Modern Poetry: From the Mid-Nineteenth to the Mid-Twentieth Century* (Evanston, Ill.: Northwestern University Press, 1974), 7–9. Subsequently, the aesthetic values proposed by Friedrich transfer into postwar German poetry via dissemination by postwar authors, notably Hans Magnus Enzensberger, ed., *Museum der modernen Poesie* (Frankfurt am Main: Suhrkamp, 1960), 770. Regarding definitions of these movements, see further Beret E. Strong, *The Poetic Avant-Garde: The Groups of Borges, Auden, and Breton* (Evanston, Ill.: Northwestern University Press, 1997), 19–30.

16. The German first edition of *Die Logik der Dichtung* (1957) differs markedly from the 1968 second edition and the English translation, *The Logic of Literature* (1973). The English-language edition is more compact, with fewer examples from German literary canon and some updated references to contemporary poetry; thus I reference both editions in my discussion. The translations into English cited as *Logic* are by Rose; those referenced directly to *Logik* are my own.

17. Here I rely on the explanation offered by Culler that defines deictics as "orientational features of language that relate to the situation of utterance, such as pronouns (I, you) or adverbials of place and time." Jonathan Culler, *Literary Theory: A Very Short Introduction* (Oxford: Oxford University Press, 1997), 31.

18. See Wolfgang Kayser, *Kleine deutsche Versschule* (Bern, Switz.: Francke, 1946), Emil Staiger, *Grundbegriffe der Poetik* (Zürich: Atlantis, 1946); Emil Staiger, *Basic Concepts of Poetry,* ed. Marianne Burkhard and Luanne T. Frank, trans. Janette C. Hudson and Luanne T. Frank (University Park: Penn State University Press, 1991); Hugo Friedrich, *Die Struktur der modernen Lyrik: Von Baudelaire bis zur Gegenwart* (Hamburg: Rowohlt, 1956); and Friedrich, *The Structure of Modern Poetry.*

19. For Hamburger, mimesis is emphatically the constructed representation of reality, not the creation of reality itself. Additionally, Hamburger treats the ballad, the role-poem, and first-person narrative as special forms. However coincidentally, the division into two genres seems to mirror distantly the Cold War politics of the 1950s since Hamburger's genre dichotomy contrasts realist modes of writing with the individuality of lyrical expression.

20. Because Käte Hamburger's career as a scholar bridges the prewar and postwar periods, it provides a particularly salient reference point. The most prominent woman Germanist of the postwar era, Hamburger completed her dissertation in 1922 (*Schillers Analyse des Menschen als Grundlegung seiner Geschichts- und Kulturphilosophie*), but as a Jew was compelled to immigrate to Sweden in 1934. Her publications include *Thomas Mann und die Romantik* (1932), *Thomas Manns Roman "Josef und seine Brüder"* (1965), *Leo Tolstoi: Gestalt und Problem* (1950), *Von Sophokles zu Sartre: Griechische Dramenfiguren antik und modern* (1962), *Rilke: Eine Einführung* (1976), *Das Mitleid* (1985), and *Ibsens Drama in seiner Zeit* (1989). See Gesa Dane, "Käte Hamburger (1896–1992)," in *Wissenschaftsgeschichte der Germanistik in Porträts,* ed. Christoph König, Hans-Harald Müller, and Werner Röcke (Berlin: Walter de Gruyter, 2000). In 1956 she returned to Germany and taught at the University of Stuttgart, an appointment that was fraught with complications that Kersting attributes to political, identity, and gender issues. See Christa Kersting, "Remigration und Wissenschaftspolitik," in *Käte Hamburger: Zur Aktualität einer Klassikerin,* ed. Johanna Bossinade and Angelika Schaser, *Querelles: Jahrbuch für Frauen- und Geschlechterforschung* (Göttingen, Ger.: Wallstein Verlag, 2003). Hamburger died in 1992 in Stuttgart.

21. See, for example, Christine Di Stefano, "Dilemmas of Difference: Feminism, Modernity, and Postmodernism," in *Feminism/Postmodernism,* ed. Linda J. Nicholson (New York: Routledge, 1990); Rita Felski, *The Gender of Modernity* (Cambridge, Mass.: Harvard University Press, 1995), 13–34; and Marsha Meskimmon, *We Weren't Modern Enough: Women Artists and the Limits of German Modernism* (Berkeley: University of California Press, 1999).

22. Although *Die Logik der Dichtung* references primarily German poetics scholars, Hamburger does cite the 1949 edition of *Theory of Literature* by René Wellek and Austin Warren; see Käte Hamburger, *Die Logik der Dichtung* (Stuttgart, Ger.: Ernst Klett Verlag, 1957), 183. Brockmann confirms the dominance of American New Criticism and German *werkimmanente Kritik* in the 1940s–1950s, cautioning rightly that "while it would surely be mistaken to identify either abstract expressionism or New Criticism solely as expressions of the cold war . . . it would be equally misguided to seek to understand such movements without the overarching historical-political context provided by the tensions between the two superpowers." See Stephen Brockmann, *German Literary Culture at the Zero Hour* (Rochester, N.Y.: Camden House, 2004), 150. Relevant to the present discussion of the lyric genre is the connection to official "reeducation" programs through sponsored journals that became important vehicles for the publication of poetry and poetry criticism (including *Der Monat, Perspektiven,* and *Encounter*), as documented in Frances Stonor

Saunders, *The Cultural Cold War: The CIA and the World of Arts and Letters* (New York: New, 1999), 30–31, 140–44, 75–77. Compare in particular articles related to American poetry, criticism, and literary history that are listed in Gerhard H. W. Zuther, *Eine Bibliographie der Aufnahme amerikanischer Literatur in deutschen Zeitschriften 1945–1960* (Munich: Dissertations Druck Franz Frank, 1965), 11–12, 14–16. It is not my intention to overlook the theoretical and historical distinctions among New Criticism, *Werkimmanent* interpretation, and hermeneutics, but rather to note the historical convergence of these methods within the cultural-political context of postwar reconstruction efforts.

23. Felski underscores the distinctive qualities of European modernism (which aligned radical aesthetics and politics) and the formalist, apolitical tendencies of Anglo-American modernism; see Felski, *The Gender of Modernity,* 23–24. What is at stake, therefore, with the importation of New Criticism after 1945 and the cultivation of hermeneutics as a mode of interpretation are fundamental assumptions about art, society, and the nature of their relationship.

24. Compare Bennett's analysis of the debate over critical authority among Staiger, Martin Heidegger, and Leo Spitzer. See Benjamin Bennett, "The Politics of the Mörike-Debate and Its Object," *Germanic Review* 68, no. 2 (1993): 67. Hamburger, like these contemporaries, proceeds from assumptions about intellectual hierarchy when she observes, "Creative artists themselves are not conscious of this logical structure or inherent order"; see Käte Hamburger, *The Logic of Literature,* trans. Marilynn J. Rose, 2nd revised ed. (Bloomington: Indiana University Press, 1973), 7. However, she parts ways with criticism based on intellectual hierarchy by insisting that anyone can learn to understand the logic of literature. To the extent that she expresses faith that readers universally have an innate capacity to interpret, she aligns her project with the work of Susanne Langer and by extension with other gestalt approaches to art interpretation, such as that of Rudolf Arnheim, *Art and Visual Perception* (Berkeley: University of California Press, 1954).

25. Hamburger's wavering argumentation is indicative of the tensions present in postwar German intellectual debate that pitted allegiance to preservation of an elite "Culture" against the commitment to social and political change. In appraising this situation, Zimmermann concludes that the ingrained dilemmas—the long-standing rift between journalistic and academic criticism, elitist notions of culture, and apolitical attitudes—left German criticism poorly equipped to deal with postwar literature with any sense of historical context. See Bernhard Zimmermann, "Literary Criticism from 1933 to the Present," in *A History of German Literary Criticism 1730–1980,* ed. Peter Uwe Hohendahl (Lincoln: University of Nebraska Press, 1988), 392–94.

26. For the purpose of gauging contemporary attitudes toward the creative process, it is instructive to compare Hamburger's *Die Logik der Dichtung* with Hans Bender's collection of statements by poets, *Mein Gedicht ist mein Messer* (*My Poem Is My Knife,* 1955). While Bender acknowledges the inevitably selective nature of his volume, its contents depict a impressively accurate panorama of writerly positions, ranging from the more traditional approach of Rudolf Hagelstange in "Die Form als erste Entscheidung" ("Form as the

First Decision") to satirist Peter Rühmkorf's "Paradoxe Existenz" ("Paradoxical Existence"). Overall, a notion of *Handwerk* (handiwork or artisanship) is emphasized, a concept that Bender connects to the poetics of Gottfried Benn, traditional poetic forms, and pragmatic American concepts of writing. See Hans Bender, ed., *Mein Gedicht ist mein Messer* (Munich: List, 1964), 10–11. In the same volume, on the other hand, Enzensberger emphasizes the transformative value of poetry, writing, "So poems are not consumer goods, but rather means of production, with the help of which the reader can succeed in producing truth" ("Gedichte sind also nicht Konsumgüter, sondern Produktionsmittel, mit deren Hilfe es dem Leser gelingen kann, Wahrheit zu produzieren"). See Hans Magnus Enzensberger, "Scherenschleifer und Poeten," in *Mein Gedicht ist mein Messer*, ed. Hans Bender (Munich: List, 1964), 146–47. Concerning the variable role of satire, wit, humor, and experimentalism in postwar poetry, see also Hillebrand, "Ende des orphischen Gesangs—Gedanken zur Tonlosigkeit der deutschen Lyrik nach 1945."

27. The relationship of these terms to postwar literature is detailed in Korte, *Geschichte der deutschen Lyrik seit 1945*, 1–17; Brockmann, *German Literary Culture at the Zero Hour*, 21–70; Melin, *Poetic Maneuvers*, 35–54; and Schnell, *Geschichte der deutschsprachigen Literatur seit 1945*, 88–93.

28. Both categories implicitly take issue with Gottfried Benn's conception of poetry as the monologic creation of an isolated writer whose concern lies in creating an "absolute poem" that exists on a level of timelessness and abstraction. See Gottfried Benn, *Probleme der Lyrik* (Wiesbaden, Ger.: Limes, 1951), 39.

29. Hamburger employs dense syntactical constructions in explaining this concept, formulations that are difficult to render into English: "Zwischen dem lyrischen Ich und dem historischen bzw. theoretischen oder praktischen aber läuft, nur dem Blicke der Logik erkennbar, die Grenze, die wir als Kontext bezeichneten, der den Willen eines Aussagesubjekts kundgibt, ein lyrisches Ich zu sein." Marilynn J. Rose translates *Aussagesubjekt* as "statement-subject," a formulation that cites Hamburger's theory in philosophical argumentation. In departing from this translation, I have chosen to acknowledge Hamburger's investment in explaining the lyric genre in nontechnical terms as well.

30. It is worth noting that Hamburger in the 1957 German edition refers to what from current perspective appears to be an eclectic, at times idiosyncratic, canon. In addition to Nelly Sachs and Virginia Woolf, she cites a range of women authors writing in German and English, including Agnes Miegel (whose patriotic poetry, written under Nazism, resulted in her eventual disappearance from accounts of twentieth-century German literature). In addition to Susanne Langer, Hamburger also refers to René Wellek and Austin Warren, *Theory of Literature* (New York: Harcourt Brace, 1949).

31. I stress this contrast in my translation to emphasize the centrality of this distinction to Hamburger's argument. In German, this formulation states, "Die lyrische Form ist der Ausdruck für den Willen des Aussagesubjekts, seine Aussage *nicht* als seine Aussage zu verstehen, die auf einen Wirklichkeitzusammenhang gerichtet ist, sei dieser ein historischer, theoretischer oder praktischer." Although stressing subjectivity as the essence of poetry, Hamburger does also

treat several examples of poems that are less purely lyrical, including texts used in religious contexts (*Logik,* 167). More interested in developing a comprehensive theory of poetry than in dividing literature from other forms of discourse, such as scientific inquiry, she also acknowledges the proximity of natural philosophy to poetry in Goethe's time (167).

32. Tightly arguing her point, Hamburger also dismisses the notion that poetry is simply about the medium of language. See Hamburger, *Logik,* 182.

33. See Korte, *Geschichte der deutschen Lyrik seit 1945,* 66–70.

34. See also the review by Käte Hamburger, "Hilde Domin: *Wozu Lyrik heute,*" *Poetica* 3 (1970).

35. A 1966 essay by Hamburger revives this unresolved problem by stating that modern interpretation—unlike positivistic criticism from a naively biographical approach—insists on completely separating poem and the person of the poet, a solution clearly aligned with the interpretive practices of New Criticism. Hamburger proposes that the proper, though paradoxical, relationship of the two is to assert that as soon as the lyrical *I* is declared, any reference of it to the person of the poet must be sublated. See Käte Hamburger, "Das tranzendierende Ich. Zur Lyrik von Nelly Sachs," in *Kleine Schriften zur Literatur und Geistesgeschichte* (Stuttgart, Ger.: Hans-Dieter Heinz Akademischer Verlag, 1986), 265. An extensive footnote in the English translation responds to René Wellek, who criticized her reasoning, and reaffirms Hamburger's assertion that the concept of *Wirklichkeitsaussage* (reality statement) doesn't equate speaker with utterance. In a further attempt to refine this line of thinking, Hamburger argues we should be primarily concerned with the constitutive capacities of language. This argumentation aims to render poetic expression abstract, yet as we will see, Hamburger's definition of subjectivity makes even this abstraction extremely problematic. See Hamburger, *Logic,* 241–42, 362–63.

36. Of course, paraliterary elements, not just texts, shape poetic persona and reputation. For example, Barry argues, based on the case of Robert Lowell, that "the personhood of the author—the poet, the bard—normally contributes more meaning to his or her works than does that of the artist who works in nonlinguistic media." See Jackson Barry, "The Meaning of the Author: Robert Lowell as Image of an Age," in *Art, Culture, and the Semiotics of Meaning* (New York: St. Martin's, 1999), 87.

37. The label *Fräuleinwunder* (roughly translated, "Girl Wonder") was coined by Volker Hage in an article for the March 22, 1999, issue of the German magazine *Der Spiegel*. For discussion of its currency and limitations see Stuart Taberner, *German Literature of the 1990s and Beyond: Normalization and the Berlin Republic* (Rochester, N.Y.: Camden House, 2005), 16–23.

38. My analysis refers primarily to the West German environment and its defining influence on the literary climate in other German-speaking countries. The complex cultural, social, and political dynamics that influenced the intellectual climate in East Germany, Austria, and Switzerland warrant separate consideration that cannot be undertaken within the scope of the current study.

39. Pointing out that literary histories for this period define literature without taking into account reading audiences, censorship, and commercial publications,

Häntzschel proposes to remedy this oversight by surveying a broader spectrum of the postwar book market. See Günter Häntzschel, "Die Präsenz weiblicher Autoren auf dem Buchmarkt 1945 und 1950: Vorläufige Skizze eines Projekts," in *Erfahrung nach dem Krieg: Autorinnen im Literaturbetrieb 1945–1950 BRD, DDR, Österreich, Schweiz,* ed. Christiane Caemmerer, Walter Delabar, Elke Ramm, and Marion Schulz (Frankfurt am Main: Peter Lang, 2002), 215–17. Häntzschel's conclusions are borne out in Hermann Korte's list of poetry publications, which selectively acknowledges volumes by Kaschnitz, Langgässer, and Sachs (1947), Lavant and Sachs (1949), Kaschnitz (1950), and Bachmann (1953). See Korte, *Geschichte der deutschen Lyrik seit 1945,* 209–11.

40. Writing about poetry in the early modern period, Watanabe-O'Kelly makes an observation applicable to the twentieth century: poetry was "the pre-eminent genre employed by women because it could be easily practiced without censure in private by individuals, as opposed to drama." See Helen Watanabe-O'Kelly, "Women's Writing in the Early Modern Period," in *A History of Women's Writing in Germany, Austria and Switzerland,* ed. Jo Catling (Cambridge, Eng.: Cambridge University Press, 2000), 33. Clearly private/public distinctions played a role in shaping the literary terrain after 1945, but the separation of spheres alone should not be accepted uncritically as an explanation of the dynamics operating in the literary environment.

Chapter Two

1. Domin refers here to the novelist Christa Wolf (1929–) and the poet Annette von Droste-Hülshoff (1797–1848).

2. See also Marion Tauschwitz, *"Das ich sein kann, wie ich bin": Hilde Domin: Die Biografie* (Heidelberg, Ger.: Palmyra Verlag, 2009), 372–73, 92.

3. Feminism, of course, has a long history as a social and political movement. In using the term "prefeminist," I refer to both the level of Domin's self-identification with feminism and to her position relative to the historical iteration of feminism in the postwar women's liberation movement.

4. Translation of the word *Augenblick* from the title of this lecture series itself suggests these representational and discursive complications. *Augenblick* means literally "blink of the eye," in other words, a brief second, but in postwar aesthetic discourse, the noun is also linked with photography and poetic texts that seek to capture the moment.

5. On Jens's role as an early proponent of Domin's work, see Tauschwitz, *"Das ich sein kann, wie ich bin": Hilde Domin: Die Biografie,* 328–29.

6. The phrase "drehen nicht den Kopf" could also be translated as "do not turn the head" or "do not turn anyone's head." However, Domin cites this poem as an example of how poems seem to write themselves rapidly for her and then become separate entities, hence the focus in this translation on autonomy. Here for the poet, words go forward, never looking back. See Hilde Domin, *Das Gedicht als Augenblick von Freiheit: Frankfurt Poetik-Vorlesungen 1987/1988* (Munich: Piper, 1988), 44.

7. In addition to Tauschwitz's authoritative biography, which draws on Domin's literary bequest to the Deutsches Literaturarchiv in Marbach am Neckar,

see Ilka Scheidgen, *Hilde Domin: Dichterin des Dennoch* (Lahr, Ger.: Kaufmann Verlag, 2006); and Irma Hildebrandt, "Heimat in der deutschen Sprache: Hilde Domin (1909–2006)," in *Prägende Gestalten der Bundesrepublik* (Munich: Diederichs Verlag, 2009).

8. Braun provides a survey of Domin criticism in Birgit Lermen and Michael Braun, *Hilde Domin "Hand in Hand mit der Sprache"* (Bonn: Bouvier, 1997), 7–11.

9. See Walter Höllerer, "Thesen zum langen Gedicht," *Akzente* 12, no. 2 (1965); and Karl Krolow, "Das Problem des langen und kurzen Gedichts Heute," *Akzente* 13, no. 3 (1966). For discussion of German-American literary relations pertinent to this exchange, see Hans Galinsky, *Wegbereiter moderner amerikanischer Lyrik: Interpretations- und Rezeptionsstudien zu Emily Dickinson und William Carlos Williams* (Heidelberg, Ger.: Carl Winter, 1968); Charlotte Melin, "Williams, Enzensberger, and Recent German Poetry," *Comparative Literature Studies* 29, no. 1 (1992); and Agnes C. Mueller, *Lyrik "Made in USA": Vermittlung und Rezeption in der Bundesrepublik* (Amsterdam: Rodopi, 1999).

10. It would eventually cause Celan to withdraw from the project. See Hilde Domin, *Doppelinterpretationen: Das zeitgenössische deutsche Gedicht zwischen Autor und Leser* (Frankfurt am Main: Athenäum, 1966), 340; and Domin, *Gedicht als Augenblick*, 28–29. Concerning the many personal and political tensions behind *Doppelinterpretationen*, see further Tauschwitz, *"Das ich sein kann, wie ich bin": Hilde Domin: Die Biografie*, 403–6.

11. Documentation of Gruppe 47 participants (writers who read, critics, and others) shows that only twelve of the poets in *Doppelinterpretationen*, including Domin herself, were not affiliated with the group. See Reinhard Lettau, ed., *Die Gruppe 47: Bericht, Kritik, Polemik: Ein Handbuch* (Neuwied, Ger.: Luchterhand, 1967), 527–47. Concerning political and programmatic tensions, particularly surrounding the meeting in Sweden in 1964, see Stephan Braese, ed., *Bestandsaufnahme: Studien zur Gruppe 47* (Berlin: Erich Schmidt, 1999).

12. The enormous success of the book, which was widely discussed in the press and republished in multiple editions, is noted in Scheidgen, *Hilde Domin: Dichterin des Dennoch*, 153–54.

13. Domin in fact refers to Stefan George in her introduction (*Doppelinterpretationen*, 22) and in a 1991 interview comments that Palm was a member of the George school. Hilde Domin, "'Wortwechsel' Interview Mit Christa Schulze-Rohr," in *Vokabular der Erinnerungen: Zum Werk von Hilde Domin*, ed. Bettina von Wangenheim (Frankfurt am Main: Fischer, 1998), 204.

14. Enzensberger, for example, still asserts in 1963 that "in Germany 1933 and 1945 are not merely dates of political history. These years are total, like the régime whose dominion they mark"; Hans Magnus Enzensberger, "In Search of the Lost Language," *Encounter* 21, no. 3 (1963): 44. Yet even in the 1950s, an undercurrent of ambivalence about this construct began to surface. See, for example, Christian Ferber, "Die Legende vom Kahlschlag," *Die Literatur* 1, no. 6 (1952). For an account from the perspective of one of the era's most important editors of poetry anthologies see Hans Bender, "Letter from Germany:

The Myth of 'Kahlschlag,'" *Dimension 5*, no. 3 (1972). Critical discussion is found in Frank Trommler, "Der 'Nullpunkt 1945' und seine Verbindlichkeit für die Literaturgeschichte," *Basis: Jahrbuch für deutsche Gegenwartsliteratur* 1 (1970); Trommler, "Nachkriegsliteratur—eine neue deutsche Literatur?" in *Literaturmagazin 7: Nachkriegsliteratur*, ed. Nicolas Born and Jürgen Manthey (Hamburg: Rowohlt, 1977); Hermann Korte, *Geschichte der deutschen Lyrik seit 1945* (Stuttgart, Ger.: Metzler, 1989); and Ralf Schnell, *Geschichte der deutschsprachigen Literatur seit 1945* (Stuttgart, Ger.: Metzler, 1993).

15. Nonetheless, Domin acknowledges the canonical status of Friedrich's work in "Ein Drehpunk der Lyrikinterpretation" (1968) in Hilde Domin, *Gesammelte Essays* (Munich: Piper, 1992), 308–32.

16. Domin was one of the translators whose work was included in *Museum der modernen Poesie*, and she frequently cites Enzensberger in *Doppelinterpretationen* and other works. Christian Enzensberger, his brother, was also a contributor to Domin's collection.

17. This mode of creative-critical reading puts into practice the interpretive procedures articulated in Hans Georg Gadamer, *Wahrheit und Methode*, 2nd ed. (Tübingen, Ger.: Mohr, 1965). Domin is also influenced by Anglo-American interpretive approaches, especially New Criticism, and cites Cleanth Brooks, as well as René Wellek and Austin Warren; see Domin, *Doppelinterpretationen*, 22, 34. Having spent 1964 on a reading tour that took her to the United States, Mexico, and England, Domin would have had opportunities to become familiar with New Criticism. See Tauschwitz, *"Das ich sein kann, wie ich bin": Hilde Domin: Die Biografie*, 391–415.

18. Here Domin's concern with the experiential qualities of poetry (appeal to eye and ear, breath as the determiner of line and a component of performance, and an openness to nonrational inspiration) hints at reasons for her critical interest in the work of Herbert Marcuse.

19. Domin's excursus on the visual and acoustical properties of poetry stands as a reminder that these issues have been a recurrent concern in German aesthetics, most famously during the Enlightenment with Gotthold Ephraim Lessing's essay "Laokoön" (1766). See Gotthold Ephraim Lessing, *Laocoön: An Essay on the Limits of Painting and Poetry*, trans. Edward Allen McCormick (Baltimore: Johns Hopkins University Press, 1984).

20. See Charlotte Melin, *Poetic Maneuvers: Hans Magnus Enzensberger and the Lyric Genre* (Evanston, Ill.: Northwestern University Press, 2003), 89–90. As Marjorie Perloff notes, Olson's interest in poetic line varied by breath length, focus on images, and attention to spoken discourse is shared by Allen Ginsberg and Robert Creeley. See Marjorie Perloff, *Poetry On and Off the Page: Essays for Emergent Occasions* (Evanston, Ill.: Northwestern University Press, 1998), 151–53.

21. Domin explains that she found she was able to write "Wen es trifft" ("Whom it concerns") after the year she spent in the United States, commenting that Frost's poetry gave her a sense of how to control the length of breath required for long poems; Domin, *Gedicht als Augenblick*, 35–36. Frost is a surprising source for two reasons. Only a handful of his poems were translated

into German in the 1940s–1950s; compare Gerhard H. W. Zuther, *Eine Bibliographie der Aufnahme amerikanischer Literatur in deutschen Zeitschriften 1945–1960* (Munich: Dissertations Druck Franz Frank, 1965), 57. Secondly, discussions of breath and line in Germany developed largely in relation to American poets who were received as avant-garde models for long poem forms in the 1960s (Williams, Olson, Ginsberg, and to a lesser extent Pound, due to his political views). Frost, as a traditionalist in terms of subject matter and form, is an anomalous point of reference in this context.

22. This passage furthermore echoes Rainer Maria Rilke's poetic cycle *Die Sonette an Orpheus* (*The Sonnets to Orpheus*) and Gotthold Ephraim Lessing's famous essay "Laokoön."

23. These discourses focused their attention on poetic methods, subject matter, and legitimacy. For further discussion see Hans Magnus Enzensberger, "Scherenschleifer und Poeten," in *Mein Gedicht ist mein Messer,* ed. Hans Bender (Munich: List, 1964); Melin, *Poetic Maneuvers.* Then around 1960, interest in the visual capacities of poetry was renewed as German poets labored to transform the lyric genre into a more viable medium for contemporary expression. This discourse facilitates rejection of a conception of poetry as a reflection of static memory (*Erinnerung*), a notion asserted by Emil Staiger in *Grundbegriffe der Poetik* (1946). Terms like *Augenblick* (blink of the eye) and *Momentaufnahme* (snapshot of the moment), which embody an aesthetic focused on the present, gradually gained currency among German poets as they moved from the style of *Trümmerlyrik* (rubble poetry) of the early postwar years into what they conceived of as a more universal and modern style. See Emil Staiger, *Grundbegriffe der Poetik* (Zürich: Atlantis, 1946); Melin, *Poetic Maneuvers,* 6–13; and Benjamin Bennett, "The Politics of the Mörike-Debate and Its Object," *Germanic Review* 68, no. 2 (1993). For further discussion see Enzensberger, "Scherenschleifer und Poeten"; Melin, *Poetic Maneuvers;* and Bender, ed., *Mein Gedicht ist mein Messer.*

24. On the stylistic continuities between pre- and post-1968 literature see Cettina Rapisarda, "Women's Writing, 1968–1980," in *Post-War Women's Writing in German: Feminist Critical Approaches,* ed. Chris Weedon (Providence, R.I.: Berghahn, 1997).

25. Her notion of dynamic poetry is strikingly similar to the discussion of open poems provided in Hans Magnus Enzensberger, *Poems for People Who Don't Read Poems,* trans. Jerome Rothenberg, Michael Hamburger, and H. M. Enzensberger (New York: Atheneum, 1968), 163. Presumably Domin, like Enzensberger, has in mind Susan Sontag's 1964 essay "Against Interpretation," which called for a charged erotics of art (a term that *Erregung* echoes) to replace enervated hermeneutics. Compare Susan Sontag, "Against Interpretation," in *Against Interpretation and Other Essays* (New York: Farrar, Straus and Giroux, 1966), 14.

26. These sections include "Die Prinzipien der Wort- und Bildwahl" or "The Principles of Word and Image Selection" (based on an essay from 1962), "Über die 'unspezifische Genauigkeit' als Merkmal der Lyrik" ("On the 'Imprecise Precision' as a Distinguishing Feature of Poetry," an expanded version of a

newspaper article from 1965), "Lyriker und Text: Zur Terminologie" ("Poet and Text: On Terminology"), first published in 1965 in the *Fischer-Almanach*, and Domin's "Offener Brief an Nelly Sachs" ("An Open Letter to Nelly Sachs"), which appeared in a collection on the occasion of that author's seventy-fifth birthday.

27. I am not, however, arguing that Domin should be viewed through a narrow lens of political activity, as for example the Marxist position that informs Dagmar C. Stern, "Hilde Domin's Personal and Social Ideals," *Modern Language Studies* 9, no. 2 (1979).

28. This essay appeared in the influential journal *Merkur* with a dedication to Herbert Marcuse.

29. What Enzensberger actually disparages is the lack of a literature capable of transforming society, which he envisions as possible through the cultivation of politicized literacy; Hans Magnus Enzensberger, "Gemeinplätze, die Neueste Literatur betreffend," *Kursbuch* 15 (1968): 197. See Melin, *Poetic Maneuvers,* 103.

30. In a later characterization of the revival of German poetry between 1955 and 1965 in *Nachkrieg und Unfrieden* (*Postwar and Unpeace,* 1970), Domin singles out Marcuse as one of the defining thinkers for writers of the period; Hilde Domin, *Nachkrieg und Unfrieden: Gedichte als Index 1945–1970* (Neuwied, Ger.: Luchterhand, 1970), 145–50.

31. See further chapter 3 for Ulla Hahn's revival of the phrase "seismograph of the time" to describe poetry. Both Wolfdietrich Schnurre and Christoph Meckel refer to poetry as a seismograph in Karl H. Van D'Elden, *West German Poets on Society and Politics* (Detroit: Wayne State University Press, 1979), 33, 131, 209. Likewise Domin's poetry is characterized as functioning as a seismographic representation of reality in Scheidgen, *Hilde Domin: Dichterin des Dennoch,* 174.

32. Marcuse, according to Tauschwitz, gave Domin a copy of *Eros and Civilization* after her 1964 reading at Harvard University. See Tauschwitz, *"Das ich sein kann, wie ich bin": Hilde Domin: Die Biografie,* 398–99.

33. It should be noted that Bovenschen also finds Marcuse's ideas inspirational, though she is much more skeptical of the leveling effects of his reasoning than Domin. See Silvia Bovenschen, "Über die Frage: Gibt es eine 'weibliche' Aesthetik?," *Aesthetik und Kommunikation* 25 (1976): 66–67.

34. The ambivalence Domin displays toward feminism almost certainly has a biographical component. Domin and her husband had a complex relationship that was punctuated by separations and Palm's jealousy of her literary aspirations. See Tauschwitz, *"Das ich sein kann, wie ich bin": Hilde Domin: Die Biografie,* 39, 162, 251, 67. See also Jan Bürger and Frank Druffner, eds., *Hilde Domin: Die Liebe im Exil: Briefe an Erwin Walter Palm aus den Jahren 1931–1959* (Frankfurt am Main: S. Fischer Verlag, 2009).

35. In German this reads as "Literarische Meinungsbildung. Die Dialektik von Urteil, Vor-Urteil und Schaffensprozeß in der gesteuerten Gesellschaft."

36. A parallel phenomenon occurs with the sexual revolution, as Herzog details: "By the late 1960s, West Germany had been inundated by the commodification of sex in every facet of existence—from highly sexualized advertising

to easily available hard-core pornography, from a constant stream of news reportage about sexual matters to sex enlightenment films and curricula and a culturewide discussion of nudity, adultery, and group sex. Market-driven voyeurism had become the inescapable part of everyday life in the West." Dagmar Herzog, *Sex After Fascism. Memory and Morality in Twentieth-Century Germany* (Princeton, N.J.: Princeton University Press, 2005), 192–93.

37. In a recent study of German literary culture from 1945 to 1950, however, Marianne Vogel persuasively argues that "the structure and climate of Gruppe 47 did not make available to women a position that could be taken seriously, something that is unsatisfactorily reflected in the later reception"; see Marianne Vogel, "Platz, Position, Profilierung: Geschlechteraspekte des deutschen Literaturbetriebs 1945–1950 unter anderem am Beispiel der Gruppe 47," in *Erfahrung nach dem Krieg: Autorinnen im Literaturbetrieb 1945–1950 BRD, DDR, Österreich, Schweiz,* ed. Christiane Caemmerer, Walter Delabar, Elke Ramm, and Marion Schulz (Frankfurt am Main: Peter Lang, 2002), 226. Domin's reticence on this point may be attributed both to the tenor of intellectual debate in 1968 and to her own conclusion at that point that she herself was well treated in these settings. Tauschwitz, however, notes that although Domin followed Gruppe 47 matters with interest, the perception existed that she would not fare well in the intense atmosphere of its readings and critiques. In fact, in 1962 Domin opted to travel with her husband rather than to attend one of the group's meetings. Tauschwitz, *"Das ich sein kann, wie ich bin": Hilde Domin: Die Biografie,* 276–77, 376–77.

38. See Walter Benjamin, "Das Kunstwerk im Zeitalter seiner technischen Reproduzierbarkeit," in *Illuminationen: Ausgewählte Schriften* (Frankfurt am Main: Suhrkamp, 1977). The attention given to experimental writing and concrete poetry in the mid-1960s stands as background to Domin's treatment of automatic forms of writing. Max Bense (a poet whose academic education was in the fields of mathematics, physics, and philosophy) is included in *Doppelinterpretationen.* Compare also Enzensberger's fascination with computer-generated poetry in Hans Magnus Enzensberger, *Einladung zu einem Poesie-Automaten* (Frankfurt am Main: Suhrkamp, 2000).

39. Domin appears to be responding to rhetoric of the day that strove to assert in metaphorically deprecating terms that revolutionary work was not *Kochkunst* (the art of cooking). In this regard, it is worth noting that during the Cold War era, domesticity carried a double-edged meaning. On the one hand, modern conveniences mirrored the technological inventions devised to combat enemies, thereby offering power and freedom. On the other, the maintenance of strictly assigned gender roles depended on continued feminization and subordination of women at home. Compare discussion of the 1949 feature in *The Ladies Home Journal* in Camille Roman, *Elizabeth Bishop's World War II—Cold War View* (New York: Palgrave, 2001), 89–96.

40. Domin describes the circumstances of this display in Karl H. Van D'Elden, "Hilde Domin," in *West German Poets on Society and Politics* (Detroit: Wayne State University Press, 1979), 88–91. Compare Braun's discussion in Lermen and Braun, *Hilde Domin "Hand in Hand mit der Sprache,"* 115–20; and Karl

Krolow, "Zivilcourage des Wortes: 'Drei Arten Gedichte aufzuschreiben 2,' " in *Heimkehr ins Wort: Materialien zu Hilde Domin,* ed. Bettina v. Wangenheim (Frankfurt am Main: Fischer, 1982).

41. For an alternate translation, see Agnes Stein, ed., *Four German Poets* (New York: Red Dust, 1979), 80–81.

42. See Stefan George, "Komm in den totgesagten park und schau," in *Werke* (Munich: Helmut Kupper, 1958).

43. Braun's interpretation of the scene as a futuristic is not sustained by the details of the poem. See Lermen and Braun, *Hilde Domin "Hand in Hand mit der Sprache,"* 116.

44. The poem begins "Wie man zum Stein spricht, wie / du" (239), and "Die hellen Steine" opens with the lines "DIE HELLEN / STEINE gehn durch die Luft, die hell- / weißen, die Licht- / bringer." See Paul Celan, *Gedichte I* (Frankfurt am Main: Suhrkamp, 1975), 255.

45. Braun relates the description of precise letters to the poetics of Gottfried Benn in Lermen and Braun, *Hilde Domin "Hand in Hand mit der Sprache,"* 116.

46. "Daß Auf-Schreiben ein eminenter Akt des Festhaltens und zugleich des Fließens (der Worte, der Wirklichkeit) ist . . ."

47. Not only is Droste-Hülshoff an important touchstone for postwar German women's writers, but also this poem in particular is a particularly inspiring example of the poetic experience that inspires other writers like Helga M. Novak in "ach ich stand an der Quelle"; Helga M. Novak, *Margarete mit dem Schrank* (Berlin: Rotbuch Verlag, 1978), 29.

48. Fried is among the poets included in *Doppelinterpretationen* and Domin also recalls in the Frankfurt lectures that around 1972 he joined her in approaching *Die Zeit* about publishing poems on a regular basis. Although the project was declined, the concept eventually was realized with the beginning of the *Frankfurter Anthologie* in 1974 by Marcel Reich-Ranicki, an effort that Domin credits with spurring the subsequent comeback of poetry after years of decline on the German literary scene. See Domin, *Gedicht als Augenblick,* 19–20.

49. The statement explicitly links civil courage with the action of women in relationship to men; she also observes here that women often find it convenient to take sides with men in attacking other women.

50. For examples of persistent small acts of courage, see Domin's tribute to Else Lasker-Schüler, Hilde Domin, "'Nur Ewigkeit ist kein Exil,' " in *Gesammelte Essays* (Munich: Piper, 1992).

51. Hans Magnus Enzensberger, *Landessprache* (Frankfurt am Main: Suhrkamp, 1960); Ingeborg Bachmann, *Sämtliche Gedichte* (Munich: Piper, 1978), 124.

52. Advertising slogans for Coke from 1963 to 1968 increasingly stressed the overlap between material goods and happiness as the campaign "Things Go Better with Coke" was transformed into slogans touting the beverage as the "Real Thing" in October 1969. See Mark Pendergrast, *For God, Country, and Coca-Cola* (New York: Scribner, 1993), 295.

53. Though Domin evokes the persuasiveness of advertising slogans, their negative overtones lie close at hand. German professional model Uschi

Obermaier, for example, became an icon for solipsistic consumer culture and as Herzog observes, "Obermaier was notoriously apolitical, given to declaring nonchalantly that she was far more interested in drinking Coca-Cola than reading Marx"; in Herzog, *Sex After Fascism*, 257.

54. About the presentation and broadcast of these lectures, see Tauschwitz, *"Das ich sein kann, wie ich bin": Hilde Domin: Die Biografie*, 454–55.

55. Hartung also flags this year as a significant change in the literary climate. See Harald Hartung, *Deutsche Lyrik seit 1965* (Munich: Piper, 1985), 11. Concerning the roles of Domin, Erich Fried, and Reich-Ranicki role in trying to revive newspaper publication of poetry, see Hilde Domin, "Marcel Reich-Ranicki und die Lyrik," in *Gesammelte Essays* (Munich: Piper, 1992), 355; and Marcel Reich-Ranicki, *The Author of Himself: The Life of Marcel Reich-Ranicki*, trans. Ewald Osers (London: Weidenfeld and Nicolson, 2001), 344–52.

56. In March 1974 Marcuse also delivered his lecture "Marxism and Feminism," further indication of the attention given to feminism by intellectuals with whom Domin shared common interests. See Herbert Marcuse, "Marxism and Feminism," in *Herbert Marcuse. The New Left and the 1960s*, ed. Douglas Kellner (London: Routledge, 2005).

57. With regard to the general literary climate for women, it is interesting to note that Domin also published interpretations of poems by Marie Luise Kaschnitz and Elizabeth Borchers in the *Frankfurter Allgemeine Zeitung* in 1975. See Domin, *Gesammelte Essays*, 341–46. Translations of two poems by Denise Levertov from *O Taste and See* (1960–61) appear in Hilde Domin, *Gesammelte Gedichte* (Frankfurt am Main: S. Fischer, 1987), 392–99. According to Tauschwitz, Domin encountered Levertov's work while in exile in London. See Tauschwitz, *"Das ich sein kann, wie ich bin": Hilde Domin: Die Biografie*, 211.

58. See Christa Wolf, *Voraussetzungen einer Erzählung: Kassandra: Frankfurter Poetik-Vorlesungen* (Darmstadt, Ger.: Luchterhand, 1983); and Judith Ryan, "Poetik als Experiment: Christa Wolf, *Voraussetzungen einer Erzählung: Kassandra* (1983), in *Poetik der Autoren: Beiträge zur deutschsprachigen Gegenwartsliteratur*, ed. Paul Michael Lützeler (Frankfurt am Main: Fischer, 1994).

59. Still, she takes note of many contemporary writers, including Ulla Hahn (51) and Else Lasker-Schüler, whom she terms the one writer whose work is the "Meßlatte" (gold standard) regardless of gender (52). On Hahn's 1992 tribute to Domin, see Tauschwitz, *"Das ich sein kann, wie ich bin": Hilde Domin: Die Biografie*, 426–27.

60. Enzensberger writes polemically that "poems are not consumer goods, but instead means of production, with whose help the reader can succeed in producing the truth," in Bender, ed., *Mein Gedicht ist mein Messer*, 146–47.

61. There can be no question of Domin's admiration for Enzensberger, despite problematical moments in their exchanges; cf. Tauschwitz, *"Das ich sein kann, wie ich bin": Hilde Domin: Die Biografie*, 331–32. Contact between the two authors dated to her first years in Germany in the 1950s, according to Domin, and Domin became a contributor to the 1960 anthology *Museum der modernen Poesie*; see Hans Magnus Enzensberger, ed., *Museum der modernen Poesie* (Frankfurt am Main: Suhrkamp, 1960). Her autobiographical writings wryly comment that

Enzensberger and the lushly photographed travel magazine *Merian* popularized the Caribbean area where she spent her exile years; Hilde Domin, "Meine Wohnungen—'Mis Moradas,'" in *Gesammelte autobiographische Schriften* (Munich: Piper, 1992), 95. In addition, in her fictive interview with Heinrich Heine (1972), Domin quips in an aside that even Enzensberger believes that poetry is not simply written for political ends, commenting, "I gladly turn to Enzensberger, he is canonized, I am not." See Domin, "Hilde Domin Interviewt Heinrich Heine 1972 in Heidelberg," in *Gesammelte autobiographische Schriften* (Munich: Piper, 1992), 237. In *Doppelinterpretationen,* Enzensberger is called upon as the example of the poet who speaks loudest about issues that concern Domin and to prove that even writers with highly rationalized programs do not mechanically reproduce these ideas in poetry. See Domin, *Doppelinterpretationen,* 16, 33. Moreover, she frequently cites Enzensberger, particularly in writings that concern political poetry, leftist positions, and the discipline (or intellectual training) that occurs in the writing of poetry. In *Nachkrieg und Unfrieden: Gedichte als Index 1945–1970,* Domin references positions Enzensberger articulated in *Kursbuch* and his long poem "Schaum" from *Landessprache* (1960). In her autobiographical prose, collected in *Aber die Hoffnung* (1982), she acknowledges his crucial role in promoting Nelly Sachs, a forgotten poet before his intervention. "From his first appearance and throughout two decades he was one of the shapers—and also destroyers—of our literary landscape"; see Hilde Domin, "'Daß nicht Einer Tod meine, wenn er Leben sagt': Die Dichtung der Nelly Sachs," in *Aber die Hoffnung* (Munich: Piper, 1982), 144.

Chapter Three

1. Domin asserts reader coauthorship as "the reader is on the way to authorship, that is to becoming one with the poem in which the author himself has already 'disappeared,' when it is a good poem." See Hilde Domin, *Doppelinterpretationen: Das zeitgenössische deutsche Gedicht zwischen Autor und Leser* (Frankfurt am Main: Athenäum, 1966), 41.

2. The collection includes equal numbers of poems by Hahn and Ingeborg Bachmann; only Sarah Kirsch has greater prominence in the collection.

3. Her 1991 novel *Ein Mann im Haus* (*A Man in the House*) received some praise. See Susanne Baackmann, "Zu Ulla Hahns *Ein Mann im Haus,*" in *Erklär mir Liebe: Weibliche Schreibweisen von Liebe in der Gegenwartsliteratur* (Hamburg: Argument, 1995). Subsequent novels, *Das verborgene Wort* (*The Hidden Word,* 2001), *Unscharfe Bilder* (*Unfocused Pictures,* 2003), and *Aufbruch* (*Breaking Away,* 2009), and the short-story collection *Liebesarten* (*Types of Love,* 2006), established Hahn's credentials as a fiction writer. Cf. Elizabeth Boa, "Telling It How It Wasn't: Familial Allegories of Wish-Fulfillment in Postunification Germany," in *German Memory Contests: The Quest for Identity in Literature, Film, and Discourse Since 1990,* ed. Anne Fuchs, Mary Crossgrove, and George Grote (Rochester, N.Y.: Camden House, 2006).

4. In German the lines echo Goethe's famous use of profanity in the Storm and Stress drama *Götz von Berlichingen* and read, "Ihr könnt mich mal / mir hängt mein Grinsen schon längst zum Maul raus ich / geh lieber in die Binsen."

5. Sontag attracted attention as a critic of U.S. Vietnam policy in German press reports on the Gruppe 47 meeting in Princeton, New Jersey, in 1966. See Reinhard Lettau, ed., *Die Gruppe 47: Bericht, Kritik, Polemik: Ein Handbuch* (Neuwied, Ger.: Luchterhand, 1967), 218–47; and Heinz Ludwig Arnold, *Die Gruppe 47* (Reinbek bei Hamburg, Ger.: Rowohlt, 2004), 123. Enzensberger, who participated in the meeting, subsequently appropriated the concept of an "erotics of art" from Sontag's essay "Against Interpretation." See Charlotte Melin, *Poetic Maneuvers: Hans Magnus Enzensberger and the Lyric Genre* (Evanston, Ill.: Northwestern University Press, 2003), 89. Sontag was interviewed and published in Germany beginning in the 1970s in venues familiar to Hahn.

6. Similarly, Hahn emphasizes three objective motivations for her prose texts: reflection about praxis, connection to other writers, and critical appreciation in Ulla Hahn, *Dichter in der Welt: Mein Schreiben und Lesen* (Munich: Deutsche Verlags-Anstalt, 2006), 11.

7. Hahn indexes Heinrich von Kleist's "Über das Marionettentheater" and Jean Genet rather than the famous *Seiltänzer* described in Friedrich Nietzsche, *Also Sprach Zarathustra* (Baden-Baden, Ger.: Insel, 1982), 16.

8. In German the line reads, "Du mußt dein Leben ändern"; Rainer Maria Rilke, "Archaïscher Torso Apollos," in *Der ausgewählten Gedichte erster Teil* (Wiesbaden, Ger.: Insel, 1951), 60.

9. "Anständiges Sonett" bears an epigraph by Hermlin. In light of this reference, Demetz reads "Für einen Flieger" as honoring Hermlin in Marcel Reich-Ranicki, ed., *Frauen dichten anders* (Frankfurt am Main: Insel, 1998), 756–58.

10. Hahn's interpretations of poems by Lasker-Schüler, Kirsch, Bachmann, and Runge in *Frauen dichten anders* and her laudation for Christa Reinig will not be treated in the present study.

11. Hahn, in fact, asserts that the expressive capacities of the lyric genre constitute a unique form of thought: "In the poem the paradoxical succeeds: the rules of analytical understanding are suspended in a condition of supreme presence of mind"; Ulla Hahn, "Wer Sprache benutzt, um zu verharmlosen, handelt lebensgefährdend," in *Literatur und Politik* (Frankfurt am Main: Schriftenreihe Börsenverein des Deutschen Buchhandels, 1988), 64.

12. This notion also motivates the discussion of *Gebrauchslyrik* by Domin, Enzensberger, and other writers, noted in chapter 2. Her engagement with Domin is further evidenced in the tribute she pays to Domin in naming the main protagonist in the novel *Aufbruch* Hildegard Palm (156) and registering this character's interest in poetry by Domin (338). See Ulla Hahn, *Aufbruch* (Munich: Deutsche Verlags-Anstalt, 2009).

13. On confessionalism, see Alex Preminger and T. V. F. Brogan, eds., *The New Princeton Encyclopedia of Poetry and Poetics* (Princeton, N.J.: Princeton University Press, 1993), 61.

14. The trope refers to the fate of the Münster Anabaptists, while the title "Manche freilich" ("Many Indeed") quotes the first words of a poem by Hugo von Hofmannsthal.

15. Concerning Hahn's use of biblical language, see Karl-Josef Kuschel, "Schreiben, um die Sehnsucht wachzuhalten: Gespräch mit Ulla Hahn," in *Ich glaube nicht, daß ich Atheist bin* (Munich: Piper, 1992); and Inge Meidinger-Geise, "Hoffnung auf Liebe," *Zeitwende* 57, no. 1 (1986).

16. The sentence as rendered by Hahn retranslates as "In the male universe, I naturally adopted conceptions about women, sexuality, power from the subjective view of male poets."

17. For an interpretation, see Helmut Kiesel, "Der Blick der Liebe," in *Frauen dichten anders*, ed. Marcel Reich-Ranicki (Frankfurt am Main: Insel Verlag, 1998).

18. "Rose, oh reiner Widerspruch" ("Rose, oh pure contradiction"). See Hans Egon Holthusen, *Rainer Maria Rilke* (Reinbek bei Hamburg, Ger.: Rowohlt, 1958), 163.

19. Hahn has acknowledged the incongruity of her work. Commenting in *Poesie und Vergnügen,* Hahn confesses that as a university student she disputed academic readings. "Not to detract from the reputation of *Wolfgang Kayser* did I cite this," Hahn remarks, "but rather to underscore once more how quickly our conception of the comprehensibility of a poem changes and how much, too, professional readers can err, that is how much they are dominated by contemporary taste"; Ulla Hahn, *Poesie und Vergnügen—Poesie und Verantwortung* (Heidelberg, Ger.: C. F. Mueller Juristischer Verlag, 1994), 30–31.

Chapter Four

1. There is no straightforward translation for the term *Fremdbestimmung* in English. The term *fremd* also means "alien" or "exotic," while *Bestimmung* is both a noun used in legal formulations and a word that can be symbolically interpreted to mean "destiny."

2. See Karl Corino and Elisabeth Albertsen, eds., *Nach zwanzig Seiten waren alle Helden tot: Erste Schreibversuche deutscher Schriftsteller* (Düsseldorf, Ger.: Marion von Schröder, 1995), 65–68; and Ursula Krechel, *In Zukunft schreiben* (Salzburg, Austria: Jung und Jung, 2003), 9–10.

3. Though prolific as a writer and theorist, Krechel has received limited critical attention beyond brief reviews of her work. For discussion of her early feminism see in particular Rita Mielke, "Ursula Krechel," in *Kritisches Lexikon zur deutschsprachigen Gegenwartsliteratur* (Munich: Text und Kritik, 1986), 1–14; and Jürgen Serke, "Ursula Krechel: Kämpferin für die Frauenbewegung," in *Frauen schreiben* (Frankfurt am Main: Fischer, 1982), 347–48. See also Beth Bjorklund, "Ursula Krechel, *Rohschnitt,*" *World Literature Today* 58, no. 2 (1984): 261; Harald Hartung, "Warten auf das lange Gedicht," in *Deutsche Lyrik seit 1965: Tendenzen, Beispiele, Porträts* (Munich: Piper, 1985), 74–77; and Herbert Wiesner and Alexander von Bormann, "Ursula Krechel," in *Lexikon der deutschsprachigen Gegenwartsliteratur,* ed. Hermann Kunisch, Herbert Wiesner, and Sibylle Cramer (Munich: Nymphenburger, 1987), 346–48.

4. Krechel notes the penchant of contemporary writers, herself included, for piecing together texts from autobiographical materials, memory scraps, and quotidian snippets. See Ursula Krechel, "Meine Sätze haben schon einen Bart: Abmahnung an die neue Weiblichkeit," *Kursbuch* 73 (1983): 153.

5. See Ursula Krechel, *Verwundbar wie in den besten Zeiten* (Darmstadt, Ger.: Luchterhand, 1979); Krechel, *Rohschnitt* (Darmstadt, Ger.: Luchterhand, 1983); Krechel, *Vom Feuer lernen* (Darmstadt, Ger.: Luchterhand, 1985); Krechel, *Kakaoblau* (Salzburg, Austria: Residenz, 1989); Krechel, *Landläufiges Wunder* (Frankfurt am Main: Suhrkamp, 1995); Krechel, *Stimmen aus dem harten Kern: Gedichte* (Salzburg, Austria: Jung und Jung, 2005); Krechel, *Mittelwärts: Gedichte* (Springe, Ger.: Zu Klampen!, 2006); and Krechel, *Jäh erhellte Dunkelheit: Gedichte* (Salzburg, Austria: Jung und Jung, 2010). Krechel also demonstrates wit and facile handling of episodic construction as well in prose narratives and dramatic sketches, which will not be discussed here: *Zweite Natur* (*Second Nature*, 1981), "Roswitha" (1983), *Spiel verderben* (*Spoiling the Game*, 1984), *Die Freunde des Wetterleuchtens* (*The Friends of Sheet-Lightning*, 1990), and *Der Übergriff* (The Encroachment, 2001), alongside numerous uncollected fictional works. *Stimmen aus dem harten Kern* has been translated as Krechel, *Voices from the Bitter Core*, trans. Amy Kepple Strawser (Austin, Tex.: Host, 2010).

6. Ursula Krechel, "Erika: Ein Stück," *Theaterheute* 15, no. 8 (1974).

7. See Ursula Krechel, *Selbsterfahrung und Fremdbestimmung: Bericht aus der Neuen Frauenbewegung* (Darmstadt, Ger.: Luchterhand, 1975/1983).

8. Sontag is an abiding point of reference in Krechel's work, and her book *Illness as Metaphor* (1978) is cited in Krechel, *In Zukunft schreiben*, 197.

9. Krechel's trenchant critique of the unreflected chronicling of existence in writing, which she finds very unrewarding, could easily be applied to what are today common forms of social networking.

10. Dada poet and painter Hans Arp had, in fact, reconnected postwar poetry with prewar avant-garde traditions through collections published beginning in the early 1950s. See Liselotte Gumpel, *"Concrete" Poetry from East and West Germany: The Language of Exemplarism and Experimentalism* (New Haven, Conn.: Yale University Press, 1976).

11. The latter collection assembles essays written in the previous fourteen years. See Ursula Krechel, *Mit dem Körper des Vaters spielen: Essays* (Frankfurt am Main: Suhrkamp, 1992), 257.

12. Quirinus Kuhlmann (1651–1689) was a German baroque writer known for his highly experimental use of language. He experienced mystical visions and was burned at the stake for heresy. Rolf Bossert (1952–1986), a poet, journalist, and editor, belonged to the German-speaking minority in Romania and suffered political persecution. He committed suicide shortly after immigrating with his family to West Germany. Karoline von Günderode (1780–1806) was the author of prose and fiction admired by Goethe and that shared stylistic affinities with German romantic writers. Her correspondence with Bettina von Arnim is considered the first literary exchange between German women writers.

13. Conversely, Krechel states that male writers save up biographical details for later use as they develop a mature sense of self from mother-child bonds. Krechel, *Körper*, 69–70.

14. The word play of the title is difficult to capture in English. *Auslassung*, a noun, can mean "omission," "rambling remark," "ellipses," or "elision."

15. As the co-creator of a limited-edition art book of poems and graphic prints produced with Irmgard Flemming (*Äusserst Innen,* 1993), Krechel's references to print technique fit with her direct experience in this art form.

16. Ironically, Krechel writes that artists should be dissuaded from subject matter like sunflowers or felt (a reference to conceptual artist Joseph Beuys) in Krechel, *In Zukunft schreiben,* 147–48.

17. Krechel draws inspiration from Friedrich Hölderlin's "Emilie vor ihrem Brauttag" ("Emilie Before Her Wedding Day"). See Ursula Krechel, *Verbeugungen vor der Luft* (Salzburg, Austria: Residenz, 1999), 102. Compare phrasing in Friedrich Hölderlin, *Sämtliche Werke* (Berlin: Tempel Verlag, 1963), 188–205.

18. Her terminology points to the theories of Hans Georg Gadamer and Wolfgang Iser.

19. Krechel also references other sources on this subject, adding an extensive footnote on Hemingway's description of a dog corpse extracted from an account given by William Carlos Williams in his autobiography. See Krechel, *In Zukunft schreiben,* 36, 198.

Chapter Five

1. Julia Virginia is a pseudonym for Julie Virginie Scheuermann.

2. Bender positions one project as displaying the restart of German poetry after fascism; Hans Bender, ed., *Widerspiel* (Munich: Hanser 1962), 9. For a later anthology that concentrates on defining four decades of German poetry, see Hans Bender, ed., *In diesem Lande leben wir* (Frankfurt am Main: Fischer, 1978), 260. A subsequent collection published immediately prior to the 1989 fall of the Berlin Wall is, however, framed as representing the autonomy of individual poems and the plurality of voices in German-speaking countries; Bender, ed., *Was sind das für Zeiten* (Munich: Hanser, 1988), 243. Drews expresses concern both with the dates that have marked historical epochs in the lyric genre in Germany and aesthetic quality as a determinant of canon; see Jörg Drews, *Das bleibt: Deutsche Gedichte 1945–1995* (Leipzig: Reclam, 1995), 250–51. For a recent discussion of the concept of *Kulturnation* see Andrew Piper, "Rethinking the Printed Object: Goethe and the Book of Everything," *PMLA* 121, no. 1 (2006).

3. See Hans Magnus Enzensberger, "Wie ich fünfzig Jahre lang versuchte, Amerika zu entdecken," in *Der Zorn altert, die Ironie ist unsterblich: Über Hans Magnus Enzensberger,* ed. Rainer Wieland (Frankfurt am Main: Suhrkamp, 1999), 100; Krechel, *In Zukunft schreiben,* 111–14; and Frances Stonor Saunders, *The Cultural Cold War: The CIA and the World of Arts and Letters* (New York: New, 1999).

4. The case of Ezra Pound was the subject of an article in *Wort und Wahrheit* already in 1952, and Zuther reports twenty-four publications by or about Pound from 1945 to 1959, several related to the German publication of *ABC of Reading.* See Gerhard H. W. Zuther, *Eine Bibliographie der Aufnahme amerikanischer Literatur in deutschen Zeitschriften 1945–1960* (Munich: Dissertations Druck Franz Frank, 1965), 103–5. For a description of Rainer Maria Gerhard's plans for similar anthologies, inspired by correspondence with Robert

Creeley and Charles Olson, see Franz Josef Knape, . . . *Zugeritten in manchen Sprachen . . . Über Werk und Wirkung des Dichters und Vermittlers Rainer Maria Gerhardt* (Würzburg, Ger.: Königshausen und Neumann, 1995), 181.

5. The program of relearning that informs *Museum der modernen Poesie* is boldly outlined in Hans Magnus Enzensberger, "In Search of the Lost Language," *Encounter* 21, no. 3 (1963).

6. See, for example, Bender, ed., *Widerspiel*. This marginalization continues; compare Georgina Paul, "Ismene at the Crossroads: Gender and Poetic Influence," *German Life and Letters* 60, no. 3 (2007): 430–31.

7. In the field of translation, by contrast, women were relatively well represented; Eva Hesse, for instance, undertook the difficult task of translating Pound for German audiences. For translations by the most prominent authors and translators, see especially Hans Magnus Enzensberger, ed., *Museum der modernen Poesie* (Frankfurt am Main: Suhrkamp, 1960).

8. The authors' pictures (copies of engravings and photographs) are mounted on reddish brown paper and inserted in alphabetical position. Nine pages at the end of the book advertise other poetry and prose publications by women authors.

9. *Frauenlyrik unserer Zeit* shows practically no overlap with the later anthologies examined here. Only Huch is also included in the collections edited by Reich-Ranicki and Hahn.

10. The wording echoes lines from Goethe's play *Torquato Tasso* that also serve as an epigraph for a poem: "Und wenn der Mensch in seiner Qual verstummt / Gab mir ein Gott zu sagen, was ich leide" ("And when man in his agony falls silent / A god gave me voice to say, what I suffer"). See Johann Wolfgang von Goethe, "Elegie," in *Gedichte,* ed. Erich Trunz (Munich: C. H. Beck, 1974), 381.

11. The poets are Susy Clemens, Elisabeth Wenzlik, Gabriele Weingartner, Martina Born, Brigitte Wolf, Claudia Pütz, Birgit Welz, and Jutta Glaser. None of these authors appears in the other anthologies under consideration.

12. Biographies of each of the included poets are set on separate pages, followed by poems, also printed one to a page, or on facing pages in the case of longer texts.

13. This historical focus is reinforced by the cover illustration, which depicts a woman in eighteenth-century dress poised to write with an implement that looks like a knitting needle.

14. A shift in literary canon is also not evident in electronic publications after 2000. A "top-10 list" published in the journal *Das Gedicht* (Fall 1999–Summer 2000) names only Ingeborg Bachmann and Friederike Mayröcker to the group of most important German poets of the twentieth century; see "Hitliste der Jahrhundertdichter," Anton G. Leitner Verlag, http://www.dasgedicht .de/hits.htm. For a dynamic literary map based on readers' interests that also includes few German women poets, see Marek Gibney, "Literature-Map," http://www.literature-map.com/.

15. The sections are entitled "Ars poetica," "Eine Frauenfrage" ("A Women's Question"), "Nachruf" ("Obituary"), "Zwei versuchen miteinander zu reden"

("Two Attempt to Talk with Each Other"), "An mich" ("To Myself"), "Für Alle" ("For Everyone"), "Die Wüste hat zwölf Ding" ("The Desert Has a Dozen Things"), and "Dennoch schauen" ("And Yet, Look").

16. Hahn also expresses understanding that the tradeoff for access to education (*Bildung*) became a suppression of sensuality (*Sinnlichkeit*), a dichotomy (mind/body) that has Western origins. Ulla Hahn, ed., *Stechäpfel: Gedichte von Frauen aus drei Jahrtausenden* (Stuttgart, Ger.: Reclam, 1992), 382.

17. The verb *dichten* means both "to write" in general and "to compose" or "make poetry."

18. Reich-Ranicki is, clearly, rarely a neutral critic. His rhetoric and confidence in traditions is even mirrored in the presentation of the anthology. The 2000 special edition of the collection, in fact, featured a head-shot portrait of Reich-Ranicki himself on the cover.

19. Klüger applies the term *Apokoinu* to this practice, a term also used by Enzensberger in a discussion of the possibilities of creating an open poetic language. His frame of reference is the work of William Carlos Williams. See Charlotte Melin, *Poetic Maneuvers: Hans Magnus Enzensberger and the Lyric Genre* (Evanston, Ill.: Northwestern University Press, 2003), 91.

20. Paul productively analyzes the problem of influence in women's writing, critiquing Bloom's Oedipal model and acknowledging the problem of exceptionality for the woman poet. As she points out, there are multiple lines of influence to be discovered, as, for example, allusions to Ingeborg Bachmann in the poetry of Ulrike Draesner. See Paul, "Ismene at the Crossroads: Gender and Poetic Influence," 435–36.

Conclusion

1. Leeder, in fact, cites "performed" poetry as one of the most important developments of the 1990s. See Karen Leeder, "Introduction. 'Schreiben am Schnittpunkt': The Place of Contemporary Poetry," in *Schaltstelle: Neue Lyrik im Dialog,* ed. Karen Leeder (Amsterdam: Rodopi, 2007), 7.

2. Similarly, Ostriker recognizes in poetry by Sylvia Plath a "deliberately antibelletristic, deliberately naïve" way of writing that in the American tradition enables a rejection of convention. Alicia Ostriker, *Writing Like a Woman* (Ann Arbor: University of Michigan Press, 1983), 45–46.

3. Hilde Domin in a recollection of life in Rome in the 1930s also recalls the comfort of a heater that carried the name Habakuk. See Hilde Domin, *Gesammelte autobiographische Schriften* (Munich: Piper, 1992), 86.

4. See also Charlotte Melin, "Renderings of *Alice in Wonderland* in Postwar German Literature," in *Women in German Yearbook,* ed. Sara Friedrichsmeyer and Patricia Herminghouse (Lincoln: University of Nebraska Press, 1996).

Adorno, Theodor W. 1955a. "Kulturkritik und Gesellschaft." In *Prismen,* 7–31. Berlin: Suhrkamp.

———. 1955b. "Valéry Proust Museum." In *Prismen,* 215–31. Berlin: Suhrkamp.

———. 1991. "On Lyric Poetry and Society." In *Notes to Literature.* Vol. I. Edited by Rolf Tiedemann. Translated by Shierry Weber Nicholsen, 37–54. New York: Columbia University Press.

Alexander, Elisabeth. 1982. "Frauenlyrik als Wegweiser." *Der Literat* 24, no. 5: 115–16.

Ames, Christopher. 1992. "Modernism and Tradition: The Legacies of Belatedness." *Studies in the Literary Imagination* 25, no. 2: 39–62.

Anz, Thomas. 1996. "Postmoderne Poetik." In *Frankfurter Anthologie: Gedichte und Interpretationen.* Edited by Marcel Reich-Ranicki, 241–44. Frankfurt am Main: Insel.

Arnheim, Rudolf. 1954. *Art and Visual Perception.* Berkeley: University of California Press.

Arnold, Heinz Ludwig. 2004. *Die Gruppe 47.* Reinbek bei Hamburg, Ger.: Rowohlt.

Baackmann, Susanne. 1995. "Zu Ulla Hahns *Ein Mann im Haus.*" In *Erklär mir Liebe: Weibliche Schreibweisen von Liebe in der Gegenwartsliteratur,* 189–97. Hamburg: Argument.

Bachmann, Ingeborg. 1978. *Sämtliche Gedichte.* Munich: Piper.

Bammer, Angelika. 2000. "Feminism, *Frauenliteratur,* and Women's Writing of the 1970s and 1980s." In *A History of Women's Writing in Germany, Austria and Switzerland.* Edited by Jo Catling, 216–21. Cambridge, Eng.: Cambridge University Press.

Barry, Jackson. 1999. "The Meaning of the Author: Robert Lowell as Image of an Age." In *Art, Culture, and the Semiotics of Meaning,* 77–87. New York: St. Martin's.

Belenky, Mary Field, Blythe McVicker Clinchy, Nancy Rule Goldberger, and Jill Mattuck Tarule. 1986. *Women's Ways of Knowing.* New York: Basic Books.

Bender, Hans, ed. 1962. *Widerspiel.* Munich: Hanser.

———, ed. 1964. *Mein Gedicht ist mein Messer.* Munich: List.

———. 1972. "Letter from Germany: The Myth of 'Kahlschlag.'" *Dimension* 5, no. 3: 395–401.

———, ed. 1978. *In diesem Lande leben wir.* Frankfurt am Main: Fischer.

———, ed. 1988. *Was sind das für Zeiten.* Munich: Hanser.

Benjamin, Walter. 1977. "Das Kunstwerk im Zeitalter seiner technischen Re-produzierbarkeit." *Illuminationen: Ausgewählte Schriften.* Frankfurt am Main: Suhrkamp.

Benn, Gottfried. 1951. *Probleme der Lyrik.* Wiesbaden, Ger.: Limes.

———. 1970. "Mann und Frau gehen durch die Krebsbaracke." In *Selected Poems.* Edited by Friedrich Wilhelm Wodtke, 51–52. London: Oxford University Press.

Bennett, Benjamin. 1993. "The Politics of the Mörike-Debate and Its Object." *Germanic Review* 68, no. 2:60–68.

Bernikow, Louise, ed. 1974. *The World Split Open: Four Centuries of Women Poets in England and America, 1552–1950.* New York: Vintage.

Bjorklund, Beth. 1984. "Ursula Krechel, *Rohschnitt.*" *World Literature Today* 58, no. 2: 260–61.

Blake, William. 1972. "Ah! Sun-Flower." In *Blake Complete Writings.* Edited by Geoffrey Keynes, 215. London: Oxford University Press.

Bloom, Harold. 1973. *The Anxiety of Influence: A Theory of Poetry.* London: Oxford University Press.

Boa, Elizabeth. 2006. "Telling It How It Wasn't: Familial Allegories of Wish-Fulfillment in Postunification Germany." In *German Memory Contests: The Quest for Identity in Literature, Film, and Discourse Since 1990.* Edited by Anne Fuchs, Mary Crossgrove, and George Grote, 67–83. Rochester, N.Y.: Camden House.

Borchers, Elisabeth, ed. 1996. *Gedichte berühmter Frauen.* Frankfurt am Main: Insel.

Bossinade, Johanna, and Angelika Schaser. 2003. "Von der Außenseiterin zur Klassikerin: Käte Hamburger." In *Käte Hamburger: Zur Aktualität einer Klassikerin.* Edited by J. Bossinade and A. Schaser, 7–14. Göttingen, Ger.: Wallstein Verlag.

Bourdieu, Pierre. 1993. *The Field of Cultural Production: Essays on Art and Literature.* Edited by R. Johnson. New York: Columbia University Press.

Bovenschen, Silvia. 1976. "Über die Frage: Gibt es eine 'weibliche' Aesthetik?" *Aesthetik und Kommunikation* 25: 631–45.

Braese, Stephan, ed. 1999. *Bestandsaufnahme: Studien zur Gruppe 47.* Berlin: Erich Schmidt.

Braun, Michael. 1986a. *Der poetische Augenblick: Essays zur Gegenwartsliteratur.* Berlin: Vis-à-Vis.

———. 1986b. "Ulla Hahn." In *Kritisches Lexikon zur deutschsprachigen Gegenwartsliteratur.* Edited by Heinz Ludwig Arnold, 1–10. Munich: Text und Kritik.

———. 1992. "Weißes Rauschen." *Die Zeit,* April 17, 102.

———. 1996. "Zeichen und Wunder." *Neue Deutsche Literatur* 44, no. 2: 149–52.

Brecht, Bertolt. 1967. *Gesammelte Gedichte.* Vol. 1. Frankfurt am Main: Suhrkamp.

Brinker-Gabler, Gisela, ed. 1978. *Deutsche Dichterinnen: Vom 16. Jahrhundert bis zur Gegenwart.* Frankfurt am Main: Fischer.

Brittan, Alice. 2006. "War and the Book: The Diarist, the Cryptographer, and *The English Patient.*" *PMLA* 121, no. 1: 200–213.

Brockmann, Stephen. 2004. *German Literary Culture at the Zero Hour.* Rochester, N.Y.: Camden House.

Bühler-Dietrich, Annette. 2002. "Nelly Sachs—Dichterin von Dichterinnen? Zur Sachs-Lektüre von Aichinger, Bachmann und Domin." In *Erfahrung nach dem Krieg: Autorinnen im Literaturbetrieb 1945–1950 BRD, DDR, Österreich, Schweiz.* Edited by Christiane Caemmerer, Walter Delabar, Elke Ramm, and Marion Schulz, 95–115. Frankfurt am Main: Peter Lang.

Bürger, Jan, and Frank Druffner, eds. 2009. *Hilde Domin: Die Liebe im Exil: Briefe an Erwin Walter Palm aus den Jahren 1931–1959.* Frankfurt am Main: S. Fischer Verlag.

Bürger, Peter. 1974. *Theorie der Avantgarde.* Frankfurt am Main: Suhrkamp.

Butler, Judith. 1990. *Gender Trouble: Feminism and the Subversion of Identity.* New York: Routledge.

Celan, Paul. 1972. "Der Meridian." In *Ausgewählte Gedichte,* 133–48. Frankfurt am Main: Suhrkamp.

———. 1975. *Gedichte I.* Frankfurt am Main: Suhrkamp.

———. 1986. "Speech on the Occasion of Receiving the Literature Prize of the Free Hanseatic City of Bremen." In *Collected Prose.* Translated by Rosmarie Waldrop, 33–35. Manchester, Eng.: Carcanet.

Clune, Michael. 2005. "'Everything We Want': Frank O'Hara and the Aesthetics of Free Choice." *PMLA* 120, no. 1: 181–96.

Cofalla, Sabine. 1999. "Hans Werner Richter—Anmerkungen zum Habitus und zur sozialen Rolle des Leiters der Gruppe 47." In *Bestandsaufnahme: Studien zur Gruppe 47.* Edited by Stephan Braese, 65–85. Berlin: Erich Schmidt.

Cohn, Dorrit. 1970. "Käte Hamburger, *Die Logik der Dichtung.*" *Germanic Review* 45, no. 1: 65–67.

Corino, Karl, and Elisabeth Albertsen, eds. 1995. *Nach zwanzig Seiten waren alle Helden tot: Erste Schreibversuche deutscher Schriftsteller.* Düsseldorf, Ger.: Marion von Schröder.

Culler, Jonathan. 1997. *Literary Theory: A Very Short Introduction.* Oxford: Oxford University Press.

———. 2008. "Why Lyric?" *PMLA* 123, no. 1: 201–6.

Damerau, Burghard. 2003. "Pro und contra: Zu Käte Hamburgers Kritik der ästhetischen Wahrheit." In *Käte Hamburger: Zur Aktualität einer Klassikerin.* Edited by Johanna Bossinade and Angelika Schaser, 115–28. Göttingen, Ger.: Wallstein Verlag.

Dane, Gesa. 2000. "Käte Hamburger (1896–1992)." In *Wissenschaftsgeschichte der Germanistik in Porträts.* Edited by Christoph König, Hans-Harald Müller and Werner Röcke, 189–98. Berlin: Walter de Gruyter.

Demetz, Peter. 1970. *Postwar German Literature: A Critical Introduction.* New York: Pegasus.

———. 1986. *After the Fires.* San Diego: Harcourt Brace Jovanovich.

Di Stefano, Christine. 1990. "Dilemmas of Difference: Feminism, Modernity, and Postmodernism." In *Feminism/Postmodernism.* Edited by Linda J. Nicholson, 63–82. New York: Routledge.

Domin, Hilde. 1966. *Doppelinterpretationen: Das zeitgenössische deutsche Gedicht zwischen Autor und Leser.* Frankfurt am Main: Athenäum.

———. 1968. *Wozu Lyrik heute.* Munich: Piper.

———. 1970. *Nachkrieg und Unfrieden: Gedichte als Index 1945–1970.* Neuwied, Ger.: Luchterhand.

———. 1982. "'Daß nicht Einer Tod meine, wenn er Leben sagt': Die Dichtung der Nelly Sachs." In *Aber die Hoffnung,* 143–60. Munich: Piper.

———. 1987a. "Ausbruch von hier." In *Gesammelte Gedichte,* 359. Frankfurt am Main: S. Fischer.

———. 1987b. "Drei Arten Gedichte aufzuschreiben." In *Gesammelte Gedichte,* 333–36. Frankfurt am Main: S. Fischer.

———. 1987c. *Gesammelte Gedichte.* Frankfurt am Main: S. Fischer.

———. 1987d. "Tunnel." In *Gesammelte Gedichte,* 291. Frankfurt am Main: S. Fischer.

———. 1988a. *Das Gedicht als Augenblick von Freiheit: Frankfurt Poetik-Vorlesungen 1987/1988.* Munich: Piper.

———. 1988b. "Selbstvorstellung." In *Hilde Domin: Begleitheft zur Ausstellung der Stadt- und Universitätsbibliothek Frankfurt am Main 12. Januar–27. Februar 1988.* Edited by Bernd Koßmann and Winifred Giesen, 11–15. Frankfurt am Main: Die Bibliothek.

———. 1992a. "Engagement zu Beginn der deutschen Geschichte." In *Gesammelte Essays: Heimat in der Sprache,* 66–72. Munich: Piper.

———. 1992b. *Gesammelte autobiographische Schriften.* Munich: Piper.

———. 1992c. *Gesammelte Essays.* Munich: Piper.

———. 1992d. "Hilde Domin interviewt Heinrich Heine 1972 in Heidelberg." In *Gesammelte autobiographische Schriften,* 233–42. Munich: Piper.

———. 1992e. "Marcel Reich-Ranicki und die Lyrik." In *Gesammelte Essays,* 255–57. Munich: Piper.

———. 1992f. "Meine Wohnungen—'Mis moradas.'" In *Gesammelte autobiographische Schriften,* 71–138. Munich: Piper.

———. 1992g. "'Nur Ewigkeit ist kein Exil.'" In *Gesammelte Essays,* 80–93. Munich: Piper.

———. 1992h. "Über die Schwierigkeiten, eine berufstätige Frau zu sein." In *Gesammelte Essays,* 73–79. Munich: Piper.

———. 1992i. "Über Virginia Woolf." In *Gesammelte Essays,* 94–99. Munich: Piper.

———. 1998. "'Wortwechsel' Interview mit Christa Schulze-Rohr." In *Vokabular der Erinnerungen: Zum Werk von Hilde Domin.* Edited by Bettina von Wangenheim, 200–218. Frankfurt am Main: Fischer.

Drews, Jörg. 1977. "Selbsterfahrung und Neue Subjektivität in der Lyrik." *Akzente* 24, no. 1: 89–95.

———. 1980. *Vom "Kahlschlag" zu "movens": Über das langsame Auftauchen experimenteller Schreibweisen in der westdeutschen Literatur der fünfziger Jahre.* Munich: Edition Text und Kritik.

———. 1995. *Das bleibt: Deutsche Gedichte 1945–1995*. Leipzig: Reclam.

Droste-Hülshoff, Annette von. 1973. "Die Mergelgrube." In *Sämtliche Werke*, 45–48. Munich: Winkler.

DuPlessis, Rachel Blau. 1994. "'Corpses of Poesy': Some Modern Poets and Some Gender Ideologies of Lyric." In *Feminist Measures: Soundings in Poetry and Theory*. Edited by Lynn Keller and Christianne Miller, 69–95. Ann Arbor: University of Michigan Press.

Ecker, Gisela, ed. 1985. *Feminist Aesthetics*. Boston: Beacon.

Elm, Theo. 1999. "Weibliche Lyrik der deutschen Gegenwartsliteratur." In *Frauen Literatur Geschichte: Schreibende Frauen vom Mittelalter bis zur Gegenwart*. Edited by Hiltrud Gnüg and Renate Möhrmann, 340–51. Stuttgart, Ger.: Metzler.

Elsner, Gisela. 1983. "Autorinnen im literarischen Ghetto." *Kürbiskern* 2: 136–44.

Emmerich, Wolfgang. 1981. *Kleine Literaturgeschichte der DDR*. Darmstadt, Ger.: Luchterhand.

Engel, Peter, Anna Rheinsberg, and Christoph Schubert, eds. 1980. *Handbuch der deutschsprachigen alternativen Literatur*. Trier, Ger.: Édition Trèves.

Enzensberger, Hans Magnus. 1960a. *Landessprache*. Frankfurt am Main: Suhrkamp.

———, ed. 1960b. *Museum der modernen Poesie*. Frankfurt am Main: Suhrkamp.

———. 1963. "In Search of the Lost Language." *Encounter* 21, no. 3: 44–51.

———. 1964a. *Einzelheiten II: Poesie und Politik*. Frankfurt am Main: Suhrkamp.

———. 1964b. "Scherenschleifer und Poeten." In *Mein Gedicht ist mein Messer*. Edited by Hans Bender, 144–48. Munich: List.

———. 1968a. "Gemeinplätze, die Neueste Literatur betreffend." *Kursbuch* 15: 187–97.

———. 1968b. *Poems for People Who Don't Read Poems*. Translated by Michael Hamburger, Jerome Rothenberg, and H. M. Enzensberger. New York: Atheneum.

———. 1976. "Die Aporien der Avantgarde." In *Einzelheiten II: Poesie und Politik*, 50–80. Frankfurt am Main: Suhrkamp.

———. 1978. *Der Untergang der Titanic: Eine Kömodie*. Frankfurt am Main: Suhrkamp.

———. 1999. "Wie ich fünfzig Jahre lang versuchte, Amerika zu entdecken." In *Der Zorn altert, die Ironie ist unsterblich: Über Hans Magnus Enzensberger*. Edited by Rainer Wieland, 96–111. Frankfurt am Main: Suhrkamp.

———. 2000. *Einladung zu einem Poesie-Automaten*. Frankfurt am Main: Suhrkamp.

Falkner, Gerhard. 1993. *Über den Unwert des Gedichts: Fragmente und Reflexionen*. Berlin: Aufbau.

Farner, Geir. 1978. "Käte Hamburger und das Problem des fiktiven Erzählers." *Orbis Litterarum* 33, no. 2: 111–22.

Felski, Rita. 1995. *The Gender of Modernity*. Cambridge, Mass.: Harvard University Press.

Ferber, Christian. 1952. "Die Legende vom Kahlschlag." *Die Literatur* 1, no. 6: 1–2.

Ferry, Anne. 2001. *Tradition and the Individual Poem: An Inquiry into Anthologies.* Stanford, Calif.: Stanford University Press.

Flannery, Kathryn Thoms. 2005. *Feminist Literacies, 1968–75.* Urbana: University of Illinois Press.

Foucault, Michel. 1978. *The History of Sexuality.* Translated by Robert Hurley. Vol. 1. New York: Vintage.

Fried, Erich. 1978. "Neue Subjektivität." In *Lyrik-Katalog Bundesrepublik: Gedichte, Biographien, Statements.* Edited by Jan Hans, Uwe Herms, and Ralf Thenior, 115–16. Munich: Goldmann.

———. 1982. "Angst vor der Angst." In *Warngedichte,* 125. Frankfurt am Main: Fischer.

Friedrich, Hugo. 1956. *Die Struktur der modernen Lyrik: Von Baudelaire bis zur Gegenwart.* Hamburg: Rowohlt.

———. 1974. *The Structure of Modern Poetry: From the Mid-Nineteenth to the Mid-Twentieth Century.* Translated by Joachim Neugroschel. Evanston, Ill.: Northwestern University Press.

Gadamer, Hans Georg. 1965. *Wahrheit und Methode.* 2nd ed. Tübingen, Ger.: Mohr.

Galinsky, Hans. 1968. *Wegbereiter moderner amerikanischer Lyrik: Interpretations- und Rezeptionsstudien zu Emily Dickinson und William Carlos Williams.* Heidelberg, Ger.: Carl Winter.

George, Stefan. 1958. "Komm in den totgesagten park und schau." In *Werke,* 121. Munich: Helmut Kupper.

Gibney, Marek. 2008. literature-map, http://www.literature-map.com/.

Göbelsmann, Christel, ed. 1982. *Mörikes Lüfte sind vergiftet.* Bremen, Ger.: Schreiben Frauenliteraturverlag.

Goethe, Johann Wolfgang von. 1974. "Elegie." In *Gedichte.* Edited by Erich Trunz, 381. Munich: C. H. Beck.

Golding, Alan. 1995. *From Outlaw to Classic: Canons in American Poetry.* Madison: University of Wisconsin Press.

Graves, Peter J. 2002. "Karen Duve, Kathrin Schmidt, Judith Hermann: 'Ein literarisches Fräuleinwunder'?" *German Life and Letters* 55, no. 2: 196–207.

Guillory, John. 1993. *Cultural Capital: The Problem of Literary Canon Formation.* Chicago: University of Chicago Press.

Gumpel, Liselotte. 1976. *"Concrete" Poetry from East and West Germany: The Language of Exemplarism and Experimentalism.* New Haven, Conn.: Yale University Press.

Habermas, Jürgen. 1968. *Technik und Wissenschaft als "Ideologie."* Frankfurt am Main: Suhrkamp.

Hage, Volker. 1980. *Lyrik für Leser: Deutsche Gedichte der siebziger Jahre.* Stuttgart, Ger.: Reclam.

Hahn, Barbara. 2003. "Erratischer Block oder von der Schwierigkeit, Käte Hamburgers *Logik der Dichtung* zu lesen." In *Käte Hamburger: Zur*

Aktualität einer Klassikerin. Edited by Johanna Bossinade and Angelika Schaser, 129–39. Göttingen, Ger.: Wallstein Verlag.

Hahn, Ulla. 1978. *Literatur in der Aktion: Zur Entwicklung operativer Literaturformen in der Bundesrepublik.* Wiesbaden, Ger.: Akademische Verlagsgesellschaft Athenaion.

———. 1981a. *Herz über Kopf.* Stuttgart, Ger.: Deutsche Verlags-Anstalt.

———. 1981b. "Spätbürger und Kommunist: Stephan Hermlin, Ein Porträt." *Die Horen* 26, no. 4: 92–99.

———. 1982. "Die Dichterin Else Lasker-Schüler." In *Literarische Profile: Deutsche Dichter von Grimmelshausen bis Brecht.* Edited by Walter Hinderer, 202–15. Königstein, Ger.: Athenäum.

———. 1983a. "Nachwort." In *Gertrud Kolmar: Gedichte.* Edited by U. Hahn, 173–87. Frankfurt am Main: Suhrkamp.

———. 1983b. "Vorwort." In *Stephan Hermlin: Aufsätze, Reportagen, Reden, Interviews.* Edited by U. Hahn, 7–11. Frankfurt am Main: Fischer.

———. 1984. "'Möchte verständlich bleiben . . . ': Gespräch mit Ulla Hahn." *Der Literat* 26, no. 4: 92–93.

———. 1985a. *Begleitheft.* Edited by Walter Jens and Marcel Reich-Ranicki. *Zu Ricarda Huch: Michael Unger.* Stuttgart, Ger.: Deutscher Bücherbund.

———. 1985b. "Nachwort." In *Gertrud von Le Fort: Die Tochter Farinatas,* 95–112. Frankfurt am Main: Suhrkamp.

———. 1985c. "Ulla Hahn." In *Butzbacher Autoren-Interviews.* Edited by Hans-Joachim Müller, 160–70. Darmstadt, Ger.: Eduard Roetter.

———. 1986. "Schreiben als Sehnsucht: Abenteuer der Phantasie." *Frankfurter Allgemeine Zeitung,* October 6, 25.

———. 1987a. "Die schnippische Emily Dickinson." *Frankfurter Allgemeine Zeitung,* December 8, 9.

———. 1987b. "Seiltanz auf festen Versesfüßen." In *Seiltanz auf festen Versesfüssen: Neun Autoren in der Marburger Universität.* Edited by Wilhelm Solms, 111–19. Marburg, Ger.: Hitzeroth.

———. 1987c. "Wohnen bei den Wurzeln der Blumen: Hilde Domins Gesammelte Gedichte." *Frankfurter Allgemeine Zeitung,* June 27, n.p.

———. 1988a. *Unerhörte Nähe.* Stuttgart, Ger.: Deutsche Verlags-Anstalt.

———. 1988b. "Wer Sprache benutzt, um zu verharmlosen, handelt lebensgefährdend." In *Literatur und Politik,* 58–65. Frankfurt am Main: Schriftenreihe Börsenverein des Deutschen Buchhandels.

———. 1989a. "Die Stadt in der Literatur: Zwischen Dämonisierung und Akzeptanz." *Der Literat* 31, no. 2: 41–42.

———. 1989b. "Die Tatsache, daß ein Tisch vier Beine hat: Interview mit der Lyrikerin Ulla Hahn: Auf postmodernem Versfuß." *Stuttgarter Nachrichten.* November 25, 23.

———. 1990. "Kurzschluß aufs Leben: Wenn Biographen Moralisten werden." *Frankfurter Allgemeine Zeitung,* March 10, n.p.

———. 1992a. "Magischer Gebrauchsgegenstand: Zum achtzigsten Geburtstag der Lyrikerin Hilde Domin." *Frankfurter Allgemeine Zeitung,* July 27, 23.

———, ed. 1992b. *Stechäpfel: Gedichte von Frauen aus drei Jahrtausenden.* Stuttgart, Ger.: Reclam.

———. 1993. *Liebesgedichte.* Stuttgart, Ger.: Deutsche Verlags-Anstalt.

———. 1994. *Poesie und Vergnügen—Poesie und Verantwortung.* Heidelberg, Ger.: C. F. Mueller Juristischer Verlag.

———. 1995. *Epikurs Garten.* Stuttgart, Ger.: Deutsche Verlags-Anstalt.

———. 1997a. *Galileo und zwei Frauen: Gedichte.* Stuttgart, Ger.: Deutsche Verlags-Anstalt.

———. 1997b. "Hinter der Maske des Edelfräuleins." *Rheinischer Merkur,* January 3, 19.

———. 1997c. "'Ich habe dir nie einen Zitronenkuchen versprochen.' Gerichtstag über sich selbst: Sylvia Plath in ihren Tagebüchern." *Frankfurter Allgemeine Zeitung,* November 4, L10.

———, ed. 1999. *Gedichte fürs Gedächtnis: Zum Inwendig-Lernen und Auswendig-Sagen.* Stuttgart, Ger.: Deutsche Verlags-Anstalt.

———. 2000. "Der Fluch soll ewig währen." *Frankfurter Allgemeine Zeitung,* January 22, IV.

———. 2003. *Süßapfel rot.* Stuttgart, Ger.: Philipp Reclam jun.

———. 2004. *So offen die Welt.* Munich: Deutsche Verlags-Anstalt.

———. 2006. *Dichter in der Welt: Mein Schreiben und Lesen.* Munich: Deutsche Verlags-Anstalt.

———. 2009. *Aufbruch.* Munich: Deutsche Verlags-Anstalt.

Hall, Donald E. 2004. *Subjectivity.* New York: Routledge.

Hamburger, Käte. 1957. *Die Logik der Dichtung.* Stuttgart, Ger.: Ernst Klett Verlag.

———. 1970. "Hilde Domin: *Wozu Lyrik heute.*" *Poetica* 3: 310–15.

———. 1973. *The Logic of Literature.* Translated by Marilynn J. Rose. 2nd revised edition. Bloomington: Indiana University Press.

———. 1986. "Das tranzendierende Ich: Zur Lyrik von Nelly Sachs." In *Kleine Schriften zur Literatur und Geistesgeschichte,* 265–74. Stuttgart, Ger.: Hans-Dieter Heinz Akademischer Verlag.

Häntzschel, Günter. 2002. "Die Präsenz weiblicher Autoren auf dem Buchmarkt 1945 und 1950: Vorläufige Skizze eines Projekts." In *Erfahrung nach dem Krieg: Autorinnen im Literaturbetrieb 1945–1950 BRD, DDR, Österreich, Schweiz.* Edited by Christiane Caemmerer, Walter Delabar, Elke Ramm, and Marion Schulz, 215–24. Frankfurt am Main: Peter Lang.

Hartung, Harald. 1985a. *Deutsche Lyrik seit 1965.* Munich: Piper.

———. 1985b. "Warten auf das lange Gedicht." In *Deutsche Lyrik seit 1965: Tendenzen, Beispiele, Porträts,* 66–82. Munich: Piper.

———. 1999. "Die Sache der Hände." *Lyrik: Über Lyrik* 53, nos. 3–4: 324–31.

———. 1994. "Lyrik und Hoffnung: Hilde Domin, *Das Gedicht als Augenblick von Freiheit*" (1988). In *Poetik der Autoren: Beiträge zur deutschsprachigen Gegenwartsliteratur.* Edited by Paul Michel Lützeler, 182–93. Frankfurt am Main: Fischer.

Helfer, Martha B. 2005. "The Male Muses of Romanticism: The Poetics of Gender in Novalis, E. T. A. Hoffmann, and Eichendorff." *German Quarterly* 78, no. 3: 299–319.

Herzog, Dagmar. 1998. "'Pleasure, Sex, and Politics Belong Together': Post-Holocaust Memory and the Sexual Revolution in West Germany." *Critical Inquiry* 24, no. 2: 393–445.

———. 2005. *Sex After Fascism: Memory and Morality in Twentieth-Century Germany*. Princeton, N.J.: Princeton University Press.

Heukenkamp, Ursula. 1985. "Poetisches Subjekt und weibliche Perspektive: Zur Lyrik." In *Frauen Literatur Geschichte: Schreibende Frauen vom Mittelalter bis zur Gegenwart*. Edited by Hiltrud Gnüg and Renate Möhrmann, 354–66. Stuttgart, Ger.: Metzler.

Hildebrandt, Irma. 2009. "*Heimat in der deutschen Sprache:* Hilde Domin (1909–2006)." In *Prägende Gestalten der Bundesrepublik*, 33–52. Munich: Diederichs Verlag.

Hillebrand, Bruno. 1997. "Ende des orphischen Gesangs—Gedanken zur Tonlosigkeit der deutschen Lyrik nach 1945." In *Traditionen der Lyrik*. Edited by Wolfgang Düsing, 221–35. Tübingen, Ger.: Max Niemeyer Verlag.

Hinderer, Walter. 1994. "Verlust der Wirklichkeit: Eine Ortsbestimmung der westdeutschen Lyrik von 1945 bis 1975." In *Arbeit an der Gegenwart: Zur deutschen Literatur nach 1945*, 11–48. Würzburg, Ger.: Königshausen und Neumann.

Hitliste der Jahrhundertdichter. 2008. Anton G. Leitner Verlag. http://www.dasgedicht.de/hits.htm.

Hoffmann, Paul. 2001. *Das erneute Gedicht*. Frankfurt am Main: Suhrkamp.

Hofmannsthal, Hugo von. 1952. "Ballade des Äusseren Lebens." In *Gedichte und Lyrische Dramen*, 16. Wien: S. Fischer.

Höllerer, Walter. 1965. "Thesen zum langen Gedicht." *Akzente* 12, no. 2: 128–30.

Holthusen, Hans Egon. 1958. *Rainer Maria Rilke*. Reinbek bei Hamburg, Ger.: Rowohlt.

Howe, Patricia. 2000. "Women's Writing 1830–1890." In *A History of Women's Writing in Germany, Austria and Switzerland*. Edited by Jo Catling, 88–103. Cambridge, Eng.: Cambridge University Press.

Irigaray, Luce. 2004. *Key Writings*. London: Continuum.

Jackson, Virginia. 2005. *Dickinson's Misery: A Theory of Lyric Reading*. Princeton, N.J.: Princeton University Press.

———. 2008. "Who Reads Poetry?" *PMLA* 123, no. 1: 181–87.

Janson, H. W. 1991. *History of Art*. New York: Harry N. Abrams.

Jens, Walter. 1998. "'Vollkommenheit im Einfachen.'" In *Vokabular der Erinnerungen: Zum Werk von Hilde Domin*. Edited by Betinna von Wagenheim and Ilseluise Metz, 53–56. Frankfurt am Main: Fischer.

Kayser, Wolfgang. 1946. *Kleine deutsche Versschule*. Bern, Switz.: Francke.

Keller, Lynn, and Cristanne Miller, eds. 1994. *Feminist Measures: Soundings in Poetry and Theory*. Ann Arbor: University of Michigan Press.

Kersting, Christa. 2003. "Remigration und Wissenschaftspolitik." In *Käte Hamburger: Zur Aktualität einer Klassikerin*. Edited by Johanna Bossinade and Angelika Schaser, 50–71. Göttingen, Ger.: Wallstein Verlag.

Kiesel, Helmut. 1998. "Der Blick der Liebe." In *Frauen dichten anders*. Edited by Marcel Reich-Ranicki, 760–62. Frankfurt am Main: Insel Verlag.

Klüger, Ruth. 1996. *Frauen lesen anders*. Munich: Deutscher Taschenbuch Verlag.

———. 1998. "Die drei Türen der Verbannung." In *Frauen dichten anders*. Edited by Marcel Reich-Ranicki, 188–90. Frankfurt am Main: Insel

Knape, Franz Josef. 1995. *. . . Zugeritten in manchen sprachen . . . : Über Werk und Wirkung des Dichters und Vermittlers Rainer Maria Gerhardt*. Würzburg, Ger.: Königshausen und Neumann.

Knörrich, Otto. 1978. *Die deutsche Lyrik seit 1945*. Stuttgart, Ger.: Alfred Kröner.

Korte, Hermann. 1989. *Geschichte der deutschen Lyrik seit 1945*. Stuttgart, Ger.: Metzler.

Krechel, Ursula. 1974a. "Erika: Ein Stück." *Theaterheute* 15, no. 8: 37–46.

———. 1974b. "Wenn Frauen an einem Stück über Frauen urteilen." *Theaterheute* 15, no. 8: 34–35.

———. 1975/1983. *Selbsterfahrung und Fremdbestimmung: Bericht aus der Neuen Frauenbewegung*. Darmstadt, Ger.: Luchterhand.

———. 1979a. "Imgard Keun: Die Zerstörung der kalten Ordnung: Auch ein Versuch über das Vergessen weiblicher Kulturleistungen." In *Literaturmagazin 10: Vorbilder*. Edited by Nicolas Born, Jürgen Manthey, and Delf Schmidt, 103–28. Reinbek bei Hamburg, Ger.: Rowohlt.

———. 1979b. "Leben in Anführungszeichen: Das Authentische in der gegenwärtigen Literatur." In *Literaturmagazin 11: Schreiben oder Literatur*. Edited by Hans Christoph Buch, Jürgen Manthey, and Delf Schmidt, 80–107. Reinbek bei Hamburg, Ger.: Rowohlt.

———. 1979c. *Verwundbar wie in den besten Zeiten*. Darmstadt, Ger.: Luchterhand.

———. 1982. *Lesarten: Vom Geburt des Gedichts aus dem Nichts*. Frankfurt am Main: Luchterhand.

———. 1983a. "Kulturzerstörung: Wird der Kuchen zerstört, indem man ihn teilt und ißt?" In *"Kultur-Zerstörung?" 10. Römerberggespräche in Frankfurt am Main*. Edited by Hilmar Hoffmann, 140–42. Königstein, Ger.: Athenäum.

———. 1983b. "Meine Sätze haben schon einen Bart: Abmahnung an die neue Weiblichkeit." *Kursbuch* 73: 143–55.

———. 1983c. *Nach Mainz: Gedichte*. Munich: Deutscher Taschenbuch Verlag.

———. 1983d. *Rohschnitt*. Darmstadt, Ger.: Luchterhand.

———. 1985. *Vom Feuer lernen*. Darmstadt, Ger.: Luchterhand.

———. 1989. *Kakaoblau*. Salzburg, Austria: Residenz.

———. 1992. *Mit dem Körper des Vaters spielen: Essays*. Frankfurt am Main: Suhrkamp.

———. 1995a. "Auslassungen über das Weglassen." *Zwischen den Zeilen: Zeitschrift für Gedichte und Ihre Poetik* 3, no. 5: 60–71.

———. 1995b. *Landläufiges Wunder*. Frankfurt am Main: Suhrkamp.

———. 1995c. "Ortlosigkeit, Stucktröstung." In *Ingeborg Bachmann*. Munich: Text und Kritik.

———. 1996. "Ausgesetzt in Einfallschneisen." In *Vom Schreiben. 4: Im Ca-féhaus, oder Wo schreiben? Marbacher Magazin 74*. Edited by Rudi Kienzle, 1–16. Marbach am Neckar, Ger.: Deutsche Schillergesellschaft.

———. 1999. *Verbeugungen vor der Luft*. Salzburg, Austria: Residenz.

———. 2003. *In Zukunft schreiben*. Salzburg, Austria: Jung und Jung.

———. 2005. *Stimmen aus dem harten Kern: Gedichte*. Salzburg, Austria: Jung und Jung.

———. 2006. *Mittelwärts: Gedichte*. Springe, Ger.: Zu Klampen!

———. 2010a. *Jäh erhellte Dunkelheit: Gedichte*. Salzburg, Austria: Jung und Jung.

———. 2010b. *Voices from the Bitter Core*. Translated by Amy Kepple Strawser. Austin, Tex.: Host.

Kreutzer, Helmut. 1981. "Neue Subjektivität: Zur Literatur der siebziger Jahre in der Bundesrepublik Deutschland." In *Deutsche Gegenwartsliteratur: Ausgangspositionen und aktuelle Entwicklungen*. Edited by Manfred Durzak, 77–106. Stuttgart, Ger.: Reclam.

Kristeva, Julia. 1984. *Revolution in Poetic Language*. Translated by Margaret Waller. New York: Columbia University Press.

Krolow, Karl. 1966. "Das Problem des langen und kurzen Gedichts heute." *Akzente* 13, no. 3: 271–87.

———. 1982. "Zivilcourage des Wortes: 'Drei Arten Gedichte aufzuschreiben 2.'" In *Heimkehr ins Wort: Materialien zu Hilde Domin*. Edited by Bettina von Wangenheim, 175–77. Frankfurt am Main: Fischer.

Kuschel, Karl-Josef. 1992. "Schreiben, um die Sehnsucht wachzuhalten: Gespräch mit Ulla Hahn." In *Ich glaube nicht, daß ich Atheist bin*, 9–25. Munich: Piper.

Lämmert, Eberhard. 2003. "Käte Hamburger—Charakterzüge ihrer Wissenschaft." In *Käte Hamburger: Zur Aktualität einer Klassikerin*. Edited by Johanna Bossinade and Angelika Schaser, 15–27. Göttingen, Ger.: Wallstein Verlag.

Langer, Susanne. 1953. *Feeling and Form*. New York: Scribner.

Lanser, Susan S. 1997. "Toward a Feminist Narratology." In *Feminisms: An Anthology of Literary Theory and Criticism*. Edited by Robyn R. Warhol and Diane Price Herndl, 674–93. New Brunswick, N.J.: Rutgers University Press.

Leeder, Karen. 2000. "Post-1945 Women's Poetry from East and West." In *A History of Women's Writing in Germany, Austria, and Switzerland*. Edited by Jo Catling, 200–215. Cambridge, Eng.: Cambridge University Press.

———. 2007. "Introduction. 'Schreiben am Schnittpunkt': The Place of Contemporary Poetry." In *Schaltstelle: Neue Lyrik im Dialog*. Edited by K. Leeder, 1–30. Amsterdam: Rodopi.

Lehr-Rosenberg, Stephanie. 2003. *"Ich setze den Fuß in die Luft, und sie trug": Umgang mit Fremde und Heimat in Gedichten Hilde Domins*. Würzburg, Ger.: Königshausen und Neumann.

Lermen, Birgit, and Michael Braun. 1997. *Hilde Domin "Hand in Hand mit der Sprache."* Bonn: Bouvier.

Lersch, Barbara. 1988. "Der Ort der Leerstelle: Weiblichkeit als Poetik der Negativität und der Differenz." In *Deutsche Literatur von Frauen*. Edited by Gisela Brinker-Gabler, 487–502. Munich: Verlag C. H. Beck.

Lessing, Gotthold Ephraim. 1984. *Laocoön: An Essay on the Limits of Painting and Poetry*. Translated by Edward Allen McCormick. Baltimore: Johns Hopkins University Press.

Lettau, Reinhard, ed. 1967. *Die Gruppe 47: Bericht, Kritik, Polemik: Ein Handbuch*. Neuwied, Ger.: Luchterhand.

Levine, Michael G. 2004. "Silent Wine: Celan and the Poetics of Belatedness." *New German Critique* 91 (Winter): 151–70.

Marcuse, Herbert. 1964. *One-Dimensional Man: Studies in the Ideology of Advanced Industrial Society*. Boston: Beacon.

———. 1966. *Eros and Civilization: A Philosophical Inquiry into Freud*. Boston: Beacon.

———. 1978. *The Aesthetic Dimension: Toward a Critique of Marxist Aesthetics*. Boston: Beacon.

———. 2005. "Marxism and Feminism." In *Herbert Marcuse: The New Left and the 1960s*. Edited by Douglas Kellner, 165–72. London: Routledge.

Mattenklott, Gert. 2003. "Käte Hamburger im Kontext ihrer jüdischen Verhältnisse." In *Käte Hamburger: Zur Aktualität einer Klassikerin*. Edited by Johanna Bossinade and Angelika Schaser, 72–82. Göttingen, Ger.: Wallstein Verlag.

McQuade, Molly, ed. 2000. *By Herself: Women Reclaim Poetry*. St. Paul, Minn.: Graywolf.

Meidinger-Geise, Inge. 1986. "Hoffnung auf Liebe." *Zeitwende* 57, no. 1: 122–23.

Melin, Charlotte. 1992. "Williams, Enzensberger, and Recent German Poetry." *Comparative Literature Studies* 29, no. 1: 77–93.

———. 1996. "Renderings of *Alice in Wonderland* in Postwar German Literature." In *Women in German Yearbook*. Edited by Sara Friedrichsmeyer and Patricia Herminghouse, 149–65. Lincoln: University of Nebraska Press.

———. 1997. "Improved Versions: Feminist Poetics and Recent Work by Ulla Hahn and Ursula Krechel." *Studies in Twentieth Century Literature* 21, no. 1: 219–43.

———, ed. 1999. *German Poetry in Transition 1945–1990*. Hanover, N.H.: University Press of New England.

———. 2003. *Poetic Maneuvers: Hans Magnus Enzensberger and the Lyric Genre*. Evanston, Ill.: Northwestern University Press.

Meskimmon, Marsha. 1999. *We Weren't Modern Enough: Women Artists and the Limits of German Modernism*. Berkeley: University of California Press.

Middleton, Peter. 2005. *Distant Reading: Performance, Readership, and Consumption in Contemporary Poetry*. Tuscaloosa: University of Alabama Press.

Mielke, Rita. 1986. "Ursula Krechel." In *Kritisches Lexikon zur deutschsprachigen Gegenwartsliteratur*, 1–14. Munich: Text und Kritik.

Möhrmann, Renate. 1981. "Feministische Trends in der deutschen Gegenwartsliteratur." In *Deutsche Gegenwartsliteratur: Ausgangspositionen und aktuelle Entwicklungen.* Edited by Manfred Durzak, 336–58. Stuttgart, Ger.: Reclam.

Mörike, Eduard. 1968. "Im Frühling." In *Gedichte.* Edited by Hans Egon Holthusen, 44. Frankfurt am Main: Fischer.

Morris, Leslie. 2000. "The Ladies Lazarus: Sylvia Plath und Ingeborg Bachmann: Versuch einer vergleichenden Lektüre." In *Über die Zeit schreiben 2: Literatur- und Kulturwissenschaftliche Essays zum Werk Ingeborg Bachmanns.* Edited by Monika Albrecht and Dirk Göttsche, 75–79. Würzburg, Ger.: Königshausen und Neumann.

Mueller, Agnes C. 1999. *Lyrik "Made in USA": Vermittlung und Rezeption in der Bundesrepublik.* Amsterdam: Rodopi.

Nichols, John G. 2006. "Ezra Pound's Poetic Anthologies and the Architecture of Reading." *PMLA* 121, no. 1: 170–85.

Nietzsche, Friedrich. 1982. *Also sprach Zarathustra.* Baden-Baden, Ger.: Insel.

Notley, Alice. 2005. *Coming After: Essays on Poetry.* Ann Arbor: University of Michigan Press.

Novak, Helga M. 1978. *Margarete mit dem Schrank.* Berlin: Rotbuch Verlag.

Oleschinski, Brigitte. 1999. "Sturmzwitter." In "Lyrik: Über Lyrik," special issue, *Merkur* 53, nos. 3–4: 389–95.

Ostriker, Alicia. 1983. *Writing Like a Woman.* Ann Arbor: University of Michigan Press.

———. 1986. *Stealing the Language: The Emergence of Women's Poetry in America.* Boston: Beacon.

Parkes, Stuart. 2000. "Neue Subjektivität." In *Encyclopedia of German Literature.* Edited by Matthias Konzett, 757–58. Chicago: Fitzroy Dearborn.

Paul, Georgina. 2007. "Ismene at the Crossroads: Gender and Poetic Influence." *German Life and Letters* 60, no. 3: 430–46.

Pendergrast, Mark. 1993. *For God, Country, and Coca-Cola.* New York: Scribner.

Perloff, Marjorie. 1998. *Poetry On and Off the Page: Essays for Emergent Occasions.* Evanston, Ill.: Northwestern University Press.

Pickerodt, Gerhart. 1984. "Zur Lyrik der frühen achtziger Jahre." In *Tendenzen der deutschen Gegenwartsliteratur.* Edited by Thomas Koebner, 163–77. Stuttgart, Ger.: Alfred Kröner.

Piper, Andrew. 2006. "Rethinking the Printed Object: Goethe and the Book of Everything." *PMLA* 121, no. 1: 124–38.

Poiss, Thomas. 2000. "Scharmützel in Scherzen." *Frankfurter Allgemeine Zeitung,* March 4, V.

Preminger, Alex, and T. V. F. Brogan, eds. 1993. *The New Princeton Encyclopedia of Poetry and Poetics.* Princeton, N.J.: Princeton University Press.

Puknus, Heinz, ed. 1980. *Neue Literatur der Frauen.* Munich: C. H. Beck.

Rapisarda, Cettina. 1997. "Women's Writing, 1968–1980." In *Post-War Women's Writing in German: Feminist Critical Approaches.* Edited by Chris Weedon, 77–100. Providence, R.I.: Berghahn.

Reich-Ranicki, Marcel, ed. 1998. *Frauen dichten anders.* Frankfurt am Main: Insel.

———. 2001. *The Author of Himself: The Life of Marcel Reich-Ranicki.* Translated by Ewald Osers. London: Weidenfeld and Nicolson.

Rich, Adrienne. 1976. "Foreword." In *The Other Voice: Twentieth-Century Women's Poetry in Translation.* Edited by Joanna Bankier, Carol Cosman, Doris Earnshaw, Joan Keefe, Deirdre Lashgari, and Kathleen Weaver, xvii–xxi. New York: Norton.

———. 1979. *On Lies, Secrets, and Silence: Selected Prose 1966–1978.* New York: Norton.

Riley, Denise. 1988. *"Am I That Name?": Feminism and the Category of "Women" in History.* Minneapolis: University of Minnesota Press.

Rilke, Rainer Maria. 1951. "Archaïscher Torso Apollos." In *Der ausgewählten Gedichte erster Teil,* 60. Wiesbaden, Ger.: Insel.

Robbins, Ruth. 2005. *Subjectivity.* New York: Palgrave Macmillan.

Rohlfs, Jochen. 1993. "'. . .bis jemand ein Wort braucht das not tut und gut.' Wortspiel in der Lyrik von Ulla Hahn." *Neophilologus* 77, no. 1: 113–26.

Rolleston, James. 1997. "Introduction." In "Contemporary German Poetry," special issue, *Studies in Twentieth Century Literature* 21, no. 1: 7–8.

Roman, Camille. 2001. *Elizabeth Bishop's World War II—Cold War View.* New York: Palgrave.

Rosenkranz, Jutta, ed. 1988. *Wenn wir den Königen schreiben: Lyrikerinnen aus der DDR.* Darmstadt, Ger.: Luchterhand.

Rühmkorf, Peter. 1962. "Das lyrische Weltbild der Nachkriegsdeutschen." In *Bestandsaufnahme: Eine deutsche Bilanz 1962.* Edited by Hans Werner Richter, 447–76. Munich: Kurt Desch.

Rumold, Rainer. 2002. *The Janus Face of the German Avant-Garde: From Expressionism Toward Postmodernism.* Evanston, Ill.: Northwestern University Press.

Ryan, Judith. 1982. "'Your Life Jacket Is Under Your Skin': Reflections on German Poetry of the Seventies." *German Quarterly* 55, no. 3: 296–308.

———. 1992. "Dead Poets' Voices: Rilke's 'Lost from the Outset' and the Originality Effect." *Modern Language Quarterly* 53, no. 2: 227–45.

———. 1994. "Poetik als Experiment. Christa Wolf, *Voraussetzungen einer Erzählung: Kassandra* (1983)." In *Poetik der Autoren: Beiträge zur deutschsprachigen Gegenwartsliteratur.* Edited by Paul Michael Lützeler, 80–94. Frankfurt am Main: Fischer.

———. 1997. "'Deckname Lyrik': Poetry After 1945 and 1989." In *Wendezeiten—Zeitwenden: Positionsbestimmungen zur deutschsprachigen Literatur 1945–1995.* Edited by Robert Weniger and Brigitte Rossbacher, 37–54. Tübingen, Ger.: Stauffenburg.

Sartorius, Joachim. 1998. "'Language, Foreign: Saying You and Being Heard': On Poetry in German, 1986–1996." In "Contemporary German Poetry," special issue, *Poetry* 173, no. 1: 121–28.

Saunders, Frances Stonor. 1999. *The Cultural Cold War: The CIA and the World of Arts and Letters.* New York: New Press.

Schabert, Ina. 2004. "No Room of One's Own: Women's Studies in English Departments in Germany." *PMLA* 119, no. 1: 69–79.

Schäfer, Hans Dieter. 1981. "Zusammenhänge der deutschen Gegenwartslyrik." In *Deutsche Gegenwartsliteratur: Ausgangspositionen und aktuelle Entwicklungen.* Edited by Manfred Durzak, 166–203. Stuttgart, Ger.: Reclam.

Scheffel, Michael. 2003. "Käte Hamburgers *Logik der Dichtung*—ein 'Grundbuch' der Fiktionalitäts- und Erzähltheorie? Versuch einer Re-Lektüre." In *Käte Hamburger: Zur Aktualität einer Klassikerin.* Edited by Johanna Bossinade and Angelika Schaser, 140–55. Göttingen, Ger.: Wallstein Verlag.

Scheidgen, Ilka. 2006. *Hilde Domin: Dichterin des Dennoch.* Lahr, Ger.: Kaufmann Verlag.

Schlesier, Renate. 2003. "Was ist Interpretation in den Kulturwissenschaften?" In *Käte Hamburger: Zur Aktualität einer Klassikerin.* Edited by Johanna Bossinade and Angelika Schaser, 29–49. Göttingen, Ger.: Wallstein Verlag.

Schmitt, W. Christian. 1986. "Der Leser soll sich in ihren Geschichten wiederfinden." In *Die Buchstaben-Millionäre: Begegnungen, Gespräche und Erfahrungen mit vierzig Schriftstellern,* 68–75. Karlsruhe, Ger.: Loeper.

Schnell, Ralf. 1993. *Geschichte der deutschsprachigen Literatur seit 1945.* Stuttgart, Ger.: Metzler.

Schor, Naomi. 1987. *Reading in Detail: Aesthetics and the Feminine.* New York: Methuen.

Schrott, Raoul, ed. 1997. *Die Erfindung der Poesie: Gedichte aus den ersten viertausend Jahren.* Frankfurt am Main: Eichborn.

Schulte-Sasse, Jochen. 1984. "Foreword: Theory of Modernism versus Theory of the Avant-Garde." In *Theory of the Avant-Garde,* vii–xlvii. Minneapolis: University of Minnesota Press.

Schumacher, Horst. 1981. "Entwicklungsphasen moderner deutscher Lyrik seit 1945." *Universitas* 36, no. 7: 927–34.

Serke, Jürgen. 1982. "Ursula Krechel: Kämpferin für die Frauenbewegung." In *Frauen schreiben,* 347–48. Frankfurt am Main: Fischer.

Sontag, Susan. 1966. "Against Interpretation." In *Against Interpretation and Other Essays,* 3–14. New York: Farrar, Straus and Giroux.

Staiger, Emil. 1946. *Grundbegriffe der Poetik.* Zürich: Atlantis.

———. 1991. *Basic Concepts of Poetry.* Translated by Janette C. Hudson and Luanne T. Frank. Edited by Marianne Burkhard and L. T. Frank. University Park: Penn State University Press.

Stein, Agnes, ed. 1979. *Four German Poets.* New York: Red Dust.

Stern, Dagmar C. 1979. "Hilde Domin's Personal and Social Ideals." *Modern Language Studies* 9, no. 2: 67–79.

Stewart, Susan. 2002. *Poetry and the Fate of the Senses.* Chicago: University of Chicago Press.

Strong, Beret E. 1997. *The Poetic Avant-Garde: The Groups of Borges, Auden, and Breton.* Evanston, Ill.: Northwestern University Press.

Susman, Margarete. 1910. *Das Wesen der modernen deutschen Lyrik.* Stuttgart, Ger.: Strecker und Schröder.

Taberner, Stuart. 2005. *German Literature of the 1990s and Beyond: Normalization and the Berlin Republic*. Rochester, N.Y.: Camden House.

Tarot, Rolf. 1997. "Käte Hamburgers Lyriktheorie—eine Revision." In *Traditionen der Lyrik*. Edited by Wolfgang Düsing, 257–75. Tübingen, Ger.: Max Niemeyer Verlag.

Tauchel, Theodor. 1981. "Lyrischer März in Darmstadt." *Der Literat* 23, no. 5: 125.

Tauschwitz, Marion. 2009. *"Das ich sein kann, wie ich bin": Hilde Domin: Die Biografie*. Heidelberg, Ger.: Palmyra Verlag.

Theiß, Elisabeth, ed. 1981. *Gezeiten: Neue Frauenlyrik aus der BRD*. Rhodt unter Rietburg, Ger.: Verlag Junge Literatur.

Theobaldy, Jürgen, and Gustav Zürcher. 1976. *Veränderung der Lyrik: Über westdeutsche Gedichte seit 1965*. Munich: Edition Text und Kritik.

Threadgold, Terry. 1997. *Feminist Poetics: Poiesis, Performance, Histories*. London: Routledge.

Trakl, Georg. 1972. "Die Sonnenblumen." In *Das dichterische Werk*. Edited by Walther Killy and Hans Szklenar, 195. Munich: Deutscher Taschenbuch Verlag.

Trommler, Frank. 1970. "Der 'Nullpunkt 1945' und seine Verbindlichkeit für die Literaturgeschichte." *Basis: Jahrbuch für deutsche Gegenwartsliteratur* 1: 9–25.

———. 1977. "Nachkriegsliteratur—eine neue deutsche Literatur?" In *Literaturmagazin 7: Nachkriegsliteratur*. Edited by Nicolas Born and Jürgen Manthey, 167–86. Hamburg: Rowohlt.

Virginia, Julia, ed. 1907. *Frauenlyrik unserer Zeit*. 2nd ed. Berlin: Schuster und Loeffler.

Vogel, Marianne. 2002. "Platz, Position, Profilierung: Geschlechteraspekte des deutschen Literaturbetriebs 1945–1950 unter anderem am Beispiel der Gruppe 47." In *Erfahrung nach dem Krieg: Autorinnen im Literaturbetrieb 1945–1950 BRD, DDR, Österreich, Schweiz*. Edited by Christiane Caemmerer, Walter Delabar, Elke Ramm, and Marion Schulz, 225–42. Frankfurt am Main: Peter Lang.

Wangenheim, Bettina von, ed. 1982. *Heimkehr ins Wort: Materialien zu Hilde Domin*. Frankfurt am Main: Fischer.

Wangenheim, Bettina von, and Ilseluise Metz, eds. 1998. *Vokabular der Erinnerungen: Zum Werk von Hilde Domin*. Frankfurt am Main: Fischer.

Watanabe-O'Kelly, Helen. 2000. "Women's Writing in the Early Modern Period." In *A History of Women's Writing in Germany, Austria and Switzerland*. Edited by Jo Catling, 27–44. Cambridge, Eng.: Cambridge University Press.

Weedon, Chris, ed. 1997. *Post-War Women's Writing in German: Feminist Critical Approaches*. Providence: Berghahn, 1997.

Weimar, Klaus. 1974. "Kritische Bemerkungen zur *Logik der Dichtung*." *Deutsche Vierteljahrsschrift für Literaturwissenschaft und Geistesgeschichte* 48: 10–24.

Weissenberger, Klaus, ed. *Die deutsche Lyrik 1945–1975*. Düsseldorf: August Bagel, 1981.

Wellek, René, and Austin Warren. 1949. *Theory of Literature.* New York: Harcourt Brace.

Werner-Birkenbach, Sabine. 2000. "Trends in Writing by Women, 1910–1933." In *A History of Women's Writing in Germany, Austria and Switzerland.* Edited by Jo Catling, 128–45. Cambridge, Eng.: Cambridge University Press.

Wiesner, Herbert, and Alexander von Bormann. 1987. "Ursula Krechel." In *Lexikon der deutschsprachigen Gegenwartsliteratur.* Edited by Hermann Kunisch, Herbert Wiesner, and Sibylle Cramer, 346–48. Munich: Nymphenburger.

Wittkowski, Joachim. 1988. "Das souveräne Bekenntnis zu sich selbst: Notizen zu einem 'Fall' der bundesdeutschen Literaturkritik." *Text + Kritik: Über Literaturkritik* 100: 59–65.

———. 1991. "Ulla Hahn: Eine Karriere im Feuilleton." In *Lyrik in der Presse: Eine Untersuchung der Kritik an Wolf Biermann, Erich Fried und Ulla Hahn.* Würzburg, Ger.: Königshausen und Neumann.

Wittstock, Uwe. 1989. *Von der Stalinallee zum Prenzlauer Berg: Wege der DDR-Literatur 1949–1989.* Munich: Piper.

Wodtke, Friedrich Wilhelm. 1968. "Die Entwicklung der deutschen Lyrik seit 1945." In *Wissenschaftliches Jahrbuch der Philosophischen Fakultät der Universität.* Athens: Athinai.

Wolf, Christa. 1983. *Voraussetzungen einer Erzählung: Kassandra. Frankfurter Poetik-Vorlesungen.* Darmstadt, Ger.: Luchterhand.

Woolf, Virginia. 1977. *The Waves.* London: Granada.

Zimmermann, Bernhard. 1988. "Literary Criticism from 1933 to the Present." In *A History of German Literary Criticism 1730–1980.* Edited by Peter Uwe Hohendahl, 359–437. Lincoln: University of Nebraska Press.

Zuther, Gerhard H. W. 1965. *Eine Bibliographie der Aufnahme amerikanischer Literatur in deutschen Zeitschriften 1945–1960.* Munich: Dissertations Druck Franz Frank.